# The
# Delights
# —of—
# Terror

# The Delights of Terror

## An Aesthetics of the Tale of Terror

*Terry Heller*

University of Illinois Press
Urbana and Chicago

*This book is printed on acid-free paper.*

Library of Congress Cataloging-in-Publication Data

Heller, Terry, 1947–
  The delights of terror.

  Bibliography: p.
  Includes index.
  1. Horror tales, English—History and criticism.
  2. Horror tales, American—History and criticism.
  3. Fear in literature. 4. Horror tales—Technique.
  I. Title.
  PR830.T3H38   1987       823′.0872′09        86-27217
  ISBN 0-252-01412-X (cloth; alk. paper)
  ISBN 0-252-01475-8 (paper; alk. paper)

# Contents

# Preface

But the apparent delight with which we dwell upon objects of pure terror, where our moral feelings are not in the least concerned, and no
passion seems to be excited but the depressing one of fear, is a paradox
of the heart, much more difficult of solution.

—John Aiken and Anna Laetitia Barbauld, "On
the Pleasure Derived from Objects of Terror"

There are works of literature designed to terrify their readers, con-
triving in special ways to reach out with not so tender "claws" and to
"draw blood." Not all tales of terror truly terrify their readers. In fact,
it would seem to be against the interest of a work of literature to really
terrify its reader if by terror we mean the fear that harm will come to
oneself. If a reader should feel terror while reading, then the reading
would most likely end. For example, I have acquaintances who have
been unable to watch *Psycho* through the shower murder. I often meet
people who report that they were unable to finish a story by Stephen
King or H. P. Lovecraft. My work on *The Delights of Terror* began when
I realized that I had encountered works that not only seemed designed
to terrify me, but whose design was so artful that even though I feared
harm to myself, I did not flee, but struggled until I had successfully
read them. Three such tales are: Edgar Allan Poe's "Ligeia" and "The
Fall of the House of Usher" and Henry James's *The Turn of the Screw.*
     In the beginning, these texts haunted me. For more than a decade,
starting with my first careful readings in graduate school and contin-

uing through years of teaching them, these tales disturbed me whenever they were before my consciousness. The central problem was that there were at least two contradictory readings for each story. On the one hand, these were tales of supernatural intrusions into the lives of their narrators. The narrators were terrified and mystified by these intrusions, and we readers were to be horrified by their adventures. By horror, I mean the fear of anticipating and witnessing harm befalling others for whom we have some sympathy. On the other hand, these were not supernatural stories at all, but the ravings of hallucinating narrators. Each time I read one of these stories, reviewed the established criticism, and read more recent criticism, I would see new features of the works emerging and try to shift my position to some solid ground. I eventually discovered myself to be on a kind of circle of interpretation. The secret (the work) would sit enigmatically in the deep center of the pool, and I would skip from stone to stone around the edge, trying to achieve the final view, but without success. Then one day I found myself, as if by magic, sitting quite safe at the center with the secret. There was still no final view, but I was not "drowning" either; my problem seemed solved.

I began thinking about writing this book on the day I discovered "Ligeia" to be beautiful. For years "she" had haunted me. Then, one day, the tale returned in memory transformed, mysterious still, but coalesced. This transformation awed me. My awe was extended because the other Poe story and James's short masterpiece had also haunted me, and these works also returned to me transformed. To complete the reading of three works simultaneously with none of them before one's eyes is the sort of event that a literary critic wishes to share with others. This book is, in part, an attempt to put my experience into words.

However, in the process of thinking about how to explain this effect, I found myself explaining other tales of terror of different kinds. There seemed to be a need for a systematic attempt to explore the aesthetics of the tale of terror. What sorts of tales of terror have been written? What sorts of pleasure do they offer the reader? In view of the persistence of horror genres and of the pervasiveness of horror as an effect in modern classics, these questions are especially important. This book has become, then, an attempt to articulate the ways in which the tale of terror frightens us, when it does, and the ways it can delight, even when it frightens.

Here at the beginning, I want to raise a question implicit in the following chapters for which I have no answer yet. To explain the pleasures of terror, I have had to explore some of the central ideas about how we form our human identities. My research led me to the edges of but not far into psychoanalytic studies of feminine identity. Drawn by the exciting ideas emerging in this field, I read a little further as this book was going to press. My reading suggests that there are probably significant differences between the ways men and women respond to tales of terror. The explanations I offer seem general enough to be true for both sexes, even though I use the conventional masculine pronouns in my descriptions. Nevertheless, I suspect that my accounts are destined to be qualified and, I hope, extended by further research and thought from a specifically feminine perspective.

# Acknowledgements

I owe thanks to many people and organizations.

For permissions to reprint materials: John Wiley & Sons, Ltd., for permission to reprint Mary Rothbart's chart, "Schematic representation of affective response to sudden, intense, or discrepant stimulation," from A. J. Chapman and H. C. Foot, eds., *Humor and Laughter* (1976), p. 39; *Arizona Quarterly* for permission to reprint material from my essay, "Terror and Empathy in Faulkner's *Sanctuary*," 40 (1984): 355-64; *Gothic* for permission to reprint material from my essay, "Poe's 'Ligeia' and the Pleasures of Terror," 2 (1980): 39-48; Salem Press, Inc., for permission to reprint material from my article on Charles Brockden Brown, which appeared in *Critical Survey of Long Fiction*, 1: 312-24. Copyright, 1983, by Frank N. Magill.

For grants that helped me purchase materials and time and that helped me consult with colleagues at other colleges and universities: The National Endowment for the Humanities; The Lilly Foundation; The Mellon Foundation; and Coe College.

For moral and intellectual support, for reading and commenting on portions of the text, and for unfailing kindness and mercy when I needed them: Charles Cannon, Neal Woodruff, and the faculty of the Coe College Department of English.

For reading the manuscript at various stages and for extraordinarily helpful comments and suggestions: Hamlin Hill, Andrew Debicki, William Veeder, Barton Levi St. Armand, and, especially, J. P. Telotte and Susan L. Patterson. Ann Lowry Weir and the staff at University of

Illinois Press were unfailingly courteous and helpful. For most of these people, thank you is the only reward for their generous assistance.

For laboriously typing early versions of the manuscript: Diane Howard and Peachie Carey.

For making sure I kept my intellectual feet on the ground and for always being a friend: Ed Gerson.

For inspiration and humane teaching: Sheldon Sacks.

For loving me in spite of my insistence upon solitude on all those summer mornings when they wanted me with them: Linda and Gabriel. I did my best for them.

## CHAPTER ONE

# Introduction

## I

What sorts of tales of terror are there?

What sorts of pleasures do they offer the reader?

To answer these questions, we need to share some basic aesthetic concepts. In this introduction I outline the main concepts I am borrowing from literary theory. But first, I must issue a warning: these concepts will not remain static. Rarely do we invent concepts for the solution of one problem that remain precisely the same when we turn to another problem. Each of the theoretical concepts I use will undergo modification as I adapt it to the explanation of tales of terror, but I will make every effort to keep these concepts clear.

The theoretical concepts that seem most useful in explaining tales of terror come from Roman Ingarden's characterization of the aesthetic experience of the literary art work and from Wolfgang Iser's elaboration of the phenomenology of reading, especially in his development of the concept of the implied reader. To understand these concepts thoroughly, one must, of course, go to the writers themselves. The following summary, therefore, draws out only those aspects of these theories that seem most useful to this project but does not attempt to explain them in detail.

Most helpful is Ingarden's concept of the literary art work as a concretion, that is, as a mental experience co-created by the interaction of a reader, who adopts an aesthetic attitude toward a text that invites such a response, and of the text itself, which is a schematized set of instructions for the creation of the whole work. Although many implications of this conception will prove valuable, none is more important than the idea that we expect literary works to be wholes; we expect a feeling of completeness in our concretion of a work. One of the features of a literary work that makes it seem whole is closure. At some point at or shortly after the end of the text, we expect to see all the prominent features of the work forming a harmony that can recede in memory as we turn to other objects in the world. To end *Pride and Prejudice* after Lizzy reads Darcy's letter of explanation in response to her refusing his first proposal of marriage would turn the novel into a fragment, not because of the deficiency of any preceding part, but because the novel creates certain expectations for the completion of several kinds of patterns that must be met before the reader will feel that the novel is finished. Only when the reader feels the novel to be contained by the patterns it has promised to complete is it possible to contemplate the novel's wholeness. Jane Austen leads her readers to desire and to expect that Lizzy and Darcy will overcome their pride and prejudices to achieve marriage. Because closure, the completing of a concretion, is so important to the reader's being able to grasp the wholeness of a work, any reasonably skillful writer should be able to complete the plot of an Austen novel as has been done, for example, with *Sanditon*. We tend to tolerate various degrees of openness in fictions, but only if some form of satisfactory closure is present. Kafka's *The Castle*, though genuinely fragmentary in the sense that Kafka never completed it, still feels whole because the fundamental parable of alienation is complete. Were K. to die and the action to end, there would be a kind of conventional closure, but our understanding of the novel would remain unchanged, and our feeling of its completeness would hardly be altered. As long as the idea this novel conveys is complete, we can do without other forms of closure. In fact, given the idea of *The Castle*, a lack of conventional closure may be a positive benefit. For K.'s life to take shape and gain meaning would work against the novel's insistently unkept promise of such meaning.

Ingarden's concept of the aesthetic attitude is also important to the discussion of the tale of terror. This concept means essentially what psychical distance means to Edward Bullough. Psychical or aesthetic distance, as I call it, is distinct from the more common use of the term *distance* in literary studies. We often think of distance as the degree of identification or sympathy an author creates between reader and character, and the degree of immediacy with which scenes and events are presented in a fiction (Abrams 43-44). In this sense, distance describes the relationship between the reader and *parts* of the work. Aesthetic distance, however, describes the relationship between the reader and the *whole* work at any stage in the reading process.

Bullough defines the aesthetic mode of perceiving as involving a separation "of the object and its appeal from one's own self by putting it out of gear with practical ends and needs" (756). Bullough formulates a principle of aesthetic distance when he says that what is most desirable "both in appreciation and production" of a work of art "is the *utmost decrease of distance without its disappearance*" (758). In other words, a work of art seems best when it involves readers in it as completely as possible without their forgetting that it is a work of art and interacting with it as if it were reality. The person who flees the theater unable to endure the terrors of *Psycho* and the person who, in Bullough's example, pulls out his pistol to shoot a film villain on the screen have both lost aesthetic distance. A sophisticated reader who declines to finish a bad novel may have found that the author is unable to reduce the aesthetic distance enough to involve him in the book.

A work of art asks for a special, *disinterested* kind of attention in which the concretization (the making of a concretion) of the work becomes an end in itself, and in which the use of our imaginative faculties in that concretization is for the pleasure rather than for solving practical problems of communication (reading a telegram) or survival (dealing with a mugger). The idea that we normally look at works of art in a different way from that in which we normally look at the rest of the world seems fairly obvious, though, of course, the natures of both kinds of looking are matters of controversy.

The concept of aesthetic distance is important because it seems to be in the nature of a tale of terror to threaten aesthetic distance. The example of *Psycho* mentioned above illustrates that sometimes a tale of terror can destroy the aesthetic attitude and that some viewers find such tales to be the equivalent of a mugger, a danger to the self in the world. We need, therefore, to look closely at how successful tales of terror handle aesthetic distance.

Related to the concepts of concretion and aesthetic distance are those I adopt from Wolfgang Iser's elaboration in *The Act of Reading* of Ingarden's phenomenology of reading.

Iser has described as accurately as anyone I have read the kinds of processes I observe in myself as I move through a text, turning its words and sentences into a presented world in my imagination. Especially important is the idea that because a fictional text is always schematic and underdetermined in comparison with our experience of natural objects, we are required to fill in gaps, to create a world of depth and of whole objects out of a verbal presentation of outlines and perspectives. Therefore, as we read we engage in a process of creating provisional unities; we hypothesize wholes, practicing for the final concretization of the work. This description emphasizes the importance of wholeness to our experience of the work of art because it shows reading to consist mainly of projecting possible wholes out of the fragments given at any specific point. On the other hand, the description also reveals the unavoidable lack of wholeness in any work. Writing fiction may be conceived, by a Henry James, for example, as the art of so moving the reader through these projections as to disguise completely the presence of gaps. Or, alternatively, an artist as sophisticated as James may discover and exploit such gaps, as James said he did in writing *The Turn of the Screw*. In his preface to *The Aspern Papers*, James explains with amusement how he deliberately made the transgressions of the ghosts into blanks, which his readers then filled in with the most horrific content. His illusion was so perfect that his readers asserted that what they imagined to fill those blanks was actually put there by James (*Theory of Fiction* 173-74).

Iser's concept of the implied reader is essential to this study. Though other theorists have developed other terms, such as *inscribed reader*, *encoded reader*, and *narratee*, I prefer Iser's term. I intend, however, to use the concept in my own way, a way modified to some extent by my contact with other developments of the concept and by my thinking about tales of terror.

I have no doubt that as I read, "I" am created by the text that I read. The text includes instructions for the creation of the appropriate reader for that text, one who can make a concretion of the work that will hold up under public and professional scrutiny. The implied reader comes into being in the process of filling gaps, of making connections between the always underdetermined presented elements; this involves making a series of commitments that, though they may always be modified as a result of subsequent information, nevertheless add up not only to a picture of a world but also to a perspective on that world. The implied reader, therefore, consists of inferences about the connections between presented elements, inferences in which the reader is "invested" or to which he is committed. In *The Act of Reading* Iser calls this construct of reader and text a *role:* "Thus the concept of the implied reader designates a network of response-inviting structures, which impel the reader to grasp the text. No matter who or what he may be, the real reader is always offered a particular role to play, and it is this role that constitutes the concept of the implied reader" (34-35).

The text offers me the role of reader and gradually creates that role in various ways. It may provide values by which characters are to be judged. It may determine points of view from which I am to look. It specifies, to some degree, my world, its events, its inhabitants, its mysteries, and its culture for the duration of the reading. In the process of reading, I pretend to occupy a fictional world as an observer of and, to some degree, as an actor in that world. I construct the fictional world and myself in relation to it in much the same way that I construct myself and the so-called real world in my daily life. Two essential differences between my life in the fiction and my life in the world are that I voluntarily enter the fiction for a limited time (its anticipated duration), and I adopt an aesthetic or disinterested attitude toward the experience of the work. This attitude means, in part, that the self that the work and I create is fictional, a role that has its beginning, middle, and end. In the modern tradition of fiction up until the twentieth century, the real reader understands that the role of implied reader is to be temporary, that the role will end more or less with the last page of the text. As I suggest in my preface, some tales of terror seem not to end in any conventional way. If "Ligeia" is made to haunt its readers, then perhaps something radically different with regard to closure for the implied reader is happening there. Clearly, these concepts of Ingarden and Iser may prove crucial in understanding such an effect.

This is probably the right place for a second warning. I have presented the key theoretical concepts that I will use and, to some extent, modify as I offer my explanations of the pleasures of terror. These concepts describe what can fairly be called "natural" reading. When I read "naturally," I disengage "my" ego from the task of self-definition and give myself over to another egolike force, the work. In this way, the implied reader comes into existence. When I read critically, I try to stand back from this process and to watch (or imagine I am watching) this implied reader come into being. This is the sort of watching in which I engage in this book. Attractive as this method may be and useful as it may prove, it is only one method and it is in the hands of only one reader. I wish to emphasize that my critical attention to the implied reader *does not privilege* my readings. My reading of the implied reader and my reading as implied reader are still *my* readings with all of my limitations.

At this point I want to claim a small privilege in the interest of efficiency in terminology. To avoid too frequent repetition of *real reader* and *implied reader*, I will use the terms mainly when the distinction between the two readers seems crucial to the discussion. Generally, when I use the shorter term, *reader*, I will mean the implied reader.

In his study of Ingarden, Eugene Falk distinguishes between a kind of naive reader, which we all are sometimes, and a more sophisticated reader. The naive reader is a consumer of literature who likes to "indulge vicariously in the experiences of presented characters, to be carried away with enthusiasm, to rejoice, to hope, or to suffer with them, to gain practical lessons from these experiences" (xiv). While such experiences are clearly of great worth, the value of literature increases as we come to see how it is made, what its structures are. Then we encounter a level of aesthetic experience to which our more naive enjoyments contribute. Horror stories are considered popular literature because they satisfy naive readers but offer rather little enjoyment beyond instruction and delight to more sophisticated readers. In this book, I argue that some tales of terror are beautiful as well as enjoyable, especially those by Poe and James. In chapter 2, we will notice that the tale of terror is connected with tragedy. Indeed, some of the greatest works in the Western tradition, for example, *Oedipus, Othello,* and *Macbeth,* are noted for their terror.

# II

What sorts of tales of terror are there?

What sorts of pleasures do they offer the reader?

The answer to the first question is a matter of descriptive poetics, the second of aesthetics. The first has received a great deal of attention, and the second, not much, though during the eighteenth century it was approached by many writers concerned with the sublime. Near the end of this book, I will suggest connections between the answers I give here and the theory of the sublime. The main purpose of this book is to answer the second question, but to do so, we must have some reasonable and useful answer to the first. Indeed, an aesthetic study of tales of terror should group them according to the different varieties of pleasure they appear to offer. Therefore, I find myself choosing from among the available descriptions the one that seems most helpful to my enterprise and, inevitably, I find myself modifying it to some extent. I will come to Tzvetan Todorov's description of the fantastic and of four closely related genres by way of Walt Whitman and Edward Bullough.

> Closer yet I approach you,
> What thought you have of me now, I had as much of you—
>     I laid in my stores in advance,
> I considered long and seriously of you before you were born.
>
> Who was to know what should come home to me?
> Who knows but I am enjoying this?
> Who knows, for all the distance, but I am as good
>     as looking at you now, for all you cannot see me?

Here in part 7 of "Crossing Brooklyn Ferry," Whitman's persona completes the identification with the reader that he has been moving toward from the beginning of the poem. Whitman uses a visionary chanting re-creation of the landscape of the ferry to move in on the reader, asserting that time and distance cannot separate him from his reader. In part 4 he manipulates grammar to transcend time: "These and all else *were* to me the same as they *are* to you" (my emphasis). In part 6 he asserts that we all play the same role, that there is something more fundamental than our physical appearances that is our true identity. At the end of part 8 he maintains that he has succeeded in unifying with the reader by means of the poem:

> What is more subtle than this which ties me to the woman or man
>     that looks in my face?
> Which fuses me into you now, and pours my meaning into you?
>
> We understand then do we not?
> What I promis'd without mentioning it, have you not accepted?

Even though we know that Whitman is attempting to induce a self-transcendent vision in the reader by reducing the distance between speaker and reader, this experience is a little spooky. Whitman tries to transform his poem, which the reader approaches as an aesthetic object, into something different. He wishes to produce the practical effect of lifting the reader out of himself into unity with a transpersonal divinity. One need make only the slight effort of being unsympathetic to Whitman's transcendentalism to feel part 7 as a somewhat chilling haunting. Whitman's voice becomes the dead returned to devour the reader. One of the reasons why this distortion is so easy is that Whitman has deliberately set out to destroy Bullough's antinomy of aesthetic distance.

Bullough says that the artist generally wants to minimize without destroying the aesthetic distance between the reader and the work. The reader is always to be aware that he is contemplating a work of art, thus keeping this experience distinct from practical experiences in life. The reader is to maintain a "disinterested" attitude toward the work, as if reading the work will have no effect on his well-being or his practice of life. Bullough reflects that it is just this disinterestedness that makes that which is ugly or frightening in life, such as a fog at sea, beautiful in aesthetic experience. Our interest in the experience shifts from what effect it may have on us to what it is like to perceive it, to patterns of sensation, feeling, and thought. On the other hand, the artist wants the reader to be as completely involved in the work as is appropriate to the work. Though the novelist typically wants readers to approach the novel in an aesthetic attitude of disinterestedness, the novelist also typically wants the reader to become deeply engaged with characters and to care about their situations, values, choices, and fates. This, then, is what I understand Bullough to mean by his antinomy of aesthetic distance.

Whitman deliberately upsets this balance. He depends upon the reader approaching his text in an aesthetic attitude that Whitman can exploit by dissolving. What is involved in this exploitation?

When I take up a literary work I do so with expectations based upon what sort of work I think I am approaching. This is the beginning of the creation of the implied reader. In effect I ask myself what sort of reader this work needs. Beginning with the first word, I construct that reader, bit by bit, using whatever instructions I find in the text. The implied reader, then, is a central structure in the establishment of aesthetic distance. By taking on a role provided by the text, I create a separate or bracketed self that, in effect, stands between my "actual" self and the work. Even though I must play the role to read the text as an art work, my involvement in this role is essentially voluntary in the sense that I have chosen to read and I may choose to stop.

In a typical reading situation there are several levels of distance between the real reader and the literary work. The real reader is engaged in a constructive activity that is interesting in itself, the concretization of the work. Part of that process of concretization involves the creation of the implied reader. The way in which that role is created may move the reader closer to the story. For example the speaker of the story may address the implied reader personally and directly, as Nathaniel Hawthorne often does. Or the speaker may address no particular person and be no particular person, as in Virginia Woolf's *To the Lighthouse*. These quite different techniques tend to minimize the distance between the reader and the work; the implied reader is made a direct observer of the work. What happens in the text may be moved further from the reader by various techniques, one of which is framing, as in Joseph Conrad's *Heart of Darkness*. Aesthetic distance is extended when a frame interposes one or more personae between the implied reader and the work, requiring that the real reader construct not only an implied reader but also various tellers of and listeners to the story as well. This is especially supportive of aesthetic distance when evaluating the attitudes of each teller and listener is necessary to the reading.

Whitman begins "Crossing Brooklyn Ferry" with the minimal requirements. There is a speaking voice, and once he turns from the setting to his listener, his listener is the implied reader. As the speaker moves through the poem, he asks the reader to construct the implied reader as a part of the speaker. Insofar as he succeeds, the speaker collapses one of the barriers that separate the real reader from the work. The speaker, in the context of *Leaves of Grass*, is Whitman's transcendent soul. The arguments he presents attempt to persuade the real reader that the role of implied reader as unified with Whitman is the one true role. He asserts, for example, that he has played the same role that all souls play, the role of ordinary life in the world, but that behind that role is the transcendent "actor or actress." The speaker of the poem is Whitman's soul identified with the implied reader; this composite is the actor or actress. As a result, Whitman transforms the dead physical Whitman and the real reader into roles rather than the actors. The transcendent composite of Whitman's soul and the implied reader becomes the more fundamental reality. In creating such a complex, transforming poem, Whitman shows an intuitive awareness of how his reader will approach his text and of how that approach might be exploited to produce his desired effect.

My main reason for looking at Whitman in the light of Bullough is to establish the idea that there may be a continuum of aesthetic distance. Whitman provides one pole of the continuum in his deliberate attempt to violate the antinomy of aesthetic distance. Were a tale of terror to violate this antinomy, what would happen? We have seen that this is a constant risk of the tale of terror and that some readers (and especially film viewers) find themselves unable to sustain aesthetic distance in relation to such tales. However, one can imagine that the ideal tale of terror *would* terrify its reader, which entails dissolving aesthetic distance, and still provide an aesthetic experience, which should entail restoring the lost distance. I argue, in fact, that three tales of terror accomplish this effect: *The Turn of the Screw*, "Ligeia," and "The Fall of the House of Usher." On a continuum moving back toward more conventional fictions are tales of terror that threaten but do not dissolve aesthetic distance and so provide noticeably different aesthetic pleasures, different clearly in degree, if not in kind.

At this point Todorov's work on the fantastic becomes especially useful, for he provides a descriptive poetics of the fantastic and four related genres that together include all tales of terror. Furthermore, his description of these genres suggests ways of placing tales of terror along the continuum from "typical" fictions toward those that make the destruction of aesthetic distance part of their effect. His names for the genres are the uncanny; the marvelous; the fantastic/marvelous; the fantastic/uncanny; and the pure fantastic.

Todorov's definitions of these genres depend on his definition of the fantastic:

> The fantastic requires the fulfillment of three conditions. First, the text must oblige the reader to consider the world of the characters as a world of living persons and to hesitate between a natural and a supernatural explanation of the events described. Second, this hesitation may also be experienced by a character; thus the reader's role is so to speak entrusted to a character, and at the same time the hesitation is represented, it be-

comes one of the themes of the work—in the case of naive reading, the actual reader identifies himself with the character. Third, the reader must adopt a certain attitude with regard to the text: he will reject allegorical as well as "poetic" interpretations. (33)

The fantastic, then, is an effect experienced by the implied reader and, perhaps, by a character in the text. The effect arises from the hesitation of the implied reader between two mutually exclusive ways of understanding the events presented in the text. I find the third condition somewhat puzzling because Todorov seems so insistent upon the reader adopting a particular attitude, as if the adoption of such an attitude were extratextual. Judging from his discussion of this point, I take him to mean that the text is so constructed as to prevent the implied reader from subordinating the experience of the fantastic to allegory or to poetic metaphor as a means of resolving the hesitation. In short, the hesitation can be resolved only if the text supplies some means of doing so, and in the true fantastic, as opposed to allegory and poetry, this resolution, if it comes at all, must be in favor either of the natural or of the supernatural interpretation of the ambiguous events.

Over Todorov's genres I will superimpose three groupings of tales of terror according to aesthetic effect: uncanny horror stories; horror thrillers; and terror fantasies. Uncanny horror stories offer the reader the opportunity to pretend to experience extreme mental and physical states by identifying with characters who undergo such experiences. Stories of this type form part, though not necessarily all, of Todorov's uncanny genre. Horror thrillers offer the reader the thrill of horror mainly by creating supernatural images, usually monsters, that in various ways and with careful qualifications embody or make concrete unconscious fears that a reader brings to the texts. Though these monsters have actions to perform in their plots, they also act directly upon the reader, threatening to bring repressed fears into consciousness. Undergoing and escaping these threats causes a thrill of horror in the reader. Todorov's genres of the marvelous, the fantastic/marvelous, and the fantastic/uncanny include most horror thrillers, though some pure fantastic tales of terror are also horror thrillers. Finally, I sort out a group of fantastic tales of terror that I call terror fantasies; I explore these in chapters 6-10.

Because I work from Todorov's genres, it will be helpful to look at his descriptions in a little more detail.

Todorov sees the uncanny as a vague genre: "events are related which may be readily accounted for by the laws of reason, but which are, in one way or another, incredible, extraordinary, shocking, singular, disturbing or unexpected, and which thereby provoke in the character and in the reader a reaction which works of the fantastic have made familiar" (46). Todorov is not very satisfying in his discussion of this genre. He points out that it tends to fade away into literature generally, where we often find events of the kinds listed above. He offers stories of Ambrose Bierce and Poe's "The Fall of the House of Usher" as examples of the genre in its pure form. Neither of these examples seems appropriate, for Bierce's tales often partake of the fantastic or the marvelous, and Poe's narrator in "Usher" is in the toils of hesitation throughout his narrative. I think the tale of terror this definition brings to mind is exemplified by "The Pit and the Pendulum." There is never a serious suggestion that the supernatural is operating in this story, yet the implied reader's identification with the persecuted narrator is such that the experience of horror is not unlike that of identifying with a Gothic heroine who is apparently the victim of supernatural terror. Similar tales come to mind, each offering a kind of horror without using the fantastic: "The Cask of Amontillado," "The Tell-Tale Heart," and "Hop-Frog" are examples by Poe. We are perhaps most familiar with this type in films in which a protagonist is hunted by powers that, though natural, seem almost supernatural in their power to find and destroy. One variation of this type is *Jaws*, which presents a natural monster whose depredations approach those of a vampire.

Uncanny tales of terror, in Todorov's definition, seem the least terrifying because their terrors are not aimed at the implied reader. If there is no appearance of the fantastic or even of the marvelous in a tale of terror, it is difficult to involve the implied reader in the terror itself, and so there is no threat to aesthetic distance. The central interest seems to be the vicarious experience of extreme emotions not readily available in ordinary life. I shall begin my examination of actual tales of terror by looking at a few works that seem to belong in this category. We will see that they become more problematic aesthetically as they move toward producing hesitation in the implied reader. There is a similar pattern in Todorov's genre of the marvelous.

According to Todorov, "in the case of the marvelous, supernatural elements provoke no particular reaction either in the characters or in the implicit reader" (54). Thus, the marvelous corresponds to Eric Rabkin's description of the fairy tale (38). In a world where the supernatural is accepted as normal, there will be no hesitation about how to interpret supernatural events, and the fantastic, in Todorov's sense, will not occur. In a marvelous tale of terror, the manifest unreality of such a world may provide the author with one major additional device for sustaining aesthetic distance; there is less danger of the reader directly connecting events in the fiction with events in the extratextual world. The safest terror can take place here. As the world of the fiction becomes more similar to the reader's world, that is, a world in which natural laws are perceived to operate without arbitrary interventions of the supernatural, then the terrors of the tale can seem more real. It is at this point that I will take up an example of a marvelous tale of terror, H. P. Lovecraft's *At the Mountains of Madness*. This tale contains little, if any, of the fantastic. Once alien beings are discovered in Antarctica, we move quickly to exploring the new laws of nature that they reveal. The implied reader is not made to hesitate significantly over whether they exist.

Once there is significant hesitation in the implied reader between the natural and the supernatural, we enter one of the three genres Todorov labels fantastic. The fantastic/marvelous is "the class of narratives that are presented as fantastic and that end with an acceptance of the supernatural" (Todorov 52). This genre seems to form a part of what Rabkin calls the fantastic, the genre in which the rules of being and of causation in a given text are violated (10). Indeed, all three of Todorov's fantastic genres fall within Rabkin's definition. Because Todorov centers on the fantastic as hesitation in the implied reader, he tends to be uninterested in a text such as *Alice in Wonderland*, which is paradigmatic for Rabkin. If there is hesitation between the supernatural interpretaton of *Alice* —there is a looking-glass world—and the natural explanation—Alice dreams—this is hardly foregrounded in the experience of the text. Rabkin's emphasis on the anti-expected provides a different perspective, which sheds more light on *Alice* and similar fantasies than on *Dracula* and its relatives. Todorov's distinctions grow out of greater attention to tales of terror and, therefore, continue to prove more useful to answering questions about the sorts of tales of terror and the pleasures they provide. In his discussion of the fantastic, however, Todorov does not mean to include only tales of terror in his genres.

*Dracula* is an example of a text in which the fantastic appears, eventually to be resolved in favor of a supernatural interpretation. In this novel, as in many fantastic/marvelous texts, the presentation of the fantastic is of relatively brief duration, necessary only to insert the supernatural being into a textual world that carefully duplicates the extratextual world of the author and his original readers. By this means, among others, the supernatural monster is brought close to the implied reader. Lovecraft's monsters, though they are also placed in a representation of the real world, seem more remote, not only because they are confined to Antarctica, but also because the implied reader does not struggle through hesitation to belief in them.

The fantastic/marvelous is probably the largest of the categories of the tale of terror. Most of the popular tales of terror that have lasted over the years and that are produced today involve the appearance of some sort of supernatural being in a realistic setting. Most use some degree of hesitation in the characters, and often in the implied reader, between belief and disbelief in the reality of the supernatural being. This most common kind of tale of terror is probably also the best understood by literary theorists.

Todorov says that in the fantastic/uncanny, "events that seem supernatural throughout a story receive a rational explanation at its end" (44). This group may be second largest. It includes the Gothic romance, sometimes called the supernatural explained. Ann Radcliffe is perhaps the best and the best known of the writers in this mode. As Todorov's description suggests, such stories, before their endings, are not much different from the fantastic/marvelous. For some major portion of the narrative, the implied reader is made to hesitate between the two ways of interpreting events. The difference comes at or near the end, when the laws of nature, as we commonly understand them, are either affirmed or denied. In many works of the fantastic/marvelous and the fantastic/uncanny, even this difference of ending is of little consequence to the aesthetic effect, since the reaffirmation of natural law, which is an assertion that supernatural events do not in fact take place, is virtually the same as the defeat of the supernatural monster. When the monster is removed from the scene, the world is returned to normality, just as when apparently supernatural events are shown to have natural causes.

On our continuum the fantastic/marvelous and the fantastic/uncanny may occupy much the same space and provide much the same aesthetic pleasure. However, we will see that the most frightening of these tales turn the screw just a little, entangling the implied reader in ambiguities and hesitations that extend beyond the end of the reading of the text. I will deal in detail with one text from this area, C. B. Brown's *Wieland*, which nicely illustrates the general patterns of the fantastic/uncanny and moves beyond the central definition by so entangling the implied reader.

In the genre of the pure fantastic, the implied reader's hesitation is sustained through the end of the text. Though this group is small, it will receive the most attention in the following chapters. I will look at six tales of terror that seem to fulfill the conditions of the pure fantastic. Three of these, E. T. A. Hoffman's "The Sandman," Guy de Maupassant's "The Horla," and Poe's "The Black Cat," involve the implied reader in irresolvable hesitation between natural and supernatural interpretations of events and, as a result, have become classics of literary terror. But three others have gone beyond being merely classics of literary terror: James's *The Turn of the Screw* and Poe's two tales, "Ligeia" and "The Fall of the House of Usher." They are undisputed classics of high literature as well and are also the centers of a long and extensive literary debate over how they ought to be read. This debate in itself is primary evidence of the power of these stories to terrify readers at a level that transcends the power of most, if not all, other tales of terror. These, then, are the most complex and aesthetically problematic of the works to be examined in the subsequent chapters. If, as I have suggested, they work in a way analogous to that of "Crossing Brooklyn Ferry" to dissolve the reader's aesthetic attitude during the reading process, then, according to what we generally understand about literary works, aesthetic pleasure would seem to be foreclosed. Furthermore, if it is terror that brings an end to the aesthetic attitude, that is, if the work becomes a threat to the reader, then it would seem a mistake to talk of any kind of pleasure at all issuing from these works. And yet . . . they are acknowledged as literary classics.

Generally, then, I will move from less to more terrifying examples of tales of terror. These examples will be grouped according to the categories I have derived from Todorov: uncanny, marvelous, fantastic/marvelous, fantastic/uncanny, and pure fantastic. However, I will analyze them differently by asking what sorts of pleasures they provide (figure 1).

In figure 1, I have divided literature, according to Kathryn Hume's suggestion, into two basic modes, mimesis and fantasy. On the branching lines I have located Todorov's genres, the uncanny tale of terror branching away from mimesis and toward fantasy, the marvelous tale of terror branching away from fantasy and toward mimesis. At the point where mimetic and fantasy modes meet, I have placed Todorov's fantastic. The fantastic/uncanny tale of terror is on the mimetic side because it ultimately claims natural causes for apparently supernatural events. The fantastic/marvelous tale of terror appears on the fantasy side because in such tales apparently supernatural events prove really to be supernatural. Finally, there is the line of the pure fantastic, where the fantastic hesitation Todorov describes persists through the whole story. The three polygons group together and show the relationships between the three distinctive kinds of pleasure that tales of terror offer. The uncanny tale of terror seems closest to other literary works in which terror may appear, such as tragedy, for the reader is here most concerned with the terrifying experiences of characters. As soon as the marvelous or the apparently marvelous appears in a tale of terror, there is the new possibility of the "thrill of terror," which results from the marvelous image, the monster that seems to speak directly to the reader while also enacting its part in the plot. Marvelous, fantastic/marvelous, and fantastic/uncanny tales all share this crucial characteristic; there-

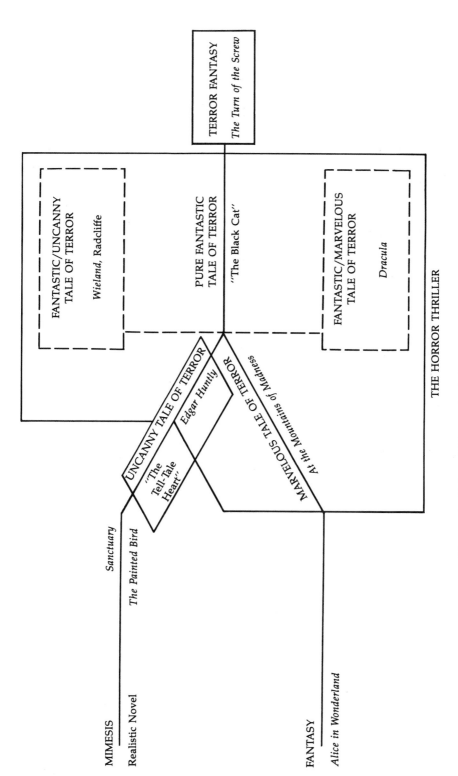

Figure 1. Tales of Terror in Relation to Literature.

fore these three genres are grouped together in a category called horror thrillers. The uncanny tales of terror and horror thrillers overlap, for the distinction between them becomes vague as uncanny tales manifest greater ambiguity concerning how they are to be read. This overlapping will be clearer when I discuss Charles Brockden Brown's *Edgar Huntly*. The pure fantastic tale of terror also divides between examples that offer the pleasure of a horror thriller and those that offer a unique pleasure. These latter are called terror fantasies. In both kinds of the pure fantastic a text creates and sustains the fantastic hesitation Todorov describes. Another sort of discomfort becomes a part of the reading experience as the reader is forced to deal with an intransigent ambiguity.

This is probably a good point for a word about what will be left out of this study. The tales I chose to discuss as examples have been determined by the breadth of my reading and the limits of my skills, interests, and tastes. Inevitably, the reader will think of better examples than I have chosen and counterexamples. That is good, for it would be a little frightening to be the first writer ever to have the last word on a literary problem. However, there is one class of works about which I will say virtually nothing: the apologue. David H. Richter defines the apologue as a work of fiction the final cause of which is "the inculcation of some doctrine or sentiment concerning the world external to the fiction" (9). Such fictions subordinate the aesthetic to the practical by seeking to directly influence attitudes of the real reader toward the real world. It is rather common for such works to use horror and terror. Voltaire's *Candide*, for example, contains many incidents that would be equally at home in Matthew Lewis's *The Monk*. The terrors suffered by the mutilated slave Candide meets in Surinam would make a sensational plot for a *Blackwood's* story, but Voltaire clearly directs the effects of this horror toward arousing indignation and toward further demonstrating the falsity of Candide's faith. The horrifying images in some twentieth-century apologues may be more disturbing, but always the horrifying image, event, or atmosphere is subordinated to the communication of ideas or feelings about the world. Though *The Castle*, *The Trial*, *Catch-22*, *The Crying of Lot 49*, and *The Lime Twig* all produce horror and, perhaps, even terror in their readers, that terror is never for its own sake, not even when the purpose of the text, as in the case of Kafka, may be to demonstrate that our extratextual world is terrifying. If Kafka, in *The Castle*, makes us feel the possibly horrifying idea that the cosmos refuses to recognize us, we feel this idea about our world, not about the work. It is not the work, but the world that becomes terrifying as a result of reading. Works that seem clearly to be apologues are so different in purpose from what we usually think of as tales of terror as to present vastly different problems of explanation from those which are the central concern of this book.

Finally, I should like to say a little more about what I mean by aesthetic pleasure. I implied in the first part of this chapter that the pleasure of experiencing a literary work consists of entering into an aesthetic attitude toward a text, working through the text to construct a concretion of that text, and completing the task. The pleasure is complete when the task is complete. Such an activity is a kind of play in which our mental faculties are engaged for the sake of using them.

Behind my concept of aesthetic pleasure then is a fairly simple and, I hope, a commonsense assumption that we humans take particular pleasure in doing those things that make us particularly human, such as using our hands, using language, constructing meaningful patterns, and constructing our identities as self-aware beings. While reading literature does not usually require much creative use of our hands, it certainly allows for and stimulates the use of all the other capabilities on this list. Reading literature is play rather than work because we intend to pretend, to use our more or less uniquely human faculties in security, fenced off from the risks involved in taking practical actions in the world.

All literature that we value and keep performs these functions and so offers aesthetic pleasure, the pleasure of using our uniquely human mental faculties without pursuing a practical goal in the world. By asking about the pleasures of terror, I am selecting for study an area of literature that seems problematic because terror is not pleasant in reality. We know that when terror happens to a character in a tragedy, we usually feel sympathy and pity, but not fear for ourselves. But some works try to terrify their readers. The pleasures offered by such works must be different. We expect such works to offer aesthetic pleasure in the general sense just described, but we expect that pleasure to have unique characteristics, as do the pleasures of tragedy and comedy. Furthermore, those unique characteristics should be related directly to the unique effect that tales of terror tend to seek, that of frightening their readers. What are the delights of terror?

## CHAPTER TWO

# Horror in Literature and the Literature of Horror

## I

THIS living hand, now warm and capable
Of earnest grasping, would, if it were cold
And in the icy silence of the tomb,
So haunt thy days and chill thy dreaming nights
That thou wouldst wish thine own heart dry of blood
So in my veins red life might stream again,
And thou be conscience-calm'd—see here it is—
I hold it towards you.

—John Keats, Untitled

This poem illustrates nicely a way in which the effect of horror may be subordinated to the larger overall effect of a work of literature. Read naively as a direct message from poet to reader, it is chilling. I am asked to imagine the poet's hand held out to me as dead and then to touch it, to imagine the touch of a stranger's corpse. But, of course, this is not what a more careful reading of the poem reveals as its probable intention. A more careful reading creates an implied speaker and an implied listener. The speaker addresses an apparently uncooperative beloved with a sort of last chance. "You spurn me now, but when I am dead, your conscience will haunt you, and you will give all your blood to bring me again to life." By creating these personae between real reader and author's text, the real reader constructs an implied reader. The real reader becomes the proper interpreter of the poem and plays the role of overhearer of a somewhat unconventional moment between lovers, imagining the possible settings and circumstances of this speech. As this concretion becomes complete, the potential mild terror of the possible naive reading becomes a rhetorical ploy of which the implied listener is the object. Not only is the experience deflected from both the real and implied reader, but it is made merely a part of a concretion rather than the effect of the whole, as it would have been in a naive reading.

In this book I distinguish between terror and horror in the following way. Terror is the fear that harm will come to oneself. Horror is the emotion one feels in anticipating and witnessing harm coming to others for whom one cares. Thus, a naive reading of Keats's poem might arouse some degree of terror in the reader, while the more appropriate reading could arouse a mild degree of horror on behalf of both speaker and listener. This example and this distinction should make clear that much of what we experience as horror in literature is only distantly related to what we experience in tales of terror proper. We tend to think of a work as a tale of terror when horror and terror dominate it. Horror (in my definition) and pity are, after all, primary emotional responses to classical tragedy. We easily recall examples of moments of terror for certain characters and moments of horror and pity in spectators. Oedipus cries out upon recognizing himself:

> O Light, may I look upon you for the last time!
> I, Oedipus,
> Oedipus, damned in his birth, in his marriage damned,
> Damned in the blood he shed with his own hand!

Mad Othello kisses the sleeping Desdemona and says:

> One more, one more!
> Be thus when thou art dead, and I will kill thee,
> And love thee after. One more and that's the last!
> So sweet was ne'er so fatal. I must weep,
> But they are cruel tears. This sorrow's heavenly;
> It strikes where it doth love.

In more modern tragic works we find similar moments of horror. Captain Ahab cries, "From hell's heart I stab at thee . . . let me tow to pieces, while still chasing thee, though tied to thee, thou damned whale! *Thus* I give up the spear!" In a work much closer to the tale of terror, Katherine Anne Porter's "Noon Wine," Mr. Thompson writes the unbearable truth in his suicide note: "It was Mr. Homer T. Hatch who came to do wrong to a harmless man. He caused all this trouble and he deserved to die but I am sorry it was me who had to kill him." The examples are numerous and various, but in every case of this kind, terror is exclusively the experience of characters in the work and horror is part of a larger response of pity for these characters and/or their victims.

When terror and horror are subordinate effects contributing to a more inclusive effect of a concretion, we are rather distant from the tale of terror. Though the moments I have recalled are as chilling as anything in literature, they are not by any means the defining moments of their works. These works were not made to leave us with the unmitigated or unqualified experiences of those moments. The terrors of these works never seriously threaten to dissolve aesthetic distance for a competent reader. We will see that uncanny tales of terror are not much different from these works in which horror and terror form subordinate parts. To illustrate this, let us look with some care at several works that might be placed along a continuum from works in which horror and terror are major but still not dominant parts to those in which such effects do dominate but that do not yet make use of the fantastic. We will begin with two modern works: William Faulkner's *Sanctuary* (1931) and Jerzy Kosinski's *The Painted Bird* (1965).

# II

In *Sanctuary*, Faulkner directly attacks the implied reader, forcing the real reader to endure psychological pain to fill the role of implied reader and to enter into an aesthetic experience of the novel. He represents horrible events, creates and violates conventional expectations, manipulates point of view, orders the representation of events and of the world in a disorienting way, and presents a virtually constant stream of powerfully disturbing images. Faulkner terrorizes the implied reader with the purpose of creating a reading experience analogous to the main characters' experiences of their world. The discomfort, even pain, of playing the role of implied reader is made to be like the pain of living in the fictional world of Temple Drake and Popeye. This technique is necessary because these characters are so deficient either in moral qualities or in perception as to be beyond sympathy and understanding for a reader who does not fully appreciate the world that produces them and their strategies of living.

In the major elements of the story and in its use of conventions, *Sanctuary* intends to shock. The central events include the corncob sodomy of a teenage girl, teenage nymphomania, mob sodomy, and immolation. These and other horrors are presented in ways calculated to maximize shock: the delayed revelation of the corncob and of the Popeye-Temple-Red relationship, the joker's revelation of how Lee Goodwin died, and Popeye's death by the hand of another joker. These events take place in an atmosphere of despair; few characters are interested in preventing the horrors, and no one effectively opposes them. Conventions of humor are violated, promising relief only to lead the reader back to the blackness that dominates color in the novel: the boys at the Negro brothel, Red spilling out of his coffin, Uncle Bud vomiting, and Popeye swinging on a punch line. Gothic conventions are also violated, as Elizabeth Kerr has shown (104-6). The reader is promised a romance that will embody an idealized mythic action, such as the rescue of a fair maiden. The novel violates this expectation and reveals an incomprehensible world where villainy may be accidental and heroism in any conventional sense impossible.

Faulkner further disorients the implied reader by manipulating point of view and using ambiguous tableaux, thus stressing a disturbing disorder in ordinary events and objects. Both Horace and the implied reader are presented at the novel's opening with moments of apparent significance that obscure point of view, do not have clear causal or thematic connection, and eschew the examination of motive. Like Benbow, the reader is forced to fill in these gaps or accept these events and actions as pointless. At the center of this problem is Popeye, whose appearance and behavior seem outside rationality. Why is he wearing city clothes with the trousers rolled and muddy? If his watch is loose in his pocket, what is at the end of his platinum watch chain? Why does a rich man carry a dollar pocket watch? And why does he squat and stare at Horace for two hours? Faulkner teases with these and other details, drawing the implied reader into a world that will not yield to his desire to understand it. This world is full of mystery. Characters materialize in scenes rather than enter them. The animate often appears inanimate and vice versa. Faulkner surprises and shocks the reader with abrupt transitions, unexpected transformations, disorienting descriptions, and unexplained gestures.

Perhaps the most pervasively disturbing technique Faulkner uses is to present the implied reader with a constant heavy barrage of repulsive, shocking, and violent images of entrapment, meaningless motion, silent screams, the world dying like beached fish, death in life, and sudden death. One of the most elaborate and pervasive of these groups of images is that of sudden death. It is presented most fully in describing the crime of a minor character who is in jail with Lee Goodwin, the man later falsely accused of raping Temple Drake. The murderer is a Negro "who had killed his wife; slashed her throat with a razor so that, her whole head tossing further and further backward from the bloody regurgitation of her bubbling throat, she ran out of the cabin door and for six or seven steps up the quiet moonlit lane" (110). Here is clearly a gratuitous assault on reader sensibility, for this detail is unnecessary except as part of a project to cause the implied reader pain. This image is repeated in multiple ways almost page by page in the novel, connecting most of the other groups of such images. There are images of decapitation, stabbing, and threats with knives on at least a dozen different pages in this novel of about 300 pages. Images of the regurgitation of blood including bleeding wounds appear on seventeen different occasions. Images of drinking blood and eating human flesh appear six times. Repulsive spitting, phlegm, and drooling appear at least eight times. Vomiting and the impulse to vomit appear at least eleven times. Such a rough count only suggests the pervasiveness of these images. Their intensity may be suggested by the places where they tend to center. When Temple is raped, she repeats a version of the murder, screaming silently, "voiding the words like hot silent bubbles into the bright silence" (99). This set of images is placed in a context of suggestion by Horace's first brush with Popeye: "He smells black, Benbow thought; he smells like that black stuff that ran out of Bovary's mouth and down upon her bridal veil when they raised her head" (7).

It is difficult to exaggerate the frequency of such images and their echoes in *Sanctuary*. The reader can hardly turn a page without encountering an image of violence, filth, threat of pain, or death. To play the reader-role offered by this novel is to feel moment by moment something of the terror its characters experience.

Why does Faulkner want the reader to share this experience so fully? A glance at two of the main characters, Temple and Popeye, makes this fairly clear. By most any conventional standard of judgment, they are despicable. The sexually impotent Popeye rapes Temple with a corncob, then takes her to Memphis where he sets her up in a brothel and observes her sexual relations with Red, a local bouncer. Temple enjoys this, except that she resents the restraint on her freedom. It may be hard to conceive why Faulkner would want his readers to care about such characters, especially when the rather noble Ruby Lamar and the well-meaning Horace Benbow are so clearly good, to some degree, according to conventional standards of judgment. The answer appears to be that Faulkner really does not wish to provide a Gothic experience in which more or less purely evil monsters are temporarily loosed in the world, as Dracula is in Stoker's novel. Temple and Popeye are neither supernatural nor symbolic. Rather, they are the quintessential products of their world. They are versions of what we would all be if the forces operating in this fictional world could completely replace traditional moral ideals. According to Lewis Simpson, these two are products of a "historicist" view of history in which events are a mere succession without intrinsic or transcendent meaning (132). Faulkner seems to want the reader to understand this connection, to see that

Temple and Popeye are human beings like us, with desires like ours, but without souls, without any commitments to values or any understanding of how to make such commitments. They are arrested in loveless childhoods.

Faulkner uses other means to minimize the natural distance between the reader and such morally empty characters. He carefully sets Temple up as a more or less innocent victim before her rape. He prepares for her shocking transformation after the rape both by showing her potential for such transformation and by making the experience of the implied reader parallel with her experience of terror at the Frenchman's before the rape. Therefore, when the reader sees the transformation, he is in the best position to see her, even then, as a victim. Faulkner uses the last chapter to "renovate" Popeye, a strategy that has offended critics who believe Popeye is a representation of "pure evil." Faulkner has prepared for this, however, by renovating Temple in advance, so to speak, and by carefully setting up a series of images associating Popeye with Temple, as a childlike victim of seemingly impersonal forces. The last chapter makes clear that Popeye, in his attraction to women like Reba, Ruby, his mother, and Temple, has been pursuing meaning. When other men find a woman valuable, Popeye takes her if he can. His childhood experiments with particularly vital live animals further suggest that he is seeking vitality—in *Requiem for a Nun* his last name is given as Vitelli. Whatever it is that makes other people want to live, he wants. However, he is never able to find the secret of "using" those "objects" when he gets them, hence his despairing acceptance of death in the novel's last chapter. Popeye emerges as a man in search of meaning at the most minimal level, but deprived of the equipment to succeed at any level. Faulkner wants the reader to pity these characters; he improves his chance of succeeding by terrorizing the implied reader.

In *Sanctuary*, the process of creating the implied reader is at least mildly terrifying, for it involves subjection to disorientation, shock, and constant repetition of the ugly, repulsive, violent, and murderous. However, undergoing this experience helps to sensitize the implied reader to the terrifying quality of everyday existence for the main characters. Thus, terror becomes a primary means by which Faulkner creates a meaningful fictional work about characters who are extreme victims of a culture that has lost faith in any spiritual reality. Terrorizing the implied reader becomes a means of reaching across the distance between the reader and unsympathetic main characters, to draw them together.

In *The Painted Bird*, Kosinski uses terror in a similar way to establish a high degree of identification between the implied reader and the child protagonist. This identification helps to sustain empathy through the last chapters, when the child becomes monstrous, and to give great significance to his final act of recovering his lost voice.

Kosinski treats his boy narrator somewhat in the way Faulkner treats Temple Drake, except that the boy is unequivocally innocent when he is abandoned in a world of terror and the comparative lawlessness of Nazi-occupied territory. Even though the boy is narrating his own story from a fairly distant prospect, even though a key element of this retrospective view is a gift for metaphor that calls attention to itself by the incongruities it suggests, and even though the narrative develops with the intensity and pace of a fairy tale that stretches credibility, still the implied reader is required to hover spellbound over the events of the narrative. Kosinski's aim is to so completely erase distance between the implied reader and the boy as actor that they will become almost indistinguishable. This purpose is revealed in the visionary quality of the earliest horrors: the deaths of the pigeon, the squirrel, Marta, Ludmilla, and the carpenter; the sufferings of the ploughboy, the painted birds, Lehk, and the lost horse. These events fall upon the boy's soul, and there is little indication of how they affect him. This is the primary gap or blank that the reader is required to fill, for the reader must construct the impressions these events make and, to do so, must pour some version of himself into the "empty vessel" of the boy's personality.

The construction of the boy's inner self is the central function of the implied reader in the first one-third of the novel. This construction does not proceed without qualificatons, but these are few by comparison with earlier novels of similar form, such as *Great Expectations*. These qualifications tend to come from what little one is able to perceive about the speaking voice. The boy learns the tricks of survival. He discovers and tests some of his special powers as a "Gypsy Jew bastard" among highly superstitious "Aryan" people. He learns to fear death and to value his vision. But the core of his experience is his wonder at the world he sees, conveyed in the metaphors he constructs from his mature perspective and in the clarity of his memory. Of Marta's burning he recalls, "The flames sparkled like a Christmas tree, and burst into a high blaze, forming a peaked hat of fire on Marta's head" (9). When the rats devour the carpenter, the boy remembers them fighting for pieces of the body, "panting, twitching their tails, their teeth gleaming under half-opened snouts, their eyes reflecting the daylight as if they were the beads of a rosary" (55).

The middle third of the novel is inaugurated with the boy's experiencing empathy, which leads him to understand and desire justice, to feel responsibility, and finally to take actions to secure justice for himself. His attempt (and failure) to save the injured horse he finds shows him for the first time identifying with the sufferings of another, filling the dumb blank of the horse's consciousness with his own awareness of pain. The boy now becomes what the implied reader has already become in the first seven chapters. Given the virtual identity of mind of the boy with that of the implied reader, the boy's development in the middle of the book, as he questions various orders and adopts and abandons various stances, proceeds largely in parallel with the implied reader's development. The implied reader sees the world through the boy's eyes with little irony, and this identification continues, even though there is at least one cause of irony that is perpetually present.

As a motif, the painted bird pervades the book. Virtually every being that distinguishes itself in any way from its kind or within its customary environment is destroyed in chapters 1-14. The boy is distinguished in two ways, by his physical features and by the peculiar growth of his imagination. The reader is constantly reminded in these chapters that the boy's attempts to join his kind are doomed, yet this irony does not significantly reduce the identification between implied reader and character. Opposite to this irony is the continued imaginative sympathy of those few people who protect and preserve him despite their prejudices. It is finally imagination that "saves" the boy. His imagination leads him, in the last chapter, to see that it is another like himself at the other end of the telephone wire. Realizing that another person like himself wishes to speak to him, he makes the effort of speech and regains his lost voice. This effort can be seen as leading directly to his telling his story and, thereby, presenting us with this novel. The painted bird may find his way back into the flock by means of imagination that leads to sympathy and to speech.

The implied reader's close identification with the character who is terrorized leads to a deep sympathetic involvement in his struggles to master his world, even with the ethic of revenge that dominates the boy's thoughts after the end of the war and his return to urban life. The reader feels the degree to which the boy has learned to live in a world different from the daylight world of his city. His night and silent self belongs to his life as an outcast, a life in which to identify with others is to offer oneself for sacrifice and in which silence is a means of complete self-containment. In such a world justice means the cancellation of debts without thought of reconciliation. Working against this development in the boy and in the implied reader is the imagination born out of the boy's terror.

The effect of terror upon imagination in this novel is made clear quite early. When the boy is staying with Olga, he develops a fever, which may be prelude to an attack of the plague decimating the village. Her treatment includes burying him up to his neck in the ground overnight. In the morning, he is attacked by a flock of ravens that pluck out his hair. His final mental response to them is: "I gave up. I was myself now a bird. I was trying to free my chilled wings from the earth. Stretching my limbs, I joined the flock of ravens. Borne abruptly up in a gust of fresh, reviving wind, I soared straight into a ray of sunshine that lay taut on the horizon like a drawn bowstring and my joyous cawing was mimicked by my winged companions" (22).

Granted, there is an ominousness to this identification with his destroyers, which reaches a climax in his desire to be the beautiful, fair SS officer whom he encounters later, but finally, empathy and communication prove of greater value to him than power and vengeance. In a world filled with April sunshine, at the end of his story, he again emerges from unconsciousness at the call of another, "perhaps a man like myself," and begins to speak the events of his life (213). Terror forces the boy to leap out of himself into the other. From these leaps he develops the capacity for sympathy. Terror isolates him in muteness and an ethic of revenge, but new calls to his primary imagination cause him to leap out of himself again and to risk speech. He reopens his dialogue with his kind, a dialogue that, as the last one-third of the novel has shown, need not be doomed. Finally, the boy adopts a perspective in which the self he has achieved becomes visible to himself and he is liberated from that self. Although that new perspective is not the direct result of terror, his particular power to adopt that perspective has been enhanced by his own experience of terror. The implied reader has been so close to the boy in the account of his terrors that the reader experiences with great immediacy the boy's entrapment in his outcast's role and the liberation in the release of his voice.

The sensational terror of *The Painted Bird* is one important means by which Kosinski maximizes identification of the implied reader and the developing boy. Likewise, Faulkner uses sensational terror in *Sanctuary* to narrow the gap between his characters and the implied reader. Though horror is a major effect, and even though the terror of the characters is conveyed rather directly to the implied reader, these two novels are not examples of the tale of terror. Though criticism has not ignored relationships between these works and the traditions of tales of terror and though critics have been troubled about the functions of horror and terror in them, no scholar has argued that these works belong to the same genre as "The Pit and the Pendulum" and "The Tell-Tale Heart." It is apparent to all who read with care that the final purpose of these novels is not to horrify or terrify their readers. Though some critics have argued that terror threatens the aesthetic attitude of the reader, it seems clear that most readers of these texts manage to maintain their aesthetic relation to them. Horror and terror are used as prods to sympathy and understanding. Still, even in "The Pit and the Pendulum" and to a large degree in "The Tell-Tale Heart" terror and horror are so fully contained within the tale that aesthetic distance remains unaffected. If this is true, then the pleasure of reading such works is not greatly different from that of reading more conventional fiction.

# III

The uncanny tale of terror at its simplest is exemplified by the sensation stories that appeared in *Blackwood's Edinburgh Magazine,* such as William Maginn's "The Man in the Bell" (1821) and William Mudford's "The Iron Shroud" (1830). Both of these stories are thought to have influenced Poe, the latter providing ideas for "The Pit and the Pendulum." Poe also parodies such tales several times, notably in "The Premature Burial." These stories place an individual in a horrible situation and then detail his sensations. In "The Iron Shroud," a man is condemned to an ingeniously designed dungeon that compresses, apparently from four sides, over seven days, until he is crushed and canned in his bed. The prisoner experiences varieties of anguish, from despair and loneliness at being placed forever in solitary confinement, through the terror of discovering the nature of his cell, to the experience of being crushed. Mudford uses an almost clinical third-person narration, which opens considerable psychological distance between the reader and the protagonist. This story creates an implied reader who is highly sympathetic to the unfortunate young man's sufferings. Vivenzio is presented as a hero, "the noble and generous, the fearless in battle, and the pride of Naples in her sunny hours of peace" (*Romantic Gothic Tales* 186). He becomes the innocent victim of a tyrant, and the reader is horrified by his fate. One reason for calling this a sensation story is the degree to which it presents the "sensations" of the protagonist. What is it like to realize that one is abandoned and helpless, that one is in a machine that will slowly crush him, and to feel the walls closing in? Insofar as the story conveys these impressions and successfully encourages the reader to imagine his feelings in this situation, it provides a vicarious experience of terror. This experience can be made more intense if the psychological distance between reader and protagonist is reduced, as is the case with "The Man in the Bell."

The structure of "The Man in the Bell" gives greatest play to a brief experience of terror. The narrator explains that by accident one Sunday he found himself in a tiny belfry when the noon ringing began. As a result, he was confined for about a half hour directly under the giant bell, within inches of it, on a weak lath floor. The bulk of the tale describes his entrapment: twenty minutes of ringing, followed by a five-minute silence and a chance to escape that he is unable to use, and then a final five minutes of ringing. He moves from fear of falling through the flimsy floor to fear of being struck by the bell, to a vibration between fear of these two opposing eventualities. He appreciates the irony that he need only be still to be safe, but the noise and the terror make holding still difficult. The noise is so great that it benumbs his mind and he begins to hallucinate. The bell takes the forms of various monsters that may tear and devour him. The motion of the air convinces him he is in a sea storm. Supernatural beings appear to him, including, finally, the devil who offers salvation in return for worship. When he screams for help, he is unheard, but his words are uncannily echoed back to him by the bell. His greatest fear becomes that he will lose control of himself and move into the bell's path. This story, more fully than "The Iron Shroud," details the sensations of the sufferer and, thereby, more fully stimulates the reader's imagination of what it must be like to be in this situation. Though the tale is completely free of supernatural occurrences, it gains some of the advantages of using such occurrences in the narrator's hallucinations. Natural terror evokes the experience of the supernatural. Indeed, it could be unclear whether the devil really does appear to tempt him, but the narrator seems quite sure that this was another hallucination. Though this tale may be more effective than "The Iron Shroud" in providing an opportunity to "play at" being in danger, the effect of both seems much the same.

"The Iron Shroud" is like *Sanctuary* and *The Painted Bird* in that, for the most part, terror is the experience of the protagonist. The implied reader is instructed to feel horror at the protagonist's sufferings. However, insofar as the tale offers the reader an opportunity to construct an implied reader imaginatively sharing the protagonist's situation, "The Iron Shroud" moves away from tragedy toward terror, where the reader may experience fear for its own sake. "The Man in the Bell" moves further toward terror by removing the causes of horror. There is little horror for the reader to experience because the reassuring voice of the narrator is always present, reminding the reader that the terrifying experience was only an aberration. The narrator, speaking fifty years after the event, is virtually free of harm from his adventure. Quite understandably, he sometimes finds the sound of bells disturbing, but on the whole, he is a stable and secure elderly raconteur. Assured as we are of the safety of the teller, virtually all of our imaginative energy is free to place ourselves with him in his terrific adventure, to concentrate on its details and to fill them in as we are inclined.

The special pleasure offered by this sort of tale seems clear and simple. We are invited to play at being in danger. The danger is essentially physical, though we can see that physical dangers lead to psychological fears that may, in turn, increase the physical danger. Indeed, for the reader who never has experienced and most likely never will experience just these situations, the psychological fear is of more importance than the physical danger. Though most people will never be trapped in a belfry or in a contracting prison cell, many will find themselves in analogous situations: traffic accidents, muggings, fires, and diseases. These stories, then, seem related to many kinds of human play in which we practice for encountering the various difficulties and dangers of human life. One of the useful functions of literature is to provide this kind of play, though I do not believe it is the primary reason for valuing literature. Indeed, the main special pleasure of the sensational tale of terror seems to be safely experiencing feelings unavailable in the normal course of events. We seek out such stories primarily to exercise our uniquely human psychological equipment, to explore, insofar as we safely can, the psychological extremes that arise from physical danger.

Our pleasure in such experiences might come, then, from at least three different sources. First, we may be aware of the survival value of practicing for the terrifying; hence, we take pleasure in doing what is good for us. Second, as humans, we are especially endowed with the ability to self-consciously explore our mental states; hence, we enjoy the self-examination that these tales make possible. Finally, we take pleasure in the safe, distanced, experience of extreme emotions. This last is the specific aesthetic pleasure these tales offer. Each of the other kinds of pleasure may be seen to contribute directly to this aesthetic pleasure. Both of these tales place terror and horror within highly controlled aesthetic wholes. There is little danger that a real reader will encounter in such a tale any terror so formidable as to dissolve aesthetic experience. We enter such tales in a spirit of aesthetic play and the tales do nothing to violate that spirit. Like most fictions, then, they offer themselves to us for concretization, and they make the process easy. As a result, the containment of any terrors they may present is comparatively easy. This containment is easier, certainly, than in *Sanctuary*, where the terror of the fictional world, though it belongs to that world, persists after the text ends, in part, because the fictional world claims to be a representation of our world. Sensational tales of terror are unique in that within their aesthetically closed forms, they encourage the entertainment of catastrophe. The reader can pretend to be terrified without the risk of a really terrifying experience. The play of art makes a dangerous part of the world available to imagination.

The uncanny tale of terror seems to become more effectively horrifying as it moves toward greater psychological complexity and as ambiguity is introduced at various levels of concretization. For example, Poe's "The Pit and the Pendulum" partakes of the effects of the sensation stories but introduces greater psychological complexity in the central character and confronts the implied reader with ambiguity in interpreting the events.

The first-person narrator of "The Pit and the Pendulum" tells of his condemnation to death by some inquisition, of the diabolical modes by which he is threatened with various horrible deaths, and of his last minute escape from the final threat. He gives detailed, clinical descriptions of his circumstances and his situation. However, these are complicated by a delirium that distorts his perception and makes his experience dreamlike and nightmarish. In these features, the story is not greatly different from a sensation story, nor is it different in the particular terrors the narrator experiences. Upon awakening in his utterly dark cell, he fears he has been buried alive. His exploration of the cell proves him mistaken, but reveals that the darkness is a trap, which is to lead him to fall into the pit in the center of his cell. His senses are very limited in the darkness and, as a result, he is unable to form an accurate picture of his cell. This disorientation is remedied when he accidentally escapes the pit and so is subjected to the pendulum. Having avoided the pit by luck, he avoids the pendulum by pluck, more or less. Though in fear and despair he finds it difficult to reason, he is eventually able to do so when the threat of death is most immediate. He then works out how he is bound and how he may use the numerous rats in his cell to sever the bonds. For this to work, he must endure the sensations of rats, which have been waiting to eat him, crawling on his body. Finally, the unavoidable folding of heated iron walls forces him toward the pit that, in the course of his tortures, he has learned to dread above all the forms of death he has encountered. From this death, he is rescued neither by luck nor by pluck but by a fortuitous external force, a political revolution.

The psychological complexity of the narrator encourages a closer identification with him than with the main characters of the other two sensation stories. Because he is so actively engaged in trying to keep control of his faculties and to deal with his situation, he draws the reader more fully into participation in his situation. He is more than a convenient admission into extreme experience. Furthermore, the narrator has a motive for telling his story, which goes beyond his qualifications as one who has experienced something extraordinary, for he now has evidence of the immortality of his consciousness. Early in the story, he speculates about two stages of awakening, "first that of the sense of mental or spiritual; secondly, that of the sense of physical existence." He reflects that if one could carry the memory of that first sense through the second stage of awakening, he might gain knowledge in this life of "the gulf beyond" (51). The narrator's suffering, which has pushed him to the limits of mental and physical endurance, has given him an especially rich awareness of the boundary between normal consciousness and what he calls madness, "the madness of a memory which busies itself among forbidden things" (51). The pit may be a literal representation of the gulf he wishes to know; by leading to his death, the pit would provide the knowledge he seeks, but not in the form he seeks it, for he prefers clearly to have it both ways, to remain in this world while obtaining knowledge of the other world. By putting his adventure into words, he captures, insofar as he can, what he values in his harrowing experience. That this suffering has benefited him makes it no less terrifying for him or horrifying for the reader. In fact, the story seems more horrifying than the sensation stories at least in part because the narrator is more complex. Terror is more significant because it happens to a more developed character about whom we care.

Another element that contributes to the greater effectiveness of horror in this tale is the first-person narration, which makes the narrator's perceptions ambiguous. Poe creates a slight ambiguity, which unsettles the reader, making the implied reader more difficult to constitute. Once the narrator sinks into nightmare, near the opening of the story, it is never perfectly clear that he awakens. He records the experiences of awakening and swooning, but the events on both sides of this barrier, insofar as they are shown, seem adequately described as "the madness of a memory which busies itself among forbidden things." Though it is possible to make much—or even too much—of this ambiguity, it is a relatively minor feature of the tale. The narrator himself expresses little serious doubt about distinguishing between waking and sleeping. Resolving the issue one way or the other has little influence on the impact of the story. However, even such a slight uncertainty makes closure more difficult and, therefore, threatens to entangle the implied reader in the tale.

Such ambiguity is more apparent and perhaps more productive of horror in "The Tell-Tale Heart." The first-person narrator here, in an attempted demonstration that he is not mad, proves unequivocally that he is. This tale, like sensation stories, details horrors, the stalking, smothering, and dismembering of a victim. However, the point of view is the murderer's. The troubling ambiguity arises most clearly in the middle of the tale, when the narrator reports the groan of his victim as precisely like his own midnight groans. The narrator so fully identifies with his victim that he may be his own victim. The question, which arises here and which is never settled, is whether the narrator is a mad killer or only a mad talker. Did he murder a man, whom he took to be a representation of a part of himself, or did he, in his mind, murder that part of himself? This uncertainty is more troubling than that of "The Pit and the Pendulum" because, though resolving it would not greatly change the meaning of the story, it does seem to affect the reader's view of the narrator. But since the text offers nothing but a madman's testimony, the question cannot be answered.

One effect of a persistent ambiguity about the meaning of a text is a disturbing frustration of closure. If concretization is a fundamental process of the aesthetic experience, we cannot feel that a work is whole and the experience complete until a satisfying closure is provided. "The Tell-Tale Heart" is not a fragment, nor is closure really prevented. Closure is effected in a number of conventional ways: the confession is complete, its irony is fully realized, and the incident, from planning the crime through its detection, is whole. Poe has, however, introduced a problem that throws into question the status of this whole: is it a confession or is it revealing raving? This disturbs but does not prevent closure; it may even contribute to the tale by unnerving the reader. It is disturbing to discover that, like the narrator, we are unable clearly to distinguish between what is real and what is imagined. However, we are superior to the narrator, for we see how he is entangled in this problem as he does not. The implied reader shares the narrator's problem of perception but, from the vantage point of sanity, keeps that problem in perspective and does not allow the distinction between mental and physical events to collapse. By constructing such an implied reader, the real reader lets the ambiguity be a part of the story and so completes closure.

In each of these short stories, terror is contained within the story. Only when there is troubling ambiguity about how to interpret the events does any kind of discomfort threaten the implied reader. Indeed, tales of this kind are relatively uninterested in really horrifying readers. Rather, they seem to encourage the vicarious experience or the contemplation of the extreme mental states that result from suffering or madness. Readers are more likely to feel horror in uncanny tales of terror when characters and situations are more fully developed.

In William Godwin's *Things as They Are; or, The Adventures of Caleb Williams* (1794), for example, the horror of Caleb's sufferings is increased by his fuller development as character and narrator as well as by the fuller development of his nemesis, Falkland. This is a curiously flawed novel, which begins as an apologue to demonstrate the need for reforms in certain aspects of English law, but which, after the first volume, becomes a kind of Gothic novel of persecution that occasionally remembers its original intention. The fuller development of the two main characters allows for the creation of a suggestive psychological relationship between the two. Caleb seems impelled by a power he calls curiosity to probe Falkland until he discovers his secret guilt. Once he has discovered that guilt, Caleb continues to function as the conscience Falkland wishes to silence. There is an external drama of ambiguous persecution in which Falkland tries to insure Caleb's silence without taking his life, which seems to symbolize an internal drama in which Falkland tries to evade without eliminating the guilt resulting from his crimes. The multiple mirrorings of Caleb's situation, of Falkland's situation, and of their peculiar relationship, though Godwin may have intended them as persuasive examples of the pervasiveness of the iniquities he wishes to prevent, seem actually to produce a feeling of the uncanny (in Freud's sense). They tend to point at one possible underlying cause of a tyrant's seemingly malignant persecution of an unfortunate victim. Other authors have seen this possibility, which Godwin seems only to intuit here. For example, his daughter realizes it fully in *Frankenstein,* a "marvelous" tale of terror. There Victor clearly creates a monster that, to his mind, represents a part of himself from which he would like to escape; by refusing to own that part of himself, he invites and even "enjoys" persecution from his monster. Other similar examples appear in Simon Legree's persecution of Uncle Tom and Claggart's of Billy Budd.

As characters become more fully developed in longer fictions and so more complex, the terrors they experience may begin to point toward the unconscious. Then horrors become charged with vague and disturbing meanings and begin to cause the effects that supernatural monsters evoke. A more effective novel than *Caleb Williams* in this vein is Charles Brockden Brown's *Edgar Huntly; or Memoirs of a Sleep-Walker* (1799). Brown develops his characters fully enough to engage readers deeply on their behalf. He constructs the horrors of the tale to suggest the influence of unconscious motives, thus making them seem more significant and mysterious than the horrors of "The Iron Shroud." Furthermore, he introduces a highly disturbing ambiguity, which is left unresolved.

*Edgar Huntly* appears at first to be a clumsily episodic adventure novel, but the more closely one looks at it, the more intriguing and troubling it becomes. The protagonist-narrator writes a long letter to his betrothed, recounting a series of adventures in which he has participated. At the end of this letter appear two short ones from Huntly to his benefactor, Sarsefield, and a final short letter from Sarsefield to Huntly. This last letter suggests some of the ways in which the apparent clumsiness becomes troubling. Midway through the novel, Edgar, a poor gentleman, learns that he will probably be unable to marry his correspondent, Mary Waldegrave, for her inheritance from her recently murdered brother does not seem to belong to her. Later it appears that the return of his advantageously married benefactor once again enables him to marry, but Sarsefield's last letter raises doubts about this event, which remain unresolved. The reader never learns whether Edgar and Mary are united. The purpose of Sarsefield's letter is to chastise Edgar. To understand how this comes about, we must look briefly at Edgar's adventures.

The novel seems intended to demonstrate that one is rarely if ever fully aware of the meanings or the consequences of his actions. Edgar returns to his home shortly after the murder of his closest friend, Waldegrave, to solve the crime and bring the murderer to justice. When he sees Clithero, the mysterious servant of a neighbor, sleepwalking at the murder scene, he suspects Clithero of the murder. When he confronts Clithero, Edgar learns of his past. In Ireland Clithero rose out of obscurity to become the favorite servant of Mrs. Lorimer. His virtue eventually led to her allowing an engagement between Clithero and her beloved niece. Accidents and fatalities led Clithero, in self-defense, to kill Mrs. Lorimer's blackguard twin brother, father of his betrothed. Because Mrs. Lorimer believed her life supernaturally entwined with her brother's, she believed she would die when he did. Convinced that by killing her brother, he has, in effect, killed her, Clithero conceives, in a mad refinement of benevolence, the plan of killing her before she learns of her brother's death, thus sparing her part of the pain she can anticipate. When he fails to carry out this plan, he tells her what has happened and flees, ignorant of the consequences. Of course, Mrs. Lorimer does not die; eventually she marries Sarsefield and comes to America. Clithero's confession does not remove Edgar's suspicion, but it does push Clithero toward insanity, and it does awaken Edgar's benevolence.

Edgar's main project in the novel becomes to cure the mad Clithero, who still believes he killed Mrs. Lorimer, now Mrs. Sarsefield. By the end of his adventures, Edgar knows that Clithero is mistaken and believes that when Clithero learns the truth, he will be cured. To Edgar's surprise, when Clithero does learn the truth, he sets out again to murder his former benefactress. Edgar writes two letters to Sarsefield to warn of Clithero's impending appearance. He sends them directly to Sarsefield, knowing that his wife may well see them first, since she handles his affairs during his frequent absences from home. She does see the second letter, and she collapses and miscarries as a result.

Sarsefield chastises Edgar, then, for misdirecting the letters, even though Sarsefield knew full well from the first letter, which he luckily received himself, that the second was on its way to the same address. On one hand, Edgar's error seems almost comically trivial, especially when compared to the misguided benevolence that drives him to meddle with Clithero and thus send the murderer on his last mission. On the other hand, the consequences are quite serious, serious enough to make one wonder why Edgar *and* Sarsefield are so stupid about their handling of the letters. The reader is left wondering what to make of Edgar and Sarsefield; does either know what he is doing? This question arises repeatedly in Edgar's account of his adventures.

His benevolence awakened by the story of Clithero's life in Ireland, Edgar becomes determined to help him, for even if he is Waldegrave's murderer, he has suffered enough. Clithero retires to the wilderness of Norwalk to die after telling his story to Edgar, but Edgar pursues him to save him. After three trips filled with wilderness adventures, Edgar has a series of shocks. He meets the man who is probably the real owner of Mary's inheritance and, in consequence, loses his hope for a speedy marriage. Fatigued from his adventures in the wilderness, frustrated in his efforts to benefit Clithero, and perhaps guilty about his diverted efforts to find his friend's murderer and about prying into Clithero's life, Edgar begins to sleepwalk. His sleepwalking mirrors Clithero's in several ways, most notably in that he also hides a treasure, Waldegrave's letters, without being aware of doing so. This fascination with and then doubling with Clithero, who Edgar believes at this point is a murderer and whom he suspects of having murdered his friend, is suggestive of unconscious motivations. Sleepwalking especially suggests that there are forces at work that the characters do not themselves understand. What these are, we can guess. Clithero has eliminated a barrier to his marriage, but in the process made that marriage impossible. Edgar has not killed his friend, but he believes he has gained from that death. After he discovers that he has not, he begins to behave as if he is guilty by mirroring Clithero's behavior. Perhaps his attempts to cure Clithero are unconsciously motivated by a desire to deal with the unconscious guilt associated with benefiting from a friend's death. Whatever is happening, Edgar begins to experience terrors as soon his sleepwalking begins.

After a second episode of sleepwalking, Edgar finds himself at the bottom of a pit in a cave, with no memory of how he arrived there. Again, he is diverted from his quest for Waldegrave's murderer, but this time by some clearly unconscious force. Edgar takes three days to return to civilization, moving through a fairly clear death and rebirth pattern, which is parallel with a progress from savagery to civilization.

This pattern suggests a journey into the unconscious and back again. His adventures—drinking panther blood, rescuing a maiden, fighting "wild" Indians, losing and finding himself in rough terrain, nearly killing his friends, and successfully evading his own rescue while narrowly escaping death several times—are filled with weird mistakes and odd humor, all of which suggest encounters with psychological as well as physical problems. One example of the humorous, almost dreamlike quality of his terrors in the wilderness comes near the end. He is amazed at his physical endurance. When he finds himself within a half day's walk of home, he determines to demonstrate this endurance to himself by completing the walk in six hours, despite his three days of suffering and privation. Six hours later, he has not yet gained the necessary road, and though he knows where he is, he is no closer to home than he was six hours earlier. Though he has, indeed, endured the physical effort, he has made no progress. This incident parodies his larger quests for justice, to marry, and to cure Clithero. In each case, unexpected and uncanny factors prevent his success.

Of his earlier explorations of the wilderness, Edgar says, "My rambles were productive of incessant novelty, though they always terminated in the prospects of limits that could not be overleaped" (93). The physical nature of the wilderness is indicative of the moral nature of human life, which in his world proves so complex that while one believes he can see to the next step of his actions, he repeatedly finds that he has seen incorrectly. Edgar often finds himself doing what he never thought he could do and failing at what he believes he can easily accomplish. The complexities of his wilderness experience suggest that he knows neither himself, his fellows, nor his world. After hearing Clithero's story, Edgar wonders, "If consequences arise that cannot be foreseen, shall we find no refuge in the persuasion of our rectitude and of human frailty? Shall we deem ourselves criminal because we do not enjoy the attributes of diety? Because our power and our knowledge are confined by impassable boundaries?" (87).

In order for Edgar to be able to successfully undertake moral actions, such as finding a murderer, curing a melancholic, or marrying, he must achieve a just appreciation of his own limits. Although he can see Clithero's limitations quite clearly, Edgar cannot see his own, even after he learns he has been sleepwalking, that he has been largely mistaken about the events of an Indian raid in which he was involved, that he has mistaken his friends for his enemies, and that he has made several other errors that only by good luck did not cause his death. Even after he learns that an Indian killed his friend and that his efforts with Clithero have been largely irrelevant, indeed, even after admitting to himself that Clithero would be better off dead, he persists in his blind attempt to cure the madman, only to precipitate new disasters. Edgar cannot control his own self. He cannot deal well with even the physical illusions of being lost in strange country. Yet because he survives, he does not see his own limits. He fails to appreciate the degree to which his limitations in the wilderness point toward greater limitations in dealing with the souls of others. He certainly does not see the wilderness as symbolic of the terrain of his own unconscious, invisibly determining his choices.

Edgar does not know himself, and furthermore he may not be able to know himself sufficiently to avoid the errors he makes. Still, he should be able to appreciate that he is not qualified to meddle with another complex soul, which he must understand less well than he understands his own. Before Clithero tells Edgar his story, he says, "You boast of the beneficence of your intentions. You set yourself to do me benefit. What are the effects of your misguided zeal and random efforts? They have brought my life to a miserable close" (34-35). Though it is some time before the close actually comes, Clithero's words are prophetic. Each time Edgar confronts him, Clithero is at the point of determining to try to live out his life as best he can; each of Edgar's attempts to help drives Clithero toward the suicide he eventually commits.

Insofar as Edgar's quest is to avenge his friend's murder, he succeeds quite by accident. Insofar as it is for ethical maturity, he fails miserably, but no one in the novel succeeds. If a measure of moral maturity is the ability to know oneself, including one's unconscious impulses, and to moderate one's passions to the benefit of others, no one comes close to success. The virtuous Mrs. Lorimer cannot behave rationally toward her villainous brother; her suffering and Clithero's derive ultimately from that failure. Clithero conceives of murdering her out of misguided benevolence. Sarsefield, a physician, will let Clithero die of wounds received from Indians because he judges for himself that to Clithero, "consciousness itself is the malady, the pest, of which he only is cured who ceases to think." Edgar assents to this judgment and to it adds, "Disastrous and humiliating is the state of man! By his own hands is constructed the mass of misery and error in which his steps are forever involved" (266). In spite of these beliefs and statements, Edgar still wishes to correct some of Clithero's mistakes after Clithero recovers. In doing so, he threatens Mrs. Sarsefield and drives Clithero to his final suicide. No character understands himself, his limitations, or his actions thoroughly, and therefore, in the case of each of these characters, benevolence issues in murder, direct or indirect. One of this novel's many ironies is that among Edgar, Sarsefield, and Clithero, only Clithero is never morally responsible for a death other than his own, since he kills Mrs. Lorimer's brother in self-defense.

In *Edgar Huntly*, the stage of human action is beyond human comprehension. The foregrounded consequence of this fact is that virtue becomes criminal because of inevitable human ignorance. Edgar has asked whether men must be deemed criminal because they have not the attributes of diety. His adventures show that he must reply "yes." Indeed, as one observes how actions turn out, one may doubt the reality of virtue. Though Clithero has no idea who attacks him, the result of his defense is killing his betrothed's profligate father, an action clearly to his advantage. Perhaps it is because he cannot bear to benefit from such an act that he insanely deprives himself of any possible benefits. Edgar's ability to accept that he has unknowingly avenged the deaths of Waldegrave and also of his own parents, by single-handedly killing a band of Indians, may appear morally equivocal next to Clithero's despair. The reader may ultimately wonder whether Edgar's pursuit of Clithero is, in fact, unconscious vengeance disguised as benevolence, not unlike Sarsefield's refusal to treat Clithero's wounds. Perhaps Edgar even eliminates a rival for Sarsefield's affection and money with unconscious deliberation by misdirecting his two letters about Clithero. But if this is true, what is behind Sarsefield's failure to intercept the second letter? Does he have a reason for not wanting a child?

*Edgar Huntly* is an uncanny tale of terror in which the psychological complexity of the characters puzzles the implied reader. The mysteriousness of their motives and actions calls for close attention, which leads to a troubling ambiguity in interpreting their motives. Nearly every major choice and action seems double. The character gives one reason for what he does, and the reader sees the shadow of another hidden and horrifying reason. Hidden behind the virtue of the best people is self-interest and vice. They do not seem to intend persecution or cruelty or even to advance their self-interests at the expense of others, yet their actions repeatedly tend in these directions.

This ambiguity denies complete closure to the novel at the end of the reading of the text. A gap insistent upon being filled remains. And it is accentuated because so much is made to depend on how it is filled. What will be the final relationships of Edgar and Sarsefield and of Edgar and Mary? This gap is filled, I believe, with relative ease upon reflection. Upon accepting that the dilemma is not resolvable, that without a deeper knowledge of human nature and of these characters than we can possess, it is impossible to define their motives with either precision or certainty, we see that we occupy precisely the same position in relation to these characters as they occupy in relation to each other. The hesitation of the implied reader between two ways of interpreting these characters produces an uncertainty that mirrors their uncertainty about each other. To judge them precipitately as either good, evil, or even certainly mixed in their motives is to claim knowledge about them that they themselves are denied about each other. The implied reader's heightened confusion at the end of the novel, then, moves him closer to Edgar, closer to the bewilderment that he experiences but does not really understand. Even though he ultimately occupies a position superior in understanding to Edgar's, the implied reader shares Edgar's situation to such a degree as to feel an intensified horror both at the terrors Edgar suffers and at those he causes.

# IV

The tales and novels examined in this chapter tend to confirm Todorov's characterization of the vagueness of the uncanny genre. If "The Pit and the Pendulum" and "The Tell-Tale Heart" are taken as paradigmatic, in that they realize most fully what we usually think of as tales of terror while they avoid both the marvelous and the fantastic, then we can see relationships to them in at least three directions. Tales of sensation, such as "The Iron Shroud," seem to be relatively minor both in interest and power; perhaps they are prototypes of what Poe achieves in this vein. In the other two directions we have works that approach tragedy and works that approach the fantastic.

*Sanctuary, The Painted Bird,* and related works point away from the tale of terror toward classic literature, especially tragedy. These works illustrate highly sophisticated uses of terror to minimize the moral and psychological distance between the implied reader and the characters in the fiction. These works are especially important to this study because they show that novelists of the caliber of Faulkner have worked with techniques similar to Whitman's. Faulkner acts directly on the implied reader by the indirect means of a rhetoric of juxtaposition and images. Such techniques are different from modes of narration, such as Ernest Hemingway often uses, that appear to leave judgment completely up to the implied reader and also from the more overt modes of offering narrative judgments, such as those we see, for example, in Jane Austen's novel, where the narrator tells the implied reader precisely what to think of Emma Woodhouse. Faulkner is able, without the use of an "intrusive" narrator, to work from two directions on the implied reader, presenting the characters in action, on the one hand, while forming the implied reader's judgments with materials apparently unconnected to the characters and their actions, on the other. Faulkner thus draws on a rich Gothic tradition as well as on the central literary tradition when he discovers the value of terrifying the implied reader to reduce distance between reader and morally equivocal characters.

"The Tell-Tale Heart," with its mildly insistent ambiguity about the status of the narrator's acts, gestures in a direction that longer fictions such as Brown's *Edgar Huntly* seem to realize more fully. These fictions point toward without yet taking advantage of the possibilities of the fantastic in arousing horror and perhaps terror. In each of these, there is a hesitation between two or more ways of understanding events. This hesitation does not contribute to the fantastic, because all the suggested interpretations are natural. However, this hesitation between various natural explanations proves insistent and irresolvable. We wish to but we cannot know whether the madman actually takes another person's life. We cannot plumb the motives of Edgar and Sarsefield. In both cases the implied reader is brought closer to the characters and is made to experience a greater degree of identity with them than would have been the case without ambiguity. This greater identity serves to increase the horror of the stories by giving the implied reader just a taste of the terror of seeing the world as these characters do.

Works of this kind are especially important to this study for two reasons. First, they show sophisticated writers of the tale of terror experimenting with the possibility of frustrating and delaying closure by means of persistent and troubling ambiguity. By delaying closure, they place a special burden on the implied reader. The role must have an end that should coincide with the completion of the concretion of the work. To frustrate this completion arouses anxiety in the *real* reader. A key expectation is violated, if only momentarily, but the effect reverberates along the entire system by which the real reader participates in the work. The narrator is unable to read some major aspect of his experience. The implied reader is unable to read and judge the narrator; the real reader is unable to complete the role of implied reader in the expected and, therefore, relatively easy way. In a tale of terror such an experience, even when so brief as in these works, can be seriously shocking.

Second, the ambiguity in these works points toward the unconscious as a source of terror. Both Todorov and Rosemary Jackson have argued that fantasy gains its particular power to terrify by presenting images of the culturally forbidden, which is the "content" of our unconscious. In *Caleb Williams* as well as in "The Tell-Tale Heart" and *Edgar Huntly*, we see representations or at least suggestions of unconscious activity and the realization of forbidden unconscious wishes. These images are suggested also in the hallucinations of the man in the bell. Such representations can probably be most effectively made horrifying when the author uses the marvelous, either in a marvelous work or in some form of fantastic work. We will turn to marvelous tales in the chapter 3.

What can we say, then, about the particular pleasures of the uncanny tale of terror? We can see a kind of continuum on which the uncanny tale of terror relates to tragedy at one end and the fantastic tale of terror at the other. To move from works like *Sanctuary* to those like "The Man in the Bell" involves shifting the focus from using terror to control judgments of characters and their fates to making terror the center of the story. To move from works like "The Man in the Bell" to *Edgar Huntly* involves reducing the protective psychological distance between the characters and the implied reader. This distance is reduced by creating a disturbing ambiguity in the tales that seems akin to fantastic hesitation. The implied reader is implicated in the problems of the madman of "The Tell-Tale Heart" and of Huntly and Sarsfield and, therefore, entangled in these tales, while "The Man in the Bell" and "The Pit and the Pendulum" are careful to close off the narrators' terrifying experiences in completed aesthetic forms.

Within the uncanny tale of terror, then, we find two fairly clear divisions: sensational tales of terror and ambiguous sensational tales of terror. The simpler, unambiguous forms offer the pleasures of playing at being in danger. The implied reader is asked to identify closely with the victim in some catastrophe, not so much to pity him as to enter into his experience of danger and to share it vicariously. The play of being in danger and dealing with the resulting emotions becomes part of the concretization of the work. The story promises and delivers a risk-free excursion, for the experience of danger is vicarious and the evoked emotions are contained within a highly controlled aesthetic whole.

Poe and Brown, in the tales we have examined, tend to complicate this fairly simple form by introducing ambiguities. Among the results is increased risk. The pleasure, however, is much the same, though perhaps of a higher degree. "The Tell-Tale Heart" and *Edgar Huntly* require the reader to be more active in containing the threats posed by the stories. Their ambiguity challenges the reader's ability to complete concretions. The real reader experiences and overcomes mild anxiety when the work unexpectedly opens a problem at the point where closure is expected. This active use of our faculties for producing order is not greatly different from our activity in completing any literary work. As a practical matter, readers often experience similar kinds of anxiety because of more ordinary difficulties of a work's style or organization or because of their limitations as readers. The difference here is that these tales of terror deliberately seek to produce this anxiety and to heighten it at a particular point, at or near the end of the work.

Therefore, the reader experiences a quite specific challenge. Modern readers come to such works expecting some sort of a challenge; adult readers, I believe, though they may enjoy "The Man in the Bell," prefer "The Tell-Tale Heart," in part because it produces some measure of real risk. The pleasure of enduring and overcoming this anxiety of real risks, however small they may be, is greater than that of simply entering into the sufferings of the victim at second hand. When the reader risks something, then the challenge becomes, to an extent, first hand. The deliberate production of anxiety points toward the possibility of turning up that anxiety, by prolonging and intensifying it. This is one important possibility that really terrifying tales will take up to work their magic.

## CHAPTER THREE

# The Marvelous Horror Thriller

## I

In the marvelous tale, according to Todorov, events take place that violate the reader's conceptions of natural laws, but the characters behave as if the events were normal. Both Todorov and Rabkin point out that this is the fictional world of the fairy tale. Indeed, in "Hansel and Gretel," no one questions the existence of a rich witch in the woods who builds a house out of food to trap children or of a white bird to lead the children to her or of a duck to help ferry them back home. Likewise in Ray Bradbury's *The Martian Chronicles* (1950), there are no questions about the possibility of space travel, though it had not yet happened when the book was published. The existence of Martians, the physical conditions on Mars, the possibilities of interactions between humans and Martians—these are just as marvelous as witches and obedient wild ducks. Bringing science fiction and fantasy into the marvelous along with fairy tales shows the mode's extensiveness. We might go even further by mentioning the marvelous sympathy among some members of the Bundren family in Faulkner's *As I Lay Dying* or the marvelous power of poetic justice in Austen's *Pride and Prejudice*. Like Todorov's uncanny genre, his marvelous genre shades off into all of literature, where the marvelous appears in many guises, depending to some extent on what constitutes natural law for any particular cultural group.

The problem of defining fantasy is so vexed that a digression may clarify matters somewhat. It is difficult to construct a generalization to distinguish all of the works readers are inclined to call fantasies from the rest of literature. A fuller and more sophisticated illustration of this problem is available in the essays of Gary Wolfe, C. N. Manlove, and W. R. Irwin in Roger Schlobin's collection, *The Aesthetics of Fantasy Literature and Art*. Perhaps the simplest clarification for this study is to note that my purpose is not to define fantasy at all, though inevitably I find myself using the term. Instead, I am concerned with a group of works that seem to share the main purpose of frightening their readers. Some of these works, notably those under discussion in this chapter and in chapter 5, have characteristics, including violations of natural law as conceived by Western civilization in the late twentieth century, that would lead most readers to classify them as fantasies. For the purposes of understanding the pleasures of terror, what seems more important is that by means of such violations, authors can introduce supernatural monsters into their tales of terror. And even more important is the attitude toward these monsters (or possible monsters) that the authors create. Therefore, while it may be true, as Manlove argues, that Todorov's definitions of the fantastic and related genres are of little use to theorists of fantasy (*Aesthetics of Fantasy Literature* 27-28), these definitions are quite useful for understanding the literature of terror. Indeed, it seems finally that Todorov is not concerned with fantasy as an approach to representation so much as he is interested in the experience of *the fantastic* that appears almost exclusively in some examples of the tale of terror. Finally, it may prove helpful to observe that though the definers of fantasy tend to include marvelous and fantastic tales of terror in fantasy, these tales do not fit there comfortably. Manlove, for example, excludes from fantasy most of the Gothic tradition because the supernatural appears either to be explained as illusion or to be symbolic of unconscious fears (22).

Perhaps more to the point, when tales of terror make use of the marvelous or the apparently marvelous, they seem to take pains to insert the marvelous seamlessly into our world. The most effective marvelous tales of terror seem pointedly placed in worlds contemporary with their readers. Of course, in the early Gothic romances and in the more horrifying fairy tales, we see marvelous horrors in worlds quite distant from our own or even from the worlds of the original readers of the texts. Generally speaking, though, such tales, if they ever had much power to horrify adults, have not retained it in any great degree. H. P. Lovecraft approaches the completely otherworldly tale of terror in "Through the Gates of the Silver Key," but Randolph Carter's journey begins from a firmly established twentieth-century United States. While it ought to be possible to place a really effective marvelous tale of terror completely outside the known universe, I have not yet run across such a story (see George P. Landow in Schlobin,

*Aesthetics of Fantasy* 138-39). The reasons for this will become clearer as we look closely at more tales of terror. Preliminarily, we might guess that tales of terror do not promise the kind of direct escape from "the real" that we associate with fantasy.

Like Todorov, Rosemary Jackson is also more interested in explaining tales of terror than in treating all of fantasy in her book, *Fantasy*; this is because she wants to discuss the subversion of the real. To subvert everyday reality, one may be forced to represent it, but in such a way that its gaps appear. Jackson finds fantasies such as J. R. R. Tolkien's *The Lord of the Rings* conservative and repressive because they attempt to create myths that cover over the gaps in our linguistic constructions of reality (153-56). Kathryn Hume's anatomy of fantasy as a mode of representation in *Fantasy and Mimesis* may be more satisfying because it allows for multiple uses of fantasy: escape, introducing new realities, improving reality, and making reality unknowable, this last incorporating Jackson's function of subversion. We have seen that uncanny tales of terror take place, more or less, in our world and that they tend to become subversive as they become ambiguous. They offer novel sensations *and* the normal escape of aesthetic experience, which is always disengaged from the practical. Likewise, marvelous tales of terror, even though they present the supernatural, tend to take place in worlds represented as essentially like our own. They also become subversive as they become ambiguous.

Many tales of terror are like fairy tales. As long as there is no appearance of fantastic hesitation, the marvelous tale of terror appears to take place in a world where supernatural events are likely to be taken as normal. This is the case, for example, in many of the ghost stories of M. R. James. In "Canon Alberic's Scrap-book" and in "The Ash-tree," characters encounter supernatural monsters without ever doubting their reality. Indeed, the narrators and the reader easily enter into a world where such events, though rare, are quite possible. In this world evil takes physical forms that persist through generations. People who forget or who become skeptical about the reality of evil accidentally make themselves its victims. James's *Ghost Stories of an Antiquary* (1904) may be seen as an antiquarian's fantasy of revenge on those who either fail to respect his profession or who practice it with insufficient respect for the past. Stephen King, whose works provide a catalog of the kinds of popular horror story, comes close to this kind of story in "The Mangler" (*Night Shift*, 1978), about an ironing and folding machine that accidentally becomes possessed by a demon with a taste for human flesh. Though there is some momentary hesitation in the characters who conclude that the machine is possessed, this hesitation is not foregrounded in the story. Instead, the omniscient narrator concentrates on building the demon into a horrific power. Dramatic irony and ironic humor help to build the demon/machine into a grotesque, annihilating monster. The reader fears for the characters who will become its victims.

The tale of terror that uses the marvelous has available an opportunity for terrifying readers that the uncanny tale of terror does not; it can present supernatural monsters. In the stories we have just glanced at, except for "Hansel and Gretel," this opportunity is not exploited. M. R. James and King present such monsters primarily as physical threats; the "spiders" of "The Ash-tree" and the mangler simply destroy their victims in particularly gruesome ways. In "Hansel and Gretel" as in many fairy tales, according to Bruno Bettelheim in *The Uses of Enchantment*, we see the supernatural monster used to suggest or embody psychological evils and terrors. The witch is clearly like the wicked stepmother in her willingness to sacrifice the substance of the children to sustain her own life. By dealing with the witch, the children magically remove the stepmother and provide financial security for their family. The story takes the pattern of a forced journey into the self, represented as a land of magic, away from the world of hunger where pigeons and kittens do not wave good-by from the roof, and into a world where animals may be friendly. At the center of that world is the witch who stands for the stepmother. By exercising their customary perception and intelligence in this world, the children can dominate. What do they dominate? Apparently, the image of the stepmother. Their triumph is essentially mental, deriving from their development and use of imagination. Shirley Jackson's *The Haunting of Hill House* (1959) is a more horrific adaptation of these themes, for there Eleanor fails to escape the evil mother.

In the more complex and contemporary fairy tale with a monster, *King Kong* (1933), we see a similar journey with a similar effect. Andrew Griffin argues that Kong represents the unconscious, specifically, Ann's sexual desire "just as big as she feared it would be if she ever gave in to it" (1). I think Kong is more complex, for he is also placed in the context of consumerist capitalism, where the arousal and satisfaction of primitive sexual energy are exploited for profit. Denham, the filmmaker in the movie, is involved in creating misogynous myths that help to sustain this exploitation. He tries to harness Kong to these myths, but in the battle between Kong and the technological monsters of modern civilization over who will possess Ann, Denham destroys Kong. In this context, Griffin's conclusion about *King Kong* and monster films in general seems more provocative. He says the film shows its viewers that they are capable of handling their dangerous desires and reassures them that they need not fear "loss of control and loss of identity" in acknowledging and dealing with those desires (17). This interpretation seems on the mark with regard to the repressed lovers who escape an unhealthy, absolute repression of sexual desire in their journey to Skull Mountain and back. However, it misses the point of the second half of the film, the difficulty the lovers confront in New York, where they must maintain a healthy sexuality in the face of the repressive powers that crucify Kong on the Empire State Building.

"Hansel and Gretel," *King Kong*, and Griffin's comments shed light on the particular power that becomes available to the tale of terror when it exploits supernatural monsters. If the supernatural monster is constructed to represent the collective repressions of its viewers or readers, then the images of these monsters may transcend the immediate functions of the monsters in advancing the plot and speak directly to the reader. If the repressions they represent are powerful enough, the real reader may be terrified at what arises within himself as he imagines these monsters. Griffin suggests that modern monster films help us, at least intuitively, to acknowledge and gain control over these desires. These ideas reveal two major problems for the marvelous tale of terror once it begins to make its monsters psychologically suggestive. First, the danger of permanently alienating the reader from the text increases once one tries to address the unconscious fears of all humans and those peculiar to a given culture. Second, the question of why any reader would voluntarily read such texts becomes more insistent. Griffin shows something of what may be gained by reading these texts or viewing the movies, but we need to say more about whether and how the effect he describes contributes to aesthetic pleasure in the concretization of such works.

The writers of marvelous tales of terror usually make their monsters seem natural. Their discoverers do not question their appearance in the world because they result from a scientific experiment, as do Frankenstein's monster and Mr. Hyde, or are visitors from outer space, as are Lovecraft's Old Ones in *At the Mountains of Madness* (1939). Such monsters are not greatly different in the way they are made to seem normal from the monsters in Clara Reeve, Horace Walpole, Matthew Lewis, and Charles Maturin, who might be seen as writing a religious as opposed to a secular Gothic fiction (Jackson 23-26). Though these earlier works may suggest quite different cultural assumptions in their authors and original audiences, their effects on readers are likely to be rather similar. Critics generally agree that marvelous tales of terror share the purpose of providing "safe" terror (see, for example, Birkhead 190-91, 221).

Rosemary Jackson has brought together the best recent thought on the subject and, therefore, has helped to clarify the idea of "safe terror" (chs. 2, 3). She argues that Gothic fantasy, in general, allows the contemplation of transgressions that we naturally but unconsciously desire. We repress these desires in favor of the continuity of self and culture. This idea accounts for the more sensational themes of the Gothic tradition: sexual violence and perversion, incest, cannibalism, and Faustian power. It also accounts for the tendency of these themes to manifest themselves through supernatural agencies, for these desires, coming from our unconscious, seem to come from external sources of unlimited power. From this point of view, the thrills of the marvelous tale of terror arise from the creation and release of the tension of unconscious identification with the transgressors and their victims. Such tales promise and then give the reader an objectification of the forbidden, which one can experience vicariously through observing the actions of characters and which can be contemplated safely over distancing barriers.

Safe terror is distanced terror. In most works of the Gothic tradition, terror is the experience of characters. The implied reader's role is that of sympathetic onlooker. The general situation in these stories is familiar. A reasonably interesting character undergoes a series of adventures, many of which are terrifying. These adventures usually involve the supernatural. In the process of these adventures, the character's isolation increases, he or she comes to feel that the world that was once a home has become an alien mystery, finds his or her reason threatened, and either is victorious over opposing forces or is defeated and perhaps destroyed. This general story line shares, in all its many variations in all types of tale of terror, the intent of arousing highly intense suspense. In the marvelous tale of terror, suspense leads to a character's encounter with the terrifying, which provides the reader with the thrill of horror, which is a culmination and usually a partial release of the tension of suspense. This release is a principal element in creating the illusion of closure. Through identification with the character and often through involvement in a well-wrought mystery, the implied reader is brought as near to the terrifying occurrences as is possible, short of being exposed to them directly.

The marvelous horror thriller is especially concerned to satisfy Bullough's principle of the antinomy of aesthetic distance: "the utmost decrease of distance without its disappearance." This is, indeed, what we would expect, for should the distance between the terrific image and the implied reader collapse, the aesthetic distance between the reader and the work would be threatened and would most likely collapse. The image in the work and, therefore, the work itself would become a real threat to the real reader, and the concretization of the work would never be completed. Lovecraft's *At the Mountains of Mad-*

*ness* is especially useful as an example of the marvelous horror thriller because Lovecraft is so cautious in his creation of distance and closure.

# II

H. P. Lovecraft's *At the Mountains of Madness* is a fairly typical example of the marvelous tale of terror. We can see continuity between it and the older Gothic tradition in traces of conventions, such as the isolated castlelike setting, the repetition of the traditional story line, and the central theme of the Faustian quest for forbidden knowledge. The tale takes the form of a scientific report on an expedition to Antarctica, which warns *not* to continue the exploration of this continent. Lovecraft goes to considerable length to sustain the illusion of reading an actual scientist's report. The tale is circumstantially complete enough to bring the marvelous well into the realm of the plausible. The incredible creatures and places Dyer, the scientist, reports are remote, outside ordinary experience rather than totally unnatural. In this way, Lovecraft is able to insert the "impossible" monster into a natural world like the one we believe ourselves to inhabit. Lovecraft's method of telling the story encourages the implied reader to become a citizen of that world and to take seriously the implications of the world view at which the tale arrives. To take that world seriously within the work is to open oneself to the thrills it offers.

The story "reveals" that human beings are descended from organic matter left over from that which the original life on Earth created for its food and as a source of labor. The Old Ones came to Earth before there was any life and created the organic cells from which known life has evolved. Over a multimillion year history, marked by wars with other space beings, the Old Ones declined in technical skill and power, coming finally to occupy only a portion of Antarctica. In the last ice age they migrated into an abyss beneath their Antarctic city and were apparently subdued there by organic slaves of their own creation, the Shoggoths. It appears that the Shoggoths now rule beneath the ice-locked city of the Old Ones. In this cosmic tale of decline from power toward final extinction, human beings prove unimportant, merely the spin-off of greater events and higher civilizations. The humans who "rule the earth" are, after all, perhaps less powerful relatives of the Shoggoths. Furthermore, there is, to the west of this city, another higher mountain range that strikes terror in the "hearts" even of the Old Ones. In this tale, the meaning of that terror is only implied, but the clues add up to the idea that the Old Ones relate to that location as humans relate to the Old Ones. In those mountains of madness is an opening onto yet another universe, the inhabitants of which control the fate of the Old Ones. Dyer's discoveries hint that the Shoggoths and other beings that the Old Ones have feared are connected with these western mountains.

The general picture is of a universe of walls or frontiers. Behind each wall is an unknown world that is vitally involved in the existence and meaning of the known world, yet that may have no particular concern for the known world. To those others, the known world may be utterly inconsequential. The terrors resulting from the breaching of one of these walls are the central terrors of the tale. What might happen should we insignificant humans call attention to our presence?

Dyer's expedition from Miskatonic University enters into prehuman history when it unearths and haplessly thaws out several Old Ones who had unexplainedly entered a state of hibernation in a tunnel millions of years ago. These scientists breach a wall between universes, which provokes the horrors of the destruction of the exploring camp. Dyer and Danforth's experiences of these horrors and, then, of the various terrors at the abandoned city isolate them, replace their familiar world with an alien and threatening world, and virtually destroy their reason. They take in the forbidden knowledge of a world beyond, which, Dyer repeats, impinges blasphemously upon their own world. Danforth sees more than Dyer, more than reason can bear. While Dyer remains rational enough to write the report, Danforth breaks down.

It is helpful to look at the thrills these discoveries provide the reader from two points of view: their content and the way in which they are presented. The general tendency of the horrors Dyer and Danforth experience is to push mankind into an even smaller, even less important, even more fragile corner of the cosmic drama. Before the massacre at the western camp, they are members of a scientific expedition unlocking the secrets of a universe that they believe they understand. The power of the human mind is unquestioned. The interest of humanity in their work is electric, for they represent mankind at its most ingenious and in its most noble guise. The massacre raises questions about human nature, since the researchers believe that only human agency could reasonably account for the burial of the specimens, the raiding of the camp, the absence of one member, the careful dissection of another, and what appear to be signs of cannibalism. The discovery and exploration of the frozen city humbles the scientists. It is immediately clear that the city's builders far exceeded current human technical ability. Then they learn from the city's admirable art enough history to see that their specimens belong to the race that built the city, that those monstrous beings created beauty and strength, that they fought on a grand scale to preserve a tremendous civilization, that time and conflict weakened them, that these Old Ones were the creators of earth life as we know it, and finally that these magnificent beings are themselves the victims of powers beyond themselves that they have participated in unleashing. Humans become less important while their universe becomes alien and threatening. These scientists, as well as the Old Ones, have transgressed forbidden barriers.

The blasphemy of the discoveries is multiple. These men lose a sacred universe, not merely the universe created for humans by God, but even the indifferent universe of science, which is assumed to be open to human intelligence and manipulation. Certain mirrorings reveal other levels of blasphemy. The scientists dissect an Old One clumsily. In the massacre the Old Ones dissect a scientist clumsily, as if unfamiliar with this specimen. As the scientists collect artifacts from the tunnel, so the Old Ones collect artifacts from the camp. Dyer and Danforth's discovery of this chain of events humbles them still more, for they shift from being scientists to being specimens themselves. Furthermore, they have participated in the violation of their creators and are profaning what is in a sense a holy place, the womb of their own creation. Yet when the Old Ones show equal interest in a dog and in a man and equal lack of consideration for the self-consciousness of either, they too reveal a lack of reverence for significant life, even though they consider it their property. There is a poetic justice as well as pathos in the subsequent destruction of the Old Ones by the Shoggoth, a destruction that mirrors the previous dissections. The creature destroys the creator that awakened it to life, as do Hyde and Frankenstein's monster.

The mirrorings emphasize the blasphemous transgression, the breaching of walls. Each breach is a terror and a violation. The central image of horror in the tale is the Shoggoth itself. After its appearance, Danforth has a vision of the far western mountains, and among the suggestive words connected with that vision are "proto-shoggoths, the nameless cylinder, the primal white jelly, and the eyes in darkness" (1971:109-10). All of these terms relate to the Shoggoth and suggest that it is connected in some way, which the Old Ones may not have understood or, at least, fully appreciated, with the evil powers associated with the western mountains. If this association is plausible, it implies a monstrous breach between three separate worlds, those of the unknown powers of the West, the Old Ones of the mountains of madness, and mankind. To contemplate the effects, should mankind disturb the possibly quite fragile barriers between these worlds, is to see the necessity of preserving these walls. We, too, may be proto-Shoggoths, protected from the invasion of transforming forces only by our obscurity and lack of importance in the universe. These are the general fears that prompt Dyer to warn humanity not to approach the borderlands between the worlds.

The appearance of the Shoggoth specifies that terror. Dyer and Danforth encounter the Shoggoth in a smooth round tunnel when they attempt to catch a glimpse of the abyss in which the Old Ones may have built a new underwater city when the polar ice cap formed. When they find several Old Ones killed in the manner portrayed in pictures of a war against rebellious Shoggoths, they realize they are being pursued and flee. The men are isolated, trapped in the bowels of the earth and pursued by something that they only glimpse as they successfully evade it. It is a gigantic intelligent wormlike being of infinite plasticity that oozes through its cave as a subway train speeds through its tunnel. Its face undergoes transformations, gives off lights and sounds of the Old Ones as it bears down on them. Dyer says it moves like a piston in a cylinder and that its odor is unbearable: a "plastic column of fetid black iridescence oozed tightly onward through its fifteen-foot sinus, gathering unholy speed and driving before it a spiral, rethickening cloud of the pallid abyss vapor" (105). This image suggests transgressions of many kinds: pursuit by living excrement or by a plastic self-animated phallus or even some new birth from the womb of the earth. The Shoggoth kills by sucking off the head. Such images imply the breaking down of many kinds of barriers, especially those between the conscious and the unconscious. Monstrous desires bubble out of the unconscious to devour the ego. Identity is threatened by a a plastic ability to mimic any image.

These suggestions of nightmarish terrors could frighten the reader away from the work. But it seems clear that this is not Lovecraft's intention: even here at the climax of the story, the images are not so particularized as to *force* the reader to see all of the possible implications. Following the recommendation of Poe, his mentor, Lovecraft makes suggestions that the reader may pursue as far as he is inclined (Jacobs 174-75). Furthermore, it is not the real reader, but the implied reader who is invited to explore these images, to interpret them in relation to Dyer's warning. Since the implied reader need go no further to make sense of the tale, the greater danger is that the real reader will discover too disturbing an identity between himself and the self he creates in response to the terrifying images of the text. Then the aesthetic attitude will dissolve, and the work will be transformed from an object of aesthetic contemplation into an enemy for the real reader. Lovecraft is concerned about this possibility and makes special efforts to preserve the aesthetic attitude and to protect the real reader. He supports aesthetic distance in several ways, and he builds into the text some tools to help the implied reader resist the terrors of the final images.

The creation of suspense is itself a distancing technique. In many Gothic tales suspense is primarily on behalf of a highly sympathetic character whose well-being is threatened. In Lovecraft's tale the reader's suspense is focused more fully on mystery. These characters are in danger, but the reader is more concerned to understand the meaning of Dyer's warning not to explore Antarctica. Both sympathy and mystery, as grounds of suspense, help to keep the reader's attention on the story and to hold the terrifying images at a distance. The reader desires to see the forbidden and to understand the warning, but the vision is held off. Holding off the vision produces suspense, and suspense itself keeps the intelligence focused away from itself. On the one hand, suspense heightens thrills by exciting the reader's fears and desires; on the other hand, it insures distance by directing those fears and desires toward characters and events in the fiction. The implied reader is kept separate from the real reader.

The ways in which Lovecraft handles suspense reinforce aesthetic distance. From the beginning, the implied reader expects to be shown why Antarctica should remain unexplored, and reminders of this warning recur. The reader is conditioned to see terror and receives ample warning before each particular frightening episode. Each time a specific terror is not *the* terror, the implied reader gains experience and psychological preparation for the next terror. By the time the Shoggoth appears and Danforth has his vision—which together constitute a warning not to enter this borderland—the implied reader is ready for a shock, a thrill. In developing his suspense Lovecraft has followed established practice; however, he adds another element, which seems to suggest a desire to be especially cautious.

Lovecraft displays at least two quirks likely to irritate readers, a penchant to overuse certain words such as *blasphemous* and a need to make Dyer and Danforth look slow-witted. While the former may be a genuine defect of style, the latter contributes to the protection of the implied reader and is used by other writers, as Stoker does in the second section of *Dracula*. The scientists are almost incredibly reluctant to voice the more obvious hypotheses that their discoveries suggest. The implied reader is in a position to note the circumstances of the massacre and to infer that the specimens were alive and intelligent. He knows there is a city in the mountains belonging to these beings, takes the first hint that these beings created the life that led to human life, and . . . . In short, any good reader who successfully enters the role of implied reader is always far ahead of the scientists in his inferences and may find the narrator irritatingly slow. Dyer's motives for his slowness are adequate: scientific caution, a reluctance to cast aside his world view, and personal terror at what may be encountered. Still, the narrative can irritate the implied reader, who easily races ahead and watches the narrator fumble toward what he already knows. Insofar as it looks like incompetence, this technique may spoil the story for some real readers, but nevertheless, its purpose—to create an implied reader who is superior in comprehension to the narrator—also serves to protect the implied reader.

While shielding the reader, his superiority to the narrator also draws the reader into the marvelous world. The reader becomes committed to the scientists' inferences before the narrator states them, increasing their plausibility because they are the *reader's* discoveries. The impatient waiting for confirmation from the scientists adds to the suspense and, paradoxically, brings the reader closer to the scientists. Each time the implied reader's inferences are confirmed, he has participated in making the case. The interests of implied reader and scientists coincide more and more closely; the implied reader is drawn with the scientists into the world of the marvelous.

The reader's superiority to the scientists disposes him to look beyond what Dyer is willing to say. This pattern becomes especially important at the end, when the content of the warning must be inferred from the image of the Shoggoth, Danforth's vision, and the other patterns of the story. Lovecraft wants the reader to substantiate the content of the warning, to specify it in his own imagination. He sets up a pattern of response that makes such inferences likely. It is important to notice that this indeterminacy is resolvable, for the reader can easily connect the unconnected and make the story whole.

The implied reader's superiority to the narrator also builds confidence, which, on one hand, strengthens the implied reader against the terrors, but which, on the other hand, most likely betrays him at the end of the story. As the reader continues discovering the tale's "secrets," he meets the challenge of the warning. Foreseeing the terrors leads to power over them. Dyer, at one point, expresses fear that his tale will attract rather than repel explorers. Ironically, it does attract the reader who eagerly and rather confidently plunges into the story to savor forbidden knowledge at a comfortable distance from the borderland. Lovecraft draws the implied reader into that land and encourages prideful participation in the raid. The reader knows before Dyer that they will meet a Shoggoth but is kept from any clear conception of its appearance and, therefore, of its "meanings" until the monster becomes visible to the narrator. While Lovecraft has prepared the implied reader for shocks, he has not given away the conception of his monster and the inferences that may follow from seeing it. To understand the reason for the warning, and, thereby, to complete the role of implied reader, the reader must go on alone at the end of the text to connect Dyer's experience to his warning. Antarctica is to be left alone not because there is a monster there, but because the powers that may converge in that monster are sinister beyond human comprehension.

While the scientists are humbled, the reader gains confidence in his ability to deal with the terrors of this world. The implied reader is drawn into this world and given a semidelusive power over it. Then the reader is shocked by powerful images, which reveal the limits of the power of the mind in this fictional world. The point at which distance is most likely to break down—when the real reader is most likely to feel directly threatened by the story—is at the appearance of the Shoggoth, not because the real reader does not have numerous barriers and defenses, but because the image itself is so suggestive of feared violations. There are violations of the body that are also clear symbols of violations of the soul: rape, sodomy, being devoured, being engulfed in excrement, or being born with a monster or as a monster, perhaps from the anus. The appearance of the Shoggoth provides the greatest thrill in the story; considering it reveals something of the nature of that thrill.

From the time that the implied reader is warned, he is also promised. If he perseveres, he will see "the thing that should not be": he will share the forbidden knowledge of the narrator. This direct appeal to the Faustian motive is satisfied by the end of the tale, when the reader takes in the Shoggoth and its meaning in the story. Another element in the thrill is the satisfaction of desires generated within the story. The desire to see the forbidden within the story is analogous to the desire to witness transgressions, which Jackson and other theorists see as central to fantasy as a mode.

I want to briefly introduce the concept of trangression now. Central to the concept are the ideas developed by Jacques Lacan in his essay "The Mirror Phase as Formative of the Function of the 'I.' " Jackson summarizes Lacan's elaboration of Freud's description of the transition from primary narcissism to a recognition of the existence of others. In the mirror phase the child shifts from a perception of all objects as scattered parts of the self to a recognition of the self as an object of perception, as if seen in a mirror: "This self is the *ego*, and becomes the means of self-definition and identification. The mirror phase effects a shift from the 'body in fragments' and an 'asubjectivity of total presence' (Lacan) to the ideal of a whole body with a unified (constructed) subjectivity" (88-89). Jackson emphasizes the degree to which this idea of the ego is closer to Freud's concept of the superego, that it is a cultural construct, that is, an ideal of self offered by culture to an individual. The individual then attempts, insofar as it is possible, to become that ideal of a unified psyche in a whole body. My idea of transgression, like Jackson's, refers to a desire to "remember" or to relive vicariously the experience of the premirror stage when nothing was forbidden. From the point of view of a formed self, the experience of being unformed appears as non-linguistic polymorphous perversion. To suggest such an experience in language and symbol requires the naming of that which should not be, which has no name, which we seem inevitably to imagine in "terms" of what our culture most violently forbids. In Jackson's view, then, fantasy, insofar as it allows some form of violation of cultural norms, is subversive of those norms, a Dionysian force that can renew the Apollonian law.

Transgression is a motif in *At the Mountains of Madness*. The movement of the plot invites the implied reader to transgress human limits and takes the reader into a "holy of holies" that is explicitly an analogue of the human body and implicitly an analogue of the mind. As the reader nears the vision of the abyss where the creative/destructive powers have withdrawn, he encounters the monster that "means" transgressions as it rushes out to devour all in its path. This image can be tremendously powerful to a susceptible mind. It seems clearly related to the primal anxieties that John E. Mack, a Freudian, sees as central to the regressive nightmare, especially the overall fear of the disintegration of a weak ego in the face of an assault by a powerful other, the submerged id (209-14). Whatever the reader's level of susceptibility, as long as distance is maintained, this image may also satisfy a desire to reclaim or at least look upon images of the lost selves of the unconscious premirror phase. The story satisfies that desire in a general way with an image amorphous and inclusive enough to touch on a variety of fears of transgression and violation. Part of the thrill of the image includes this actual brush with the truly forbidden. The contents of the reader's unconscious are called into play by the suggestive image, and the reader must deal with the resulting anxiety to complete the concretization of the work.

This thrill is the goal of the most powerful of the marvelous tales of terror. We can see the theme of transgression in relatively ineffective tales such as Horace Walpole's *The Castle of Otranto* (1764). There the desires of Isabella and all other women to be free of the restraint of the males who control them is embodied in Manfred's and Frederic's overassertion of their power. The men attempt to defy God's will to gratify their lusts; their defeat teaches the women submission, but the forbidden freedom is envisioned. More effective examples center on the image of the forbidden. In James Hogg's *The Private Memoirs and*

*Confessions of a Justified Sinner*, the satanic Gil-Martin objectifies Robert Colwan's secret desires to displace the father and brother who displaced him, to be the favorite of a father figure, and to be his own parents. At the same time Gil-Martin externalizes Robert's guilt and the judgment that awaits him and, also, the barrier of fanaticism that keeps these two ideas separate in Robert's consciousness. This monster eventually displaces Robert, condemning him to hell on earth and hell hereafter. Secret wishes are given their heads for a while and then reined in. So Hyde devours Dr. Jekyll in "hideous" multiple transformations, but brings about his own death as well. The submerged and feared personality masters the body they share. Frankenstein's monster becomes what Frankenstein insists that he be, a mirror of Victor's dark inner self and therefore a persecutor of his ego. So we see the monster, after murdering Victor's wife, as he peers in at the widower's grief with a vengeful leer. Though the ending is somewhat ambiguous, there are indications that with Victor's death, the monster's monstrosity disappears. Some stories, such as Oliver Onions's "The Beckoning Fair One," are quite explicit about their presentation of the forbidden. Here the third-person narrator repeatedly judges the protagonist, Oleron, as surrendering his identity to evil out of his desire to know the ghostly possessor of his apartment. Oleron experiences a kind of regression away from a civilized self into an infantile narcissicism, which is self-destructive and, given Onions's slight toying with the fantastic, possibly murderous as well.

Powerful tales of terror that use marvelous monsters draw upon the forbidden, allowing readers to view images that point at unspeakable things. The moments at which these views are granted produce the most powerful thrills in these works. If it is true that such tales include an actual fulfillment of the reader's secret desire, then one wonders about the reader's distance from the cause of the thrill. It should be clear that such distance may vary greatly. We have noted more than once that aesthetic distance can break down in the face of such images. Now we can see more clearly why. If the individual reader encounters an image that is an especially powerful evocation of a personal terror, then, in the absence of extraordinary buffers in the work, the reading must end. The anxiety aroused by the image takes precedence over aesthetic experience. Inevitably some works will tear the fabric that veils them from some readers, by producing an image that the reader recognizes directly as belonging to his rejected "selves." If *At the Mountains of Madness* inadvertently evokes a personal fear in a particular reader, there is nothing that reader can do to recover the aesthetic experience except to deal with his own terror and, when he has done so, return to the work to see if he can now enjoy it. Lovecraft goes to considerable lengths to protect the reader from this degree of terror. His narrative strategies are designed toward this end, and so also, we may note, is his presentation of the Shoggoth as a far away, rather vague and disguised representation of ideas of transgression.

While a few readers may find the image unbearable, others may find the story hardly terrifying at all. Nothing, after all, compels the reader to perceive all that we have seen in the Shoggoth. The story becomes complete when one sees that the Shoggoths are somehow related to those inscrutable powers beyond the Old Ones and, therefore, should be left as much to themselves as possible. An adequate reading need go no further and, therefore, need only read the Shoggoth as a destroyer. We can account for this whole range of response by considering the nature of the marvelous tale of terror. Because the tale makes the presentation of psychologically suggestive images of marvelous beings its central goal, it is inevitable that there will be a range of response to these images that is determined largely by the sensitivities of individual readers. Lovecraft has clearly built the text in such a way as to minimize the number of readers at each end of the continuum, wanting indeed to provide a thrill of terror but not wanting to frighten readers away. The thrill of terror in the final events of this tale derives, as Bullough would argue, precisely in the realization of the antinomy of aesthetic distance, the maximum approach to real personal terror short of the dissolution of aesthetic distance. This concept accounts for the paradox that Lovecraft provides the reader with multiple barriers between self and terror and yet eventually represents a rather sensational, potentially transfixing image of terror in the Shoggoth. One experiences the thrill in the brush with real personal fear, not in actually experiencing it, nor in being perfectly shielded from it. The thrill is in seeing it approach across a distance without finally breaching that distance.

The author of such a tale does not desire to destroy the aesthetic distance that is essential to the success of its function. He therefore deploys screening devices to construct virtually uncrossable barriers between the reader and his desire. What one sees across those barriers belongs unequivocally to another. The distancing devices of the marvelous tale of terror are those of most realistic fiction, for example, the creation of an implied reader, the presentation of fictional characters in a fictional world, the use of suspense, the provisions for closure, and closure itself. Each of these devices, but especially closure, receives extra support in Lovecraft's tale. *At the Mountains of Madness* answers all of the major narrative questions it raises. It takes and completes the form of a warning. It promises and delivers glimpses of the unnameable.

This marvelous tale of terror completes itself and releases the real reader from his role with the feeling that he has passed a test. The special pleasure of this tale derives from successfully enduring the extreme emotions it stimulates and from the glimpses of the forbidden as belonging to another. In all other respects, Lovecraft's tale is like other works of adventure fiction. An explorer/adventurer encounters obstacles of increasing difficulty and danger while on a mission or quest. The implied reader experiences increasing wonder and suspense. This tale differs from other adventures in that the obstacles encountered are terrors. Because the protagonist encounters terrors, Lovecraft creates special support for the usual devices of aesthetic distance and closure. The presence of such devices also distinguishes this horror thriller from other types of thrillers. The result is a structure in which the real reader is granted a pleasurable experience of power over the terrifying, in addition to the usual delights of fiction.

Many are the means by which this sense of power can be provided. In Lovecraft's tale the narrator retains his sanity long enough to pen his story. In some tales the protagonist triumphs over terror, as in Ann Radcliffe's *The Italian*, a fantastic/uncanny tale; in others the protagonist is destroyed, leaving behind only a manuscript to tell the tale, as in Poe's "Ms. Found in a Bottle," a fantastic/marvelous tale. As long as the author provides a structure to preserve the aesthetic distance between real reader and text and as long as the implied and real reader are kept distinct, the work can successfully give the pleasure of controlling the threatening.

As the examples of *The Italian* and "Ms. Found in a Bottle" suggest, the special pleasures of the marvelous tale of terror probably are not greatly different from those of tales in two fantastic genres, the fantastic/marvelous and the fantastic/uncanny. All three genres tend to make the marvelous, apparently supernatural image their central experience. The protagonist and the implied reader move through suspense to the contemplation of such images. In each case, the goal of such fictions seems to be to release such images in highly controlled situations, to give them some play, and then to replace them in their proper region.

We can see this pattern fairly clearly, for example, in Ann Radcliffe. Elizabeth MacAndrew argues that in Radcliffe's two major Gothic novels the presentation of terrors is to educate the protagonists. Of *The Mysteries of Udolpho*, MacAndrew says:

> The adventure of the spirit its heroine has undergone leaves us with a picture of the eighteenth-century benevolist's view of human nature. That unspoiled nature that Emily represents grapples with what it at first sees as pure evil, an outside, diabolical force. Then it discovers the evil, Mon-

toni, is of human dimensions after all. A distortion of man's natural bent, his evil is malicious rather than malignant. This lesson learned, the figure of sensibility must then learn how to live in a fallen world by developing prudence: how, through the use of reason as well as sentiment, the good can live on earth. (136)

Emily's experience of the fantastic educates her in the nature of evil when the fantastic is resolved toward the uncanny. According to MacAndrew, this establishment of rational balance is less clear in *The Italian*, for there evil seems more absolute, less certainly an aberration resulting from distortions of a basically good human nature (139-41). Nevertheless, the Gothic experiences of the protagonists, Ellena and Vivaldi, are framed within a manuscript presented to an Englishman visiting in Italy. In each novel terror is loosed within a frame that sets boundaries to its effects. In Radcliffe's fiction, as in most of the tales we have discussed so far, terror is primarily the experience of characters; the reader experiences the horror of witnessing their sufferings.

We turn next to a brief look at an example of a fantastic/uncanny novel, Charles Brockden Brown's *Wieland*, to demonstrate the essential similarity between the effects of the marvelous tale of terror and the fantastic/uncanny tale. Indeed, it is probable that all tales of terror that use the marvelous image, whether or not it is finally resolved toward the uncanny by a natural explanation, will provide the same special component of aesthetic pleasure, for each kind can present marvelous images that are suggestive of psychological transgression.

## CHAPTER FOUR

# The Fantastic/Uncanny
# Horror Thriller

# I

Brown's *Wieland, or the Transformation* (1798) is an example of Todorov's fantastic/uncanny genre. Clara Wieland, the narrator and protagonist, hesitates between supernatural and natural explanations of
what appear to be supernatural events in her life. Though the implied
reader experiences this hesitation with her, for him this hesitation seems
clearly to be resolved toward natural explanations: her brother's visions
are symptoms of madness, and the voices they hear were produced by
the ventriloquist, Carwin. The novel is especially interesting in the
context of this study because Clara is never able to escape the fantastic;
she is unable to freely accept the natural explanations that the implied
reader accepts.

Clara's difficulty illustrates the trend MacAndrew sees at the end of
the eighteenth century and that we have already seen in our examination of *Edgar Huntly*. Writers in the Gothic tradition tended more
and more frequently to call into question the assumptions that stand
behind Emily St. Aubert's education in *The Mysteries of Udolpho*. Clara
Wieland's education follows almost precisely the same pattern, but
with a quite different result. She also moves from a secure and happy
life, for which all agree she is perfectly fitted by talent and education,
into a Gothic world of terror, which probes her weaknesses and reveals
the frailty of even the most accomplished rational virtue. It is important
to notice that Radcliffe's Emily must cross geographical borders to
encounter such experiences while Clara's Gothic terrors come to her
at home in her family. Clara emerges from this experience reaffirming

her culture's values and living by them, much as Emily does, but Clara's affirmation is disturbing and rings hollow. Brown's unusual ending places this novel, like *Edgar Huntly*, on the edge of its genre, pointing toward the more disturbing possibilities of the pure fantastic.

Like *At the Mountains of Madness, Wieland* is framed, but more elaborately. Dyer speaks in retrospect and promises a warning about exploring Antarctica. When the warning is complete, his tale is finished. Clara begins her narration in a similar way. She has experienced events that have brought her to despair. She expects to tell her tale and die. She assumes that God has determined to destroy her completely by taking away from her all that is good. To the implied reader, she promises thrills and wonder as she tells her reader, an unnamed friend, that he will wonder at her surviving what she has undergone. While she frames her opening in much the same way Dyer frames his, even to the point of promising some moral instruction, she ends her story much differently. In fact, she writes two endings. The first ending, in chapter 26, completes her initial framing. Her story is finished, she has relived her terrors for the benefit of her reader (and also the implied reader), her despair is justified, and now she can die. She writes her last paragraphs as if she were speaking aloud to a listener, though there is enough ambiguity to confuse the object of her address. She may be speaking to Carwin, *her* villain; to her listener; to "life"; to the implied reader; or to all of these together when she says: "Go, wretch! torment me not with thy presence and thy prayers.—Forgive thee? Will that avail thee when thy fateful hour shall arrive? Be thou acquitted at thy own tribunal, and thou needest not fear the verdict of others. If thy guilt be capable of blacker hues, if hitherto thy conscience be without stain, thy crime will be made more flagrant by thus violating my retreat. Take thyself away from my sight if thou wouldst not behold my death!" (263).

This extremely bitter and despairing statement, though consistent with the Clara's tone whenever she breaks her narration to speak of herself in the narrative present, is the opposite of the personality belonging to the self she presents in the narrative past. In other words, within her narrative frame, the first ending emphasizes her own transformation from a happy and accomplished young woman into a bitter recluse who welcomes her anticipated death. There are, however, so many transformations in the novel that one can hardly assert that this one is *the* transformation. The second ending presents another major transformation.

In chapter 27, Clara returns to her narrative three years after the end of the previous chapter. Needless to say, she is not dead. In fact, she is rather happy. Forced by a fire from seclusion in her house filled with memories of terror and loss, she has, over time in other scenes, gradually recovered from her despair. Fortune has brought her back together with her lost lover, and they are now married and living in Europe. Even Carwin, the horrific villain of the previous chapter, is now apparently reformed and living in virtue. Under the influence of this transformation, Clara has learned new lessons to convey.

She leads up to these lessons by telling a story parallel to her own, but somewhat distantly connected to it and to her. In other words, she is more distant from these horrors than from her own. In this story, Maxwell, a malicious gentleman has sought revenge on Stuart by compromising Stuart's virtuous wife, forcing her to flee from England to America with her infant daughter and to leave her husband with no notion of what has happened to her. Years later, after the deaths of both wife and daughter, when Stuart has learned the whole story, he challenges Maxwell to a duel, but is murdered before the duel can take place. Clara then states a rather astonishing lesson:

> That virtue should become the victim of treachery is, no doubt, a mournful consideration; but it will not escape your notice, that the evils of which Carwin and Maxwell were the authors owed their existence to the errors of the sufferers. All efforts would have been ineffectual to subvert the happiness or shorten the existence of the Stuarts, if their own frailty had not seconded these efforts. If the lady had crushed her disastrous passion in the bud, and driven the seducer from her presence when the tendency of his artifices was seen; if Stuart had not admitted the spirit of absurd revenge, we should not have to deplore this catastrophe. If Wieland had framed juster notions of moral duty and of the divine attributes, or if I had been gifted with ordinary equanimity or foresight, the double-tongued deceiver would have been baffled and repelled. (265-66)

This statement contrasts pointedly with her first paragraph in the novel, in which the moral lessons she expects her narrative to teach seem aimed at people like Maxwell and Carwin; they should avoid deceit and exercise self-control. In this passage, she blames the victims of deceit rather than the authors of their woe. She has, in relating the Maxwell and Stuart story, emphasized how perfectly prepared Mrs. Stuart was to resist Maxwell and how skilled and persistent Maxwell was in his advances: "The impulses of love are so subtle, and the influence of false reasoning, when enforced by eloquence and passion, so unbounded, that no human virtue is secure from degeneracy" (272). Which way will we have it then? Can virtue always protect itself, or will sufficient craft and persistence always prevail over any degree of virtue? Is it Stuart's fault that he is murdered after arranging a duel?

As Clara implies in the sentences about herself and Wieland, her new moral applies to her story as well as to that of Maxwell and Stuart.

Her brother has succumbed to a religious mania consisting of divine commands to murder his family. She has failed repeatedly to accurately understand the events that surrounded, but were not necessarily connected with, these murders. She says that neither of these failures would have taken place had Wieland understood God and morality better and had she possessed greater equanimity and foresight. Her language and ideas are so fuzzy and confused here that one wonders, even as she states the views that characterize her present happiness and sanity, whether she is sane. For example, how is it her *fault* that she was not *gifted* with ordinary equanimity or foresight? If Carwin is now reformed, how was he so devilish before?

We will see in examining her adventures that she does possess extraordinary equanimity and foresight, but that these qualities are simply insufficient to the extreme terrors she suffers. We will see that Wieland's ideas about God and morality are little different from those of any other "gentleperson" in the novel, that he commits his crimes, not because of unsound religious notions, but because he goes mad. We will also see that Carwin's part in the horrors is comparatively minor, and that at various moments in her ordeal Clara understands this. Yet here, at the second, "sane," ending of her narrative, she returns to making Carwin the cause of her fall.

The implied reader of *Wieland* never really enjoys the superior position granted the implied reader of *At the Mountains of Madness*. For most of the novel, it is virtually impossible for the implied reader to anticipate the truth about what is happening around Clara. Brown creates this effect, in part, to insure a close emotional and intellectual identification of the implied reader with Clara. Brown also wishes to mystify the reader, to make clear that the reality of these events, while they are taking place, is no more available to the more distant and, presumably, more collected reader than to Clara. Only after Carwin makes clear the extent of his participation in the terrors does the implied reader separate from Clara, watching from a slightly superior standpoint the stumbling of her consciousness in response to her losses.

Because through most of her ordeal, the implied reader shares her puzzlement, he must, on the whole, acquiesce in her hypotheses, even as these hypotheses repeatedly prove mistaken. That she is nearly always wrong when she reasons about her situation, despite her coolness and intelligence, forces the implied reader to realize that healthy senses and rationality are inadequate to the complexity of her situation. It becomes clear that only accident and intuition preserve her from permanent harm.

It will be helpful to begin looking at her adventures with a summary of what "really" happens. Then we may turn to what she sees happening.

The Wieland family is living happily and peacefully at Mettingen, their estate in the New World, when fantastic events begin to disturb their lives. Most of these fantastic events are caused by Carwin. He is hiding from unjust persecution and finds the estate a particularly satisfying retreat. While lurking there, he comes to know the family: Wieland; his sister, Clara; his wife, Catharine; her brother, Pleyel; a ward, Louisa; and the children. Carwin is a skilled ventriloquist; the Wielands know nothing of this art and at first know nothing of Carwin's presence. To prevent discovery, Carwin imitates Catharine's voice to draw Wieland away from him one night. This voice appears supernatural to Wieland, meshing with his interest in God's communications with men, especially his own father, who he believes was killed by divine judgment. As Carwin becomes increasingly but still secretly involved with the family, he finds other occasions to expose them to supposedly supernatural voices.

Carwin begins an affair with Clara's servant—Clara has her own house—and, through the servant, grows interested in Clara as a paragon of womanhood. He experiments with her and accidentally terrifies her, leading her to believe that someone wishes to murder her. He presents her with a "divine" voice that warns her away from supposed danger. After he has been publicly introduced into the family, he secretly learns her most private thoughts by prying into her diary. Caught in her closet one night, he invents the story that he intended to rape her to avoid having to explain his activities. Finally, he plays a kind of joke on Pleyel who has always been so sure of his senses, by counterfeiting for Pleyel's benefit, a dialogue in which it appears that Carwin is a thief and murderer and that Clara, knowing this, has become his mistress and enjoys this new state in the most depraved fashion.

Carwin's actions have several serious effects that he never foresees. Three times, Wieland hears Carwin's voice and believes he may be receiving messages from a benign spiritual being. These events move him toward accepting his later mad revelations as true divine messages. Through a series of accidents, Pleyel is completely convinced by Carwin's "joke," and Clara is utterly unable to persuade Pleyel of his error. This event is doubly terrible for Clara because she loses both her reputation and the esteem of the man she expected to propose to her. Finally, the overall effect of Carwin's acts is to persuade Clara that she is the victim of a monstrous, carefully orchestrated plot to destroy her happiness. She refers to this plot in the opening of her narrative as part of God's will. She comes to believe that Carwin is the sole agent of that plot, and she apparently has not abandoned that belief even at the end of her second ending.

Clearly, then, Carwin is not the monster Clara persists in believing him to be. Yet in another sense he is just such a monster. He has not plotted to convert the wise and benevolent Wieland into a homicidal maniac, to separate Pleyel and Clara, or to reduce Clara to despair. Failing to foresee how actions that appear quite separate to him could mesh into destructive unities for Wieland, Pleyel, and Clara, Carwin has deceived people in pursuit of his own ends, but he has not planned to destroy the family. Wieland's insanity and the accident of Pleyel's not discovering his error, as Carwin believed he would, are the real blows to Clara's happiness; neither of these events was intended by Carwin, though he contributed to each. Carwin intended only temporary, separate deceptions to cover his indiscretions and a joke that might correct a genuine defect in Pleyel's character. Clara seizes upon Carwin as the author of her woe before she knows the extent of his participation, and she is unable to give up this idea after she knows how he was involved, not even after he rescues her from Wieland. Although Carwin is not the monster who caused Clara's world to crumble, he is an excellent symbol of that monster. Clara needs to understand what has happened, to give it meaning. Carwin provides her the means of doing so. If she is afflicted by multiple losses within the space of a few months, there must be a malignant and supernatural agency behind these events. Carwin fills this need.

For the implied reader, the experience of the fantastic persists until Carwin's confession. It may even persist after the confession until there is more evidence to confirm his story, but the text seems designed to favor natural interpretations of ambiguous events. Therefore, when Carwin makes a natural explanation available, it tends to end the necessity of entertaining supernatural explanations for events such as hearing disembodied voices. Brown fairly decisively establishes the priority of natural explanations in the second chapter when he, as "editor," includes a footnote to assure the reader that the "spontaneous combustion" of Wieland's father was a natural occurrence (27). Once the implied reader has reasonably adequate natural explanations for the apparently supernatural events, the implied reader parts from Clara; instead of simply looking and thinking with Clara, one begins to look at her seeing and thinking. In her suffering and fear, she becomes the victim of the fixed idea that Carwin is a diabolical villain who may command supernatural aid. As we have seen, even after her recovery, she is unable to escape this idea.

Clara ends her book with illogical assertions that sufficient wisdom and virtue to avoid such catastrophes as she has experienced are available to us and that we need only exercise such wisdom and virtue to live happily in safety. Such piety is simply unavailable to the implied reader, for Clara has repeatedly made it clear that it is impossible for the best of us to exercise reason and virtue under the conditions that have assailed her. Virtually every character in the novel, including Pleyel and Carwin, testifies to Clara's perfection, asserting from wide experience of the world and observation of her character that she surpasses all women in her wisdom and virtue. Yet she clearly finds herself inadequate to deal with terror and acknowledges this in her narrative. For example, when she tells of her discovery of Carwin in her closet and of being persuaded that he had intended to rape her, she reflects in great detail on her thoughts and feelings. She says she once believed that she could never be raped were she rational and virtuous, for she could always take the life of her enemy. But when she found herself in what she thought was real danger, she was simply unable to resist. Her physical courage was drained, and she despaired of being able to reason with a rapist. Furthermore, later in the evening, when she believes Carwin has returned to carry out his intention, she finds herself planning to take her own life rather than be raped. Whenever any great horror threatens her, she finds herself inclined to surrender to it in some way, direct or indirect. The resolutions of virtue and wisdom, taken in peace and security, repeatedly fail her in the heat of perceived threat.

This pattern suggests that the malignant monstrosity in the world, which Clara wishes to concentrate in Carwin, is actually in herself. Carwin, by his behavior and appearance, calls to something unknown in Clara, and she is unable to resist. The insane Wieland has a similar power over her. When she first meets Carwin and hears his voice, she is inexplicably affected. She finds her thoughts confused and her behavior irrational for the first time in her brief adult life. She makes a portrait of him and is haunted by it, sleeping and waking. She finds that contemplating his image and voice leads her to depression, to thoughts about the meaninglessness of living and to a wish for death. Pleyel jokes that she is in love with Carwin and then actively seeks him out to introduce him to the family.

The causes of this effect are not specified, of course, since Clara does not understand them, but once the implied reader separates from Clara's judgments near the end of the novel, he is encouraged to range back over earlier events to understand Clara's apparent irrationality, much as we are doing now. Carwin's appearance to Clara follows close upon her admitting to herself that she has secretly wished for the death of Theresa, Pleyel's fiancée and Clara's rival. That this wish has been fulfilled is soon confirmed by a message from Germany announcing Theresa's death. As it turns out, this report is mistaken, but while Clara believes it, she suffers from unconscious guilt. Once we form the hypothesis that she connects Carwin in some way with unconscious guilt feelings, several facts begin to look like evidence.

Carwin rather nicely embodies ideas we now associate with the unconscious. He is physically distorted, his body parts seeming disproportionate to each other. He proves powerful, tricky, playful, spiteful, jealous, willful, and unrestrained in his behavior. Though his behavior seems childlike, he is very muscular and seems possessed of almost infinite knowledge. In ventriloquism, he possesses a secret power to influence people's actions. Furthermore, he seems to possess the power to alter his identity at will. Pleyel, it turns out, has met him in Spain, where they became close friends; there Carwin was an almost completely different person. And, this is, for much of the novel, the only past Carwin seems to possess; that is, in the past, he was someone else. When Clara only suspects but cannot yet see Carwin's dark side, she thinks him so talented as to be worthy of adoration yet so mysterious as to make her suspect him of evil.

It is plausible to see Carwin as representing to Clara her own unconscious intruding upon her consciousness. Acknowledging her desire for Theresa's death produces her interpretation of Carwin as her double. As her double, he can be split into good and evil, and then, when his folly compromises him, he becomes available to her as the expelled image of her unconscious desires. These desires may include, on one hand, the desire for Theresa's death and the desire for sexual union with Pleyel and perhaps with other men, even her brother. At least once she describes Wieland's love for her as more than brotherly. On the other hand, her unconscious may desire punishment for these illicit desires, the kind of punishment that accident provides at first, but that she prolongs in telling her story and in irrationally insisting upon driving herself to depression and death by remaining in her house after Wieland's death.

Of course, when she makes the "decision" to exacerbate and to perpetuate her suffering after Wieland's death, she has a good deal more on her "conscience." Though she labors to rest all guilt on Carwin, the real center, for her, of external terror is Wieland's transformation. That transformation carries meanings that she is never able to face.

In the transcript of Wieland's self-justification at his trial, we can see one central meaning of his transformation. Clara's uncle gives her this transcript to correct her idea that Carwin is wholly to blame for Wieland's fall. Wieland explains in the transcript that he loved God above all. Wishing to receive decisive acknowledgment of his love, he experienced an angel voice, which came to him at a moment when he was reflecting on his great love for his family. The angel voice commanded him to sacrifice his family to demonstrate his love for God. Wieland found a way to carry out a dark deed, to kill without feeling the pangs of conscience. When Clara's uncle assures her that such mania is relatively common, she reflects that she and Pleyel have also experienced voices—this is before Carwin's confession—and that they may suffer a similar mania at any moment: "I wondered at the change which a moment had effected in my brother's condition. Now was I stupified with tenfold wonder in contemplating myself. Was I not likewise transformed from rational and human into a creature of nameless and fearful attributes? Was I not transported to the brink of the same abyss? Ere a new day should come, my hands might be imbrued in blood, and my remaining life be consigned to a dungeon and chains" (205). Here she sees herself as she is and, prophetically, as she will be, in effect, at her first ending, yet even the repetition of this discovery in telling her narrative does not allow her to deal with it and therefore to understand how she projects this side of herself, and of all humans, onto Carwin.

Shortly before his last attempt on her life, Wieland and Clara share a brief moment of lucidity. He asserts that even though he is sorry he has murdered his family, he does not feel guilt because he believed he was acting at God's command. She finds his soul tranquil and sublime in this state and places herself infinitely beneath him: "My reason taught me that his conclusions were right; but, conscious of the impotence of reason over my own conduct, conscious of my cowardly rashness and my criminal despair, I doubted whether any one could be steadfast and wise" (254). Unable to believe in Wieland's apparent return to sanity, she expresses her opinion that Carwin is at fault. Wieland defends Carwin. However, this lucidity is instantly transformed as, between one sentence and the next, Wieland denies Carwin's fault in causing his actions and, then, affirms that Carwin has been God's agent in these actions and renews his purpose of killing Clara. Though she is reminded in several ways of Carwin's essential humanity, she persists in seeing him as a monster, not only because she needs an externalization of her own unconscious desires, but also because she needs a similar external cause for her brother's insanity. If there is an external cause, then she is not threatened with instantaneous transformation into madness and, as long as she is "gifted with ordinary equanimity and foresight," she can frustrate "the double-tongued deceiver."

# II

In this example of a fantastic/uncanny horror thriller, we see the apparently marvelous character and events becoming repositories for the unconscious of Clara and her brother. Carwin and his power are uncanny in the Freudian sense for Clara. Because they correspond so well to what we can infer about her unconscious, she is unable to resolve the uncanny effects, though she does get over the immediate consequences of her experiences with the uncanny. I have grouped together as horror thrillers those tales of terror that, while not in Todorov's pure fantastic genre, make use of the marvelous either as the accepted view of events or as an alternative view. The examination of *Wieland* suggests that this grouping is reasonable from the point of view of the aesthetic question, which is our main concern.

Both the marvelous horror thriller and the fantastic/uncanny horror thriller, when they use psychologically suggestive marvelous images, may produce the special effect of a brush with real terror. While Lovecraft constructs elaborate protective barriers between the real reader and his terrifying images, Brown relies primarily on conventional fictional devices, especially closure. The villain is unmasked, the mysteries are solved, the supernatural appearances are "naturalized," the protagonist regains her mental balance and will to live, and finally she marries the right man. During her narration, distance is sustained by Clara's own apparent distance from the events she narrates, though not from their effects. Distance is also sustained, perhaps even enhanced to some extent, by the intense focus on her as the one who experiences fantastic terrors and vacillates between the alternative interpretations and for whom the implied reader is to feel pity and fear, partly as a result of sharing her vacillation. However, as in *Edgar Huntly*, Brown complicates closure. Even though he provides several conventional signals of closure and adds the unusual double ending, he manages, by making the second ending so puzzling, to provide the reader with an experience somewhat parallel to Clara's. As Clara has difficulty reading Carwin, so we have difficulty reading her. Just when the experience of the work seems complete, when all the expected signals of closure are present, and when it appears that Clara has regained her balance, Clara metamorphoses into a blurred, double character. The implied reader has separated himself from her and has seen that rational virtue is really inadequate to real malevolence and even to sufficiently complex accidental confusion. In her second ending, she first demonstrates this truth with a second example, then denies the truth her example demonstrates and, furthermore, asserts that rational virtue is adequate to all evils, even the "diabolical" Carwin. A satisfactory explanation of this new view of Clara is possible, as we have seen, but it requires that the reading process extend for some period after the end of the text. During that rather uncomfortable period when the book refuses an easy and expected concretization, the implied reader tastes what it was like for Clara to confront Carwin in her closet after he has entered her dreams, so to speak.

We see in both Lovecraft and Brown what Christopher Craft has called the characteristic triple rhythm of the Gothic novel. Speaking of *Dracula, Frankenstein,* and *Dr. Jekyll and Mr. Hyde,* Craft says: "Each of these texts first invites or admits a monster, then entertains and is entertained by monstrosity for some extended duration, until in its closing pages it expels or repudiates the monster and all the disruption that he/she/it brings. . . . Within its extended middle, the gothic novel entertains its resident demon . . . and the monster, now ascendent in its strength, seems for a time potent enough to invert the 'natural' order and overwhelm the comforting closure of the text. That threat, of course, is contained and finally nullifed by the narrative requirement that the monster be repudiated and the world of normal relations re-stored" (107-8). Brown's equivocal ending makes the "expulsion" of the monster problematic, for the monster is not really Carwin. And Clara, still thinking Carwin is a monster, has failed to expel from her consciousness the monster she has "created." This strategy suggests a potential for entrapping the implied reader, which the pure fantastic can realize more fully, the possibility of blocking closure. Before turning to that area of exploration, however, we need to explore what special pleasures horror thrillers offer their readers.

Andrew Griffin, in his discussion of monster films, and Christopher Craft have each suggested that the horror thriller allows us in imagi-nation to entertain monsters in the highly controlled situations of lit-erary art works. We have seen how a few monsters are presented, how the situations are controlled, and how they may threaten to go out of control. What makes such works pleasurable? Let us turn now to a fantastic/marvelous horror thriller, Stoker's *Dracula,* to answer this question.

## CHAPTER FIVE

# The Aesthetics of the Horror Thriller: Stoker's *Dracula*

The horror thriller, both in its marvelous and in its uncanny forms, presents the implied reader with ideas and images of terror screened by various conventional and special techniques so that the real reader can experience power over these images and ideas. This is what we mean by safe thrills. Unless something in an individual reader leads to an anomalous response, this kind of literary structure allows the real reader to make a protected contact with that which should not be. The number of films and popular books that provide this experience in contemporary Western culture suggests that we value this kind of experience highly. Why?

We can follow the hints offered by Andrew Griffin and Christopher Craft and hypothesize that the horror thriller offers a reenactment of repression. By bringing readers into carefully controlled contact with symbolic representations of the culturally forbidden and affirming that control, the horror thriller becomes one of a culture's instruments of repression. The reader of Lovecraft or Brown becomes better at repressing the forbidden by meeting it again in another identity—the implied reader—and repeating original acts of repression. Henry James, Edgar Allan Poe, and others, including filmmakers such as Val Lewton, have helped to make us aware that horror images are most effective when minimally specified because the reader is then encouraged to read his own personal versions of cultural repressions into the images (Telotte on Lewton, 15-18). Now we may further hypothesize that works that encourage this kind of reading will be more greatly valued because the individual reader will be enabled to reenact his personal repressions. Both Lovecraft and Brown give the reader opportunities to meet the repressed and to reassert the power of identity over it. The power of choosing ourselves as individual personalities in whole bodies is one of humanity's major psychological accomplishments; it is something that, on the whole, humans do well. The main visible result of this activity is a rich variety of human cultures. It would seem natural, then, to take pleasure in "doing it again."

Contemporary culture often devalues works that seem to be instruments of cultural repression and to praise those that seem more clearly designed to subvert culture. The truth is, of course, that we need both. Culture is what humanity makes; without it we are not only less interesting, but also without anyone to be interested in us. On the other hand, culture seems to want to stop being made. Our ideas of such monolithic, static cultures appear in dystopic novels in which the differences between humanity and ants tend to disappear, e.g., George Orwell's *1984*. Therefore, culture also needs to be subverted continuously even as it is being continuously created and affirmed. Without subversion, there would be no creation.

Bram Stoker's *Dracula* (1897) is an excellent horror thriller with which to elaborate and demonstrate this hypothesis about the aesthetics of the horror thriller. It is a drama of reenacted repression that seems remarkably conscious of its purpose. By examining this text, we can see fairly clearly both how a self-conscious horror thriller deploys itself to reenact repression and the degree to which Stoker valued this reenactment.

# I

*Dracula* can be divided into four main parts. In chapters 1-4, Jonathan Harker recounts in his journal a trip to Transylvania and Count Dracula's departure from there. Chapters 5-16 center on the conflict between Dracula and a loose band of allies over Lucy Westenra. Chapters 17-23 tell of the drawing together of the loose band into an effective group of hunters as the center of conflict between them and Dracula shifts to Mina, newly wedded to Harker. Chapters 24-27 cover the pursuit and exorcism of Dracula. At the center of the plot, the point at which the hunters shift from a loose band into an organized group, is the recognition of Dracula, a protracted but absolutely crucial part of the novel. The hunters cannot conquer Dracula until they know him. Therefore, a central question of the novel becomes: who is Dracula?

Of course, Dracula is a monster, a vampire, endowed with immortality unless killed in a highly specified and ritual manner. He drinks blood, not, it appears, because he is dependent upon blood to stay alive; he seems able to live indefinitely without blood. However, consuming blood seems to invigorate him and to make him appear younger. He can also replicate himself by drinking blood, but he never actually reproduces himself. In fact, rather startlingly, Dracula is shown, in Stoker's novel, only to generate "jackals," female vampires who, on the whole, do the Count's bidding. If he need not consume blood to stay alive, if taking blood invigorates him, and if the vampiric bite gives him reproductive power that he uses to create female minions rather than true rivals, then Renfield's pronouncement that "the blood is the life" seems to mean that blood is a source of power. While popular versions of the vampire myth imply that the vampire is dependent on human hosts for physical survival, Stoker modifies this view to reduce the appearance of Dracula's dependency. The irony of the dependency of the "master" sacrificed at this point reappears on a "spiritual" level, however. Mere physical survival is not enough for Dracula; to be without blood to drink is to be impotent. His spirit needs power. When we attempt to trace Count Dracula's central characteristic, his vampirism, to its final cause in Stoker's presentation, we discover that Dracula wishes to be master. In his Transylvanian castle, he is master, but he wants to extend that mastery out of this land of dreams, of superstition, paganism, feudalism, irrationality, and of life in the night. He aspires to extend his power over Western civilization, the too-rational, Christian, waking, modern, daylight world from which Harker is an emissary. On this most obvious level, then, Dracula represents the return of the repressed, an attempt of the unconscious to assert power over and to absorb consciousness.

That Stoker encourages the implied reader to see Dracula as representing the repressed is clear from the beginning. Jonathan Harker's record of his journey to Transylvania, of his encounters with the vampires, and of his own successful resistance of the vampires is highly suggestive.

Harker's journal is addressed to Mina, his betrothed. He repeatedly refers to her, thinking of her as a judging consciousness for whom he must get recipes and before whom he must be careful in expressing his sexual interests. The memoranda he makes show that he thinks of Mina as someone to whom he must account and of the Count as a source of knowledge. As he naively puts it, "I read that every known superstition in the world is gathered into the horseshoe of the Carpathians, as if it were the centre of some sort of imaginative whirlpool; if so my stay may be very interesting. (*Mem.*, I must ask the Count all about them.)" (4, see also 9). In Harker's mind, Mina is one contact with the West, with repression. The other main contact is his work;

he travels on business. However, while his business is a constant reminder of who he is and where he comes from, it also draws him toward the Count, propelling him onward despite the warnings of the natives. In this respect, he reminds one of Nathaniel Hawthorne's Young Goodman Brown, off to the forest on night business, leaving the proper young woman behind.

East and West, Count and Mina are set up in opposition to each other in the first chapter. In the East is dark knowledge from which the West would restrain Harker. The Count possesses what Harker wants, and knowledge is not all that Harker wants. In his notes he gives special attention to primal needs, to food, drink, and sex. Though all three are significant—since he becomes a possible source of all three to his "host and hostesses"—sex probably proves most important in the novel as a whole. Repeatedly he comments on the female natives during his journey, taking note of their sexual attractiveness: "The women looked pretty, except when you got near them, but they were very clumsy about the waist. They had all full white sleeves of some kind or other, and most of them had big belts with a lot of strips of something fluttering from them like the dresses in a ballet, but of course petticoats under them" (5, this passage varies, but not significantly, in different editions). The woman who brings him a message from Dracula wears an undergarment "fitting almost too tight for modesty" (6). These women do not satisfy Harker's probing eye, but they reveal its presence. They are the opposites of Dracula's ladies, who are more attractive at close range than at a distance and who provide the sexual experience his eye seeks with the native women.

Harker goes to Castle Dracula hungering after knowledge of darkness and after sexual experience. He wants to see the repressed, to look into his own unconscious. The journey becomes explicitly a dream journey and remains so for him until Dr. Van Helsing and Mina are able to assure him, months later, that his experiences at the castle were real. In this dreamlike state, he undergoes the splitting of his identity. There are many symptoms of this split, but the most explicit one is the incident of the shaving mirror. In the "objective" mirror, there is only Harker, but in Harker's "subjective" vision there are Harker, the seer, and Dracula, the seen. Dracula's response to Harker's shaving cut, the result of a start upon seeing no Count in the mirror, is doubly or triply ironic: "Take care how you cut yourself. It is more dangerous than you think in this country" (27). The Count then discards the mirror, calling it a "foul bauble of man's vanity" (27). One meaning of his statement, of which Dracula need not be conscious, is that the mirror, in affirming the unity of the psyche, deceives the individual into a belief in his absolute individuality. After Harker is seen to be split into conscious and unconscious, the unconscious waxes ever stronger. Harker becomes weak and realizes he is Dracula's helpless prisoner. Dracula takes over Harker's identity, wearing his clothes and acting "for" him outside the castle. And Harker takes Dracula's place, climbing the outside walls of the castle, lurking in its forbidden places, and meeting his women. Finally, their exchange of identities is almost completed as Dracula departs, and Harker is left to the ladies. By implication, Dracula usurps Harker's identity and takes his unconscious to England, leaving the conscious mind behind, trapped in Dracula's castle, where Dracula himself was trapped until something about Western civilization drew him out.

Near the end of the book, Van Helsing is quite specific about what drew Dracula out. Again, he begins in terms of blood; Dracula saw rich possibilities of life among the teeming Western nations, but, of course, he could have gone to India or China. What attracts him to England and the West is the skepticism of an enlightened age. Van Helsing says, in his always interestingly ungrammatical way, that they must hunt Dracula in secret because of this skepticism: "Our toil must be in silence, and our efforts all in secret; for in this enlightened age, when men believe not even what they see, the doubting of wise men would be his greatest strength. It would be at once his sheath and his armour, and his weapons to destroy us, his enemies, who are willing to peril even our own souls for the safety of one we love" (282-84). Notice that skepticism is Dracula's sheath, his hiding place; skepticism makes Dracula invisible. Where Dracula is invisible, he sees his chance to gain mastery.

We have seen that Dracula represents the repressed unconscious. Even to Harker, Dracula suggests the unconscious. Dracula's departure for England is represented in part as a split in Harker, resulting in Harker's unconscious being incarnated and unleashed on Western civilization. What can be said about the content of that unconscious? In Harker's experience of vampires, what does one learn about what is forbidden to Harker?

Certainly the most lurid and revealing passage in Harker's journal of the Transylvanian sojourn is his encounter with Dracula's ladies. The passage has been much studied, and the "perversions" found have varied greatly. Critics have seen interest in oral sex, homosexuality, blurring of gender distinction, incest, and plain old lust. We will see evidence that all these aspects of forbidden sex are indeed present. There can be little doubt that lust arises in this passage on the approach of the "fair girl":

> I was afraid to raise my eyelids, but looked out and saw perfectly under the lashes. The fair girl went on her knees, and bent over me, fairly

gloating. There was a deliberate voluptuousness which was both thrilling and repulsive, and as she arched her neck she actually licked her lips like an animal, till I could see in the moonlight the moisture shining on the scarlet lips and on the red tongue as it lapped the white sharp teeth. Lower and lower went her head as the lips went below the range of my mouth and chin and seemed about to fasten on my throat. Then she paused, and I could hear the churning sound of her tongue as it licked her teeth and lips, and could feel the hot breath on my neck. Then the skin of my throat began to tingle as one's flesh does when the hand that is to tickle it approaches nearer—nearer. I could feel the soft, shivering touch of the lips on the supersensitive skin of my throat, and the hard dent of two sharp teeth, just touching and pausing there. I closed my eyes in a languorous ecstasy and waited—waited with a beating heart. (39-41)

Stoker reserves such detailed descriptions almost exclusively for encounters with vampires, especially the exorcism of Lucy and the blood baptism of Mina.

Though these detailed accounts are never explicitly sexual, it is hard for an alert reader to avoid noticing their sexual suggestiveness. When Harker first becomes fully aware of the ladies' presence, he thinks, "There was something about them that made me uneasy, some longing and at the same time some deadly fear. I felt in my heart a wicked, burning desire that they would kiss me with those red lips. It is not good to note this down, lest some day it should meet Mina's eyes and cause her pain; but it is the truth" (39). Harker is clearly aware of sexual desire in himself, which he feels is wicked. This very desire is then actually enacted by the fair vampire. She does kiss him with her red lips, but she represents his desire more fully than with her kiss. When they make contact, Harker plays the passive and receptive female, and the vampire takes the role of aggressive penetration. This is not simple role reversal, however, because the purpose of her penetrating him is to take rather than give fluid. Yet by taking fluid, she can "infect" him. Not only is this wicked kiss lustful, but it also confuses, perhaps even eliminates gender difference. Role reversal and confused gender point toward homosexuality, a suggestion that becomes more explicit when Dracula stops the women and claims Harker as his own. The idea of homosexuality becomes even more explicit in the conflict over Lucy, where transfusion comes to be defined as marriage and where Dracula absorbs through the medium of Lucy the blood of three men: Arthur Holmwood, Dr. Seward, and Van Helsing (Craft). Incest may be suggested when Lucy receives blood from Van Helsing (a father figure) and when Dracula "nurses" his "bride," Mina, at his bloody breast (Twitchell, *Dreadful Pleasures* 137-39). The sexual suggestions of these scenes are also predominantly oral. The penetrating teeth, the churning tongue, the voluptuous lips, the tingling throat—these are the organs of pleasure. Furthermore, sexual pleasure is connected with the other primal pleasures of sucking and eating; all three are to be gratified simultaneously.

In Harker's journal, vampirism becomes associated with sexual pleasure. Stoker makes the ladies into repulsive images of horror, but because his presentation is so suggestive of sexual pleasure, they should also be attractive to the implied reader. Stoker seems to want a reader who will recognize the attractiveness of what the ladies offer, but who will want Harker to resist, nevertheless. To resist is to be loyal to Mina and to preserve his own endangered identity. What do the ladies offer in exchange for Harker's self? Not mere sexual pleasure, but *forbidden* sexual pleasure. While Harker's society prescribes monogamy, they offer promiscuity—or at least polygamy. While Harker's society prescribes heterosexual relations with clearly differentiated gender roles, they offer the elimination of gender roles. While his society prescribes genital sexual contact, they offer at the least oral and possibly polymorphous sexual contact. The sexual alternatives the ladies promise, when taken together, suggest infantile sexuality: undifferentiated sexual pleasure orally centered, sometimes called polymorphous perversion. Finally, as Norman Holland implies in *The I,* Harker's society (perhaps all societies) prescribes the maintenance of identity (74-76). Harker is tempted at Castle Dracula to surrender his self, to accept a transformation into a preverbal, selfless state.

Who is Dracula? He is the repressed unconscious of Harker's society, especially that part concerned with infantile sexuality. He is the child in Harker (and in the other men of the novel) with which he must come to terms before he can marry. Harker becomes a solicitor just before leaving on his trip, which is presented as a rite of passage into the professional life. When (and if) he returns from this business trip, he plans to wed. On the trip he meets his own shadow in Dracula. In the form of Dracula, that infantile self, what Van Helsing calls a child brain and a criminal brain, is turned loose. Until it is recaptured and controlled, though Harker may legally marry Mina, he cannot really possess her. It is significant that the book ends with a last entry in Harker's journal, in which, among other important matters, he tells of the birth of his son and of how his son must come to understand what Harker has learned from hunting vampires.

Harker's problem is to come to terms with his own unconscious. This problem is externalized in the struggle over Lucy and Mina between Dracula and a group of good men. To succeed, Harker must repress Dracula, not by driving him back into the land of dreams, but by transforming him. We learn that it is the nature of vampires to be transformed when they are properly, ritualistically killed. By repressing

Dracula, Harker accomplishes what we usually think of as the repression of infantile sexuality in favor of genital sexuality and reproduction. What, then, is the right way to kill/transform a vampire?

The remaining three parts of the novel deal primarily with this problem, recapitulating and completing what Harker has begun. The struggle over Lucy repeats Harker's discovery of the vampire. The battle over Mina in England culminates in the recognition of the vampire. Only when the recognition is complete can the hunt succeed in the final chapters.

The discovery of the vampire in England elaborates on the wish fulfillment pattern we saw in Harker's journey to Transylvania. An especially significant addition to this pattern is feminine wishing. We saw what Harker wanted, but could not have when he met Dracula's ladies. The pattern of wish fulfillment in England reveals what Lucy and Mina want but cannot have.

In chapters 5 and 6, Mina and Lucy are placed in opposition. Mina's man is absent. She is a working woman and expects to become her husband's working partner. She has been Lucy's teacher and remembers that life with pleasure. She wishes to return to it (57) and, in making such a wish, implies her desire to be like Lucy. Lucy is surrounded by men who wish to marry her. She belongs to the leisure class and promises to be more an ornament than a working partner in the marriage she plans with Arthur, the future Lord Godalming. While Mina wishes to be like Lucy, Lucy wishes for the forbidden. She laments that she cannot marry all of the three men who propose to her on the same day. She even expresses a wish to marry *all* the men who want her. In addition to these central wishes, both Mina and Lucy wish to return to their innocent childhood, to the times they have spent together free of thoughts of marriage and womanhood. Mina also expresses a desire to travel in foreign lands with Jonathan.

These are the wishes of the women. What of the men? Quincy, Seward, and Holmwood all wish to marry Lucy. When Seward is disappointed, he wishes to dedicate himself to an unselfish cause; this desire leads him to the study of his mad patient, Renfield. All of these wishes are granted—by Dracula. By means of the vampire attack on Lucy, Mina and Lucy are drawn together again in something like their old childhood innocence. Mina is called to Hungary to care for Harker and bring him home. Lucy gets to marry, by means of transfusion, all the men who want her, and all of them, of course, get to "marry" her in the same way. Mina gets to become like Lucy in almost every way. Dracula is not apparently responsible for her ascension to the leisure class upon the death of Harker's father figure, Hawkins, but he does make it possible for her to move into the center of Lucy's group of men. His attack threatens to make her Lucy's double.

Dracula "grants" other wishes as well, but these are enough to establish the pattern. By and large, these wishes are infantile and individualistic: dreams of gratification without serious regard for the consequences to others. Gratifying those wishes gives power to the unconscious and can destroy the wishing individual. This is Lucy's fate, which also teaches those who care about her that Dracula is present. They vow to destroy him, but to do so, they must not only find him, but recognize him. Identifying and killing Dracula prove to be a single act viewed from two perspectives.

To find Dracula, the initiates or discoverers must first form a community. Van Helsing leads, first gathering the three suitors together in the revelation of Lucy as vampire and in her exorcism, then drawing Mina and John into the group. We should notice that Dracula's victory over Lucy coincides with the deaths of all the parental figures in the group except Van Helsing. After she is "dead," Van Helsing and Dracula remain as good and bad parental figures; the question of who is to be master is simplified. Will the members of the group enter adulthood under the influence of Van Helsing or Dracula? As Gregory Waller in *The Living and the Undead* and others have argued, the confrontation that follows is not, however, between Van Helsing and Dracula, but between a community of hunters and Dracula. Furthermore, Mina's gathering of the narrative fragments into a whole history is as crucial to the community's union as are Van Helsing's knowledge of tradition and the ritual of freeing Lucy (Waller 30-48). When the group is gathered, Van Helsing summarizes the nature of the conflict he sees: describing what is known of Dracula's powers as brutally evil—to be defeated by him is to become him—and listing the group's special strengths: "We have on our side power of combination—a power denied to the vampire kind; we have resources of science; we are free to act and think; and the hours of the day and the night are ours equally. In fact, so far as our powers extend, they are unfettered, and we are free to use them. We have self-devotion in a cause, and an end which is not a selfish one" (211-12).

Though they know and agree that the power of combination is central, they have the most difficulty in actually realizing this power, because they are so slow to recognize Dracula after they discover him. And one reason for this slowness is that they are unable to find the proper place for Mina in the group.

As William Patrick Day has pointed out, Mina is presented as the group's intellectual and spiritual center (*In the Circles of Fear and Desire* 57). Van Helsing, as father figure, provides the values of tradition and technical knowledge. The other men mainly provide action. Mina is the mother who provides a home and an emotional center for the men. She transforms their male bonds into domestic loyalty, which is represented as devotion to the highest ideals of Western civilization: Christianity, family affection, unity of action for the good of the community. But, very importantly, she is also the scholar. At every crucial point, from the beginning of their forming a community of vampire hunters, she is the one who by careful research and thinking solves the apparently impossible problem. She compiles the narrative that establishes Dracula's presence in England and the truth of Harker's Transylvania experience. This discovery not only makes the hunt possible, but also leads directly to curing Harker of his enervation, making him, in his words, potent again. She realizes after her baptism that she can reveal Dracula's whereabouts by being hypnotized. Mina, with Van Helsing, solves the problem of where Dracula will go when he evades them in Transylvania, and she alone reasons out his route.

When we can see so clearly in retrospect the importance of Mina to the group's success, then it becomes especially clear how mistaken the men are to try to exclude her from the hunt. Van Helsing argues that even though she has a man's brain in a woman's body, she ought not to be risked: "We men are determined—nay, are we not pledged?—to destroy this monster; but it is no part for a woman. Even if she be not harmed, her heart may fail her in so much and so many horrors; and hereafter she may suffer—both in waking, from her nerves, and in sleep, from her dreams" (209). The consequences he describes are almost precisely those that occur as a result of keeping her in the dark. As they make this resolution to repress Mina, they are repeatedly described as boyish. Their keeping her "in the dark" has at least two important meanings, in addition to the main one of failing to be a true community. They are returning to the boyish pleasure of the hunts the three young men have shared in the past. They are denying Mina's personhood and her stake in the outcome of the hunt. The consequences of repressing her make their error clear. She stays alone in her room at Seward's asylum while the boys go out hunting at night—Harker has no sooner regained his potency than he devotes it to activities other than intercourse with Mina. Left in the dark, ignorant of their activities, she pines away in uselessness. Unsatisfied natural desires—these are Dracula's domain. Therefore, the ultimate consequence of the repression of Mina is that Dracula takes possession of her; if she is repressed, she is forced to become Dracula's jackal. She is given to him. Once he takes possession, she becomes almost a parody of the domestic woman, weeping, depressed, and weak in her lonely asylum.

Because the men have been boys and have failed to make Mina a full partner in the group, they lose her to the enemy. The loss is not complete, however. In fact, it becomes a blessing because it teaches them what they did not know.

After Mina's fall, she asks what she could have done to deserve the fate of being alienated from God despite her attempts to be good. We can see that she has done nothing to deserve such a fate. Rather, on one level, she is, like all mankind, a victim of original sin. On another, she is, like all mankind, split into conscious and unconscious. Repressing her has led to making this split visible, just as it makes her original sin visible in the scar produced by the Host on her forehead. If the visible symbol for the men of what is best in their civilization is split, then, of course, so are they and their civilization.

The visibility of this split leads directly to the recognition of Dracula. Even before her fall, Mina was inclined to pity the hunted and lonely Dracula. Then she pulls back from this pity, as do all the others whom he has hurt. To them, at that point, he is merely an external enemy to be destroyed in vengeance. After her fall, the motive of revenge is even stronger, especially in Harker. But when the hunters return to Mina after Dracula escapes them and taunts them, saying he possesses their girls, Mina identifies Dracula as herself. To the angry and exasperated men, she says: "I know that you must fight—that you must destroy even as you destroyed the false Lucy so that the true Lucy might live hereafter; but it is not a work of hate. That poor soul who has wrought all this misery is the saddest case of all. Just think what will be his joy when he too is destroyed in his worser part that his better part may have spiritual immortality. You must be pitiful to him too, though it may not hold your hands from his destruction" (272). When Harker demurs, she reminds him: "Just think, my dear . . . I too may need such pity; and that some other like you—and with equal cause for anger—may deny it to me!" (273). When the men see the vampire in Mina, they can pity Dracula and can carry out the new covenant they made after discovering the Count with Mina. Though they are tempted to exclude Mina again because the Count can use her against them, they soon abandon the idea as impractical. To deal with the unconscious, we must accept its presence, and we must bring *all* of our mental faculties into play.

The proper way to kill a vampire, then, is with love. Though Lucy was exorcised with love, the men do not understand the importance of this ingredient in the ritual until after Mina's fall, for only then can they begin in any way to understand the vampire as a part of themselves. When the vampire is killed with love, he or she is not really killed at all, but transformed.

The characters in *Dracula* discover the monster in the appearance of their childish wishes. At first, they think of the monster as another being, but eventually they recognize the monster as related to themselves. Finally, the external embodiment of the monster, the incarnation of the repressed, is destroyed, its heart stopped, its head separated permanently from its body. When this ritual is complete, the repressed returns transformed or neutralized to the unconscious, and they are free. Healthy sexual relations commence, and the dark Eastern land becomes a vacation spot and a reminder of what all must go through in one form or another in order truly to love others.

*Dracula*, then, presents a reenactment of repression. The repressed is released in order that we may, in the guise of the implied reader, repress it again. Stoker explicitly, perhaps even consciously, develops this structure. Though he is not explicit about the content of the repressed, he has brought it near the surface, making it easy for critics to discover. This technique suggests that Stoker did not fear that his thrills would be too much for his audience. Though he skillfully uses conventional devices of distance and closure to maintain the separation between implied reader and real reader, he does not set up additional screening structures to the extent that Lovecraft does. Like Lovecraft, he creates an implied reader who is superior in knowledge to his narrators. Though it is possible to read the first four chapters naively, discovering Harker's position as Harker discovers it, it is impossible to miss dramatic irony while Dracula is in England. Stoker also may create a more secure distance between implied reader and text by specifying his horrors in rather great detail. The most graphically rendered scenes are confrontations with vampires: Harker's with the ladies, meeting Lucy in the graveyard and her exorcism, and the blood baptism of Mina. The latter even has the advantage of being described twice, from the outside by Seward and from the inside by Mina. Though these scenes are highly suggestive, they are definite enough to limit to some extent what may be read into them from the reader's unconscious.

This novel offers the same general pleasures of all good novels, the aesthetic pleasures of making a concretion out of the signs provided by the text. The pleasures specific to it as a horror thriller are those of reenacting repression. Just as we take pleasure in the exercise of imagination to convert language into images, images into characters and actions, characters and actions into a plot, which is a concretion of the whole in which all the prominent features we have noticed have a place, so we also enjoy the similar exercise of imagination in meeting, recognizing, and replacing some of the main repressions we have made in becoming adults. These activities of the imagination combine in the best horror thrillers to produce an especially strong feeling of mental power, of being in control of one's ego or identity. Indeed, some horror thrillers, like *Dracula* and Ann Radcliffe's *The Italian* include a kind of celebration of this feeling of power at their ends.

# II

The horror thriller, in all three of the forms we have examined, offers an opportunity to reenact repression. Examining *Dracula* suggests the possibility that this reenactment may take place at two different levels. Insofar as we perceive the monster as evocative of all that we repress during what Jacques Lacan describes as the mirror phase of the development of the self, we reenact not particular acts of repression, but the primal general discovery of repression as a means of achieving selfhood. At a less universal level, we may relive repressions specific to our individual cultures and personalities. Presumably this would take place if something in a particular image evokes a cultural repression or strikes a personal chord without destroying aesthetic distance. The primal reenactment would seem the more important because it should be universal, but unique, cultural and personal responses should add to the pleasure of completing the work. Griffin says such experiences may soothe our fears about "loss of control and loss of identity" (17). Craft suggests that some kind of "play" is taking place in this controlled release of monstrosity (107-8). In *The I*, Holland presents two arguments that suggest the seriousness of this kind of play.

First, Holland argues for an identity principle to replace Freud's idea of a death instinct to explain our compulsion to mentally repeat traumatic experiences. Drawing on the work of Heinz Lichtenstein, Holland argues that to explicate human motivation, we require not only the pleasure and reality principles, but also the identity principle. Humans, indeed all living organisms, need to maintain identity. This need is strong enough to override the pleasure principle. Hence, we will endure pain if necessary to maintain identity. Furthermore, humans will not surrender identity completely, even in brainwashing or in psychoanalytic cures (74-76).

Second, Holland develops Freud's discussion, in "Analysis Terminable and Interminable," of defense mechanisms. Repression is, of course, a defense mechanism by which we hide our unacceptable wishes from ourselves or subordinate them to acceptable wishes. Freud, as quoted by Holland, points out: "The adult's ego, with its increased strength, continues to defend itself against dangers which no longer exist in reality; indeed, it finds itself compelled to seek out those situations in reality which can serve as an approximate substitute for the original danger, so as to be able to justify, in relation to them, its maintaining its habitual modes of reaction" (109). In this passage, Freud is discussing "abnormal" behavior, but we all use the defense of repression; our concern with what our culture as a whole more or less agrees to repress seems normal. The horror thriller, then, provides most members of our culture with a game, a safe, bounded process into which we can enter. By participating in the game, we do what our less fortunate fellows, as described by Freud, do in their lives. We seek to repeat those acts by which we establish and maintain our identities. Day also argues that by making our fears and desires a source of pleasure and by asserting the imagination's power over them, the horror thriller of the Gothic tradition can be therapeutic (67-74). J. P. Telotte goes a small step further when he argues that the confrontation in art between the ego and its unconscious can be liberating insofar as it reveals the psyche's power of creating order (187-89).

In the horror thriller, we make a kind of game out of what in our lives is deadly serious, the creation and maintenance of a self in culture. The game gives a brief license to the culturally forbidden, allowing it to take form in monsters to which our responses are, inevitably, ambivalent. *Dracula* makes especially clear that these monsters come out of the self and, therefore, belong to it. This discovery becomes part of the game. Essential to maintaining the game as game are all the traditional literary conventions that sustain the aesthetic relation between reader and work. To play the role of implied reader in such a work is to volunteer for a test of strength, a comparatively easy one for most readers. The work challenges the real reader: can you play this game? Can you look on the forbidden and maintain your mental balance? At the same time that the work issues this challenge, it also provides a redundancy of safety equipment, thus making the reenactment fairly easy. To make the reenactment more difficult, perhaps even impossible, is an alternative some artists might intuitively perceive. We have seen in Brown a certain desire to disrupt the pattern by "fiddling" with the safety equipment.

Any serious use of the fantastic seems to draw the author toward such tampering. It may have struck the reader that we have said little about the presence of the fantastic in *Dracula*. Harker experiences the fantastic at Castle Dracula, wondering whether Dracula is really a monster and whether his ladies are dreams. His experience of the fantastic continues until Mina's scholarship and Van Helsing's assurances based on that scholarship convince Harker that the whole Transylvanian adventure was fact rather than dream. The implied reader's hesitation is harder to specify. As Tzvetan Todorov implies, it is quite difficult to reread fantastic texts. Coming to the text in full knowledge of how the fantastic will be resolved greatly changes how one can successfully construct the implied reader. It seems clear, however, that the "original" implied reader is to share Harker's initial confusion about his experiences. Without this confusion, it would be more difficult to notice how Dracula connects with Harker's unconscious wishes and embodies them. Therefore, the hesitation of the implied reader can hardly extend beyond Lucy's first transfusion, even though the men continue to be skeptical until Lucy's exorcism. Hesitation between two interpretations is not foregrounded in this text to the degree that it is in *Wieland* or in Radcliffe's novels. The fantastic seems more important in fantastic/uncanny horror thrillers than in fantastic/marvelous horror thrillers. Brown's "fiddling" with closure, in fact, may be seen as an effort to extend the experience of the fantastic by locating it decisively and permanently in Clara rather than in her world.

In Stoker's novel, the fantastic seems to be a means of creating mystery and suspense. It is, therefore, an important effect in the novel, but not nearly so important as in *Wieland*. The use of the fantastic primarily for the creation of mystery and suspense seems characteristic of the fantastic/marvelous horror thriller. In Théophile Gautier's "The Dead Lover," the narrator's youthful double life—priest when awake and lover when asleep—may be dream or reality. As in Stoker's novel, the vampire, Clarimonda, proves real. The implied reader's hesitation, like the narrator's, is more a source of wonder and mystery than of fear. In Algernon Blackwood's "The Willows," the fantastic hesitation of narrator and implied reader leads primarily to suspense. It is resolved by the confirmation of the intimations that he and his friend have come to the wrong place at the wrong time, thus making themselves the objects of supernatural powers.

We are ready now to turn our attention to texts that aspire toward or realize the pure fantastic, sustaining the hesitation between natural and supernatural interpretations throughout the text so that no resolution takes place. As we examine these texts and ask what sorts of pleasure they offer, we will see that they develop some of the potentials present in the uncanny tales and in the horror thrillers we have examined. We will also see that the pure fantastic seems to demand of its users experimentation with the safety equipment usually provided in this game of reenacting repression. What happens when this equipment is sabotaged or cast aside?

## CHAPTER SIX

# The Pure Fantastic Tale
# of Terror

There are few examples of the pure fantastic tale of terror. I know of only three examples of the more complex of the two forms it takes. It is rare because it is so difficult to construct and it involves great risk; hence, four of the six tales to be discussed in this and subsequent chapters are by Edgar Allan Poe and Henry James, on whom critical tradition has conferred the title of master. In this chapter, we look at the simpler of the two forms.

Tzvetan Todorov says that the pure fantastic work will sustain the hesitation of the implied reader (and perhaps of a character) between a natural and a supernatural interpretation of ambiguous events through the end of the reading experience. He names two examples of such tales, James's *The Turn of the Screw* and Prosper Mérimée's "La Vénus D'Ille" (43). When this hesitation remains unresolved, we may expect a disruption of closure similar to that in "The Tell-Tale Heart" and in Brown's novels, but this disruption will be more radical. In Poe's tale and in Brown's novels, the ambiguity that disturbs closure tends to make the real reader's relation to the work parallel to the character's relation to his or her experience. Because the character narrators exhibit this ambiguity, the implied reader receives contradictory instructions on how to complete the interpretation of the character, and the real reader finds it difficult to bring the reading to an end. The real reader's reading continues after the text ends and until some satisfactory resolution of the ambiguity is attained. In these works, the ambiguity is rather easily assimilated into a satisfactory view of the whole work, though it is troubling enough to irritate some readers. When, however, the ambiguity of the fantastic is introduced and when it is foregrounded in such a way as to make it the central issue of interpretation for the implied reader, closure is more radically challenged. A gap appears that grows in importance and remains rather than disappears at the end of the text.

We are used to the gap in fiction. As Wolfgang Iser has argued in *The Act of Reading*, the gap is central to the experience of fiction. The text always underdetermines what it presents. For Iser as for Roman Ingarden, reading is a process of projecting wholes out of always insufficient parts and then revising these constructions as we take in more of the text until we arrive at a satisfactory view of the whole work. We are also used to gaps that remain pointedly unfilled and that, therefore, stimulate controversy. Critics still argue about William Faulkner's "A Rose for Emily." Did Emily kill Homer? Why? Did she sleep with the body? Why? These questions may arise from apparent clumsiness in the author, as in Faulkner's *Sanctuary*, where improbably, all evidence of the presence of Gowan Stevens's car at the Old Frenchman's disappears. Such gaps may arise from deliberate reticence as may be the case with the problem of Stevens's car and that seems clearly to be the case when Faulkner offers no explanation of why Temple Drake appears in court to testify falsely that Lee Goodwin raped her. While such gaps stimulate controversy, they cause only minor disturbances of the reading process. Critical disagreements over these incidents are minor indeed in comparison to the volumes and volumes of critical debate over whether there really are ghosts in *The Turn of the Screw*. The pure fantastic tale of terror opens a radical gap in the reading experience, which *must* be filled if the reader is to concretize the tale, but which cannot be filled if the tale does not move either toward the marvelous or the uncanny.

We will turn first, then, to three well-known and reasonably simple examples of the pure fantastic tale of terror: E. T. A. Hoffman's "The Sand-Man," Guy de Maupassant's "The Horla," and Edgar Allan Poe's "The Black Cat." We will focus on how the fantastic is created and sustained and on the effects of the pure fantastic on the reading experience, especially closure.

# II

E. T. A. Hoffman's "The Sand-Man" (1816-17) centers on the transformation of Nathanael, who kills himself in a spell of insanity. It is impossible to determine whether this insanity is the result of external forces acting upon him, as he believes, or the result of his own perverse insistence upon giving life to visionary fantasms, as Clara, his betrothed, believes. This question is complicated by the position of the tale's narrator. Let us, for the moment, bracket the narrator to concentrate on the conflict of interpretations.

Nathanael has a view of his life history as a whole. It begins with his earliest memories of the Sand-Man's intrusion into his childhood, and it will end, as he says in a dream-poem, with the figurative loss of his eyes in madness and death. The Sand-Man is presented to him as a monster who tears out the eyes of children who keep them open when they ought to be closed in sleep. This threat with which he is sent to bed as a child becomes the determining pattern of his life. Is this pattern imposed upon him by external supernatural forces, or does he impose it upon himself? Nathanael's accounts of his evil fate are heavy with implications that suggest Clara's opinion is correct. She asserts that all people, including herself, have "the intuition of a dark power working within us to our own ruin" (192). Such a power can become an obsession and may create hallucinations; "if we have once voluntarily given ourselves up to this dark physical power, it often reproduces within us the strange forms which the outer world throws in our way, so that thus it is we ourselves who engender within ourselves the spirit which by some remarkable delusion we imagine to speak in that outer form" (192).

Nathanael's account seems to make it clear that he has arbitrarily associated the lawyer, Coppelius, with the Sand-Man, though he builds this association from the coincidence that Coppelius often arrives at his bedtime. Behind this association is an implied split in his father's image: *the good father* who is usually present at dinner and who tells wonderful stories and *the bad father*, Coppelius, who is preceded by the natural father's silence and voluminous smoking after dinner, by his mother's sadness, and by an early interruption of the family's evening together (see Freud, "The Uncanny," *On Creativity and the Unconscious* 138-39, note). Coppelius himself adapts to this role by causing these interruptions and by torturing the children psychologically when he is present at meals. This pattern continues when Nathanael spies upon a meeting of his father and Coppelius and discovers them to be working together on human figures. Caught at this analogue of the primal scene, Nathanael is nearly sacrificed by Coppelius, who threatens to take his eyes for use in their products. When the father intervenes, Coppelius painfully inspects Nathanael's hands and feet. This conflict over the child between good and evil father images is completed when Coppelius is apparently responsible for the death of Nathanael's father in a laboratory explosion. As Freud suggests, these experiences become uncanny by permitting themselves to be so easily attached to repressions; the ground is prepared for the return of the repressed (137, 157).

Nathanael recalls his childhood terrors of Coppelius and the Sand-Man in a letter to his friend, Lothair, to explain his reaction to the peddler, Coppola, who initiates the return of the repressed by connecting himself with Coppelius. Nathanael then proceeds to reenact his childhood experience. He acts out within himself the split between the good and evil fathers, giving up his talent for writing pleasing, sparkling tales to write gloomy, unintelligible, formless, tedious works. This split is mirrored in his dual preoccupations with Coppola, the satanic image, and with Clara, his bright angel. He reenacts his spying, but this time on Olimpia, the "daughter" of his physics professor, Spalanzani. This spying leads to love for her, but it quickly becomes apparent to others that Olimpia is a cleverly constructed automaton in which Nathanael sees perfectly reflected his own view of himself. She makes him available to himself as an object of desire. Before he can consummate this desire, Coppola (or Coppelius?) appears to claim her as his own product, for the eyes, he claims, belong to him. The struggle between the benevolent and malevolent father figures is reenacted as the two men fight for possession of the mirror of Nathanael's "I." The father figures dismember the symbolic Nathanael, and Nathanael goes mad. Just as the poem in which he projects his life predicted, he recovers under Clara's care. These events replay his illness and recovery after Coppelius caught him spying in childhood. Just as that incident culminates in the death of his father and his poem ends in a vision of Clara transformed into death, so his life ends in the reappearance of Coppelius, the recurrence of Nathanael's madness, and his suicide.

In this reading of the tale, Nathanael's death results from the return of the repressed, thus confirming Clara's interpretation. He imposes meanings from his unconscious on unrelated external events. As his father split into a good and evil father, the evil then destroying the good, so Nathanael splits into a light and a dark self, the dark self overwhelming and destroying the light. Apparently Nathanael has been prevented by childhood terrors from unifying himself as an I. His devils emerge from the fragments of self he just barely holds together. Nathanael's problem can be understood as arising from difficulties Nathanael has in the mirror phase of his development.

Christine Brooke-Rose offers a helpful simplification of the three parts of Lacan's mirror phase of development in *A Rhetoric of the Unreal:* "recognition of the other, recognition of the other as self, recognition of the other as self but other" (161). The child, looking into the mirror or some equivalent (e.g., the gaze of others), conceives of the possibility of being a harmonious whole like those he sees around him. Then the child comes to recognize that this image of desire is the image of himself. To appropriate that image, he must symbolize it, give it graspable form. This symbolizing requires the mastery of language by which the idealized self becomes available to the child. However, in symbolizing the image, the child creates a permanent split between his self (subject) and his "I," the image that he strives to duplicate. As a product, ultimately, of language, this "I" is a social construct; its roots are in the culture that enlivens and preserves the language. The child "reads" the language of his culture and co-creates with that language his "I," the idea of the self he continually tries to be. As Juliet Mitchell argues, this ego-ideal is built up from lost love objects, and it achieves a final authority with the formation of the superego at the end of the Oedipal stage (see chapter 6).

Nathanael encounters difficulties in this phase of his development when he first identifies Coppelius as the Sand-Man, a destroyer of children's vision, and then as an evil father, the father of the creation of children. As a possible ego-ideal, his father is radically split into two persons, the one who loves him and the one who made him. It appears then that Nathanael, at least unconsciously, idealizes himself as also split in a parallel way. We have seen how he reenacts this central scene of his childhood as an adult. Though Nathanael can see harmonious wholes in Lothair and Clara, he cannot become a harmonious whole himself. To do so, it would appear that he must be seen as such a whole by the eye of love. He becomes angry with Clara when she simply declines to acknowledge the value of his dark self. Olimpia offers him what appears to be a loving gaze, but, as it turns out, she is merely a mirror, reflecting Nathanael's desire rather than offering the loving acceptance of his doubleness that might unify him. Rosemary Jackson says that the mirror phase "effects a shift from the 'body in fragments' . . . to the ideal of a whole body with a unified (constructed) subjectivity" (89). Nathanael seems not to have completed this shift. He continues to see his body and his psyche in fragments. He continues to need that unifying gaze of love to make him whole. Though Clara is sympathetic to him and willing to marry him, though she seems to understand the darkness that is within him, she does not understand his need to incorporate this darkness to be whole. It is unclear whether she could save him by taking his problems more seriously, but that remains the one untried alternative in the tale.

We have, then, a reasonably coherent psychological interpretation available. A psychoanalyst could probably correct and elaborate it into a comprehensive explanation of Nathanael. However, even then, the *tale*, as opposed to Nathanael, would not be explained. After all, Coppelius really does seem to persecute Nathanael; he appears bent on Nathanael's destruction, taking definite steps to bring it about.

Both the narrator and Spalanzani indicate that Coppola and Coppelius are the same person, so Nathanael is probably not wrong (210-11). Yet, though Coppelius appears for Nathanael's last fit of madness, there is no direct link between this fit and Coppelius's presence. Nathanael leaps from the tower upon seeing Coppelius, but his madness returns earlier, when he looks at Clara through the "magic" perspective that he obtained from Coppola and that made Olimpia appear alive to Nathanael. We may guess that the glass makes Clara look as if she were dead, since this was predicted in the poem and since he seems to call her a wooden doll. Presumably, by looking at her with the same instrument with which he saw Olimpia's ability to see him whole, he sees Clara's inability to see him whole. This repeats his response to her coldness toward his poem. Though we cannot be sure that Coppelius/Coppola intends or directly brings about Nathanael's death, he is always present at Nathanael's crises and provides the images and the instruments that help to destroy the young man. Is Coppelius an externally visible instrument of Nathanael's unconscious, or is he an independent persecuting agent who manipulates Nathanael's unconscious?

What, for example, is one to make of the circumstances by which Nathanael is given a view into Olimpia's room and provided with a perspective (in several senses) with which to view her? The view results when Nathanael's university domicile is moved after a fire. The perspective is sold him by Coppola.

While Nathaniel is visiting his friends at home, his university house burns, leaving only the outer walls standing. This fire is parallel to events taking place at home. Because the fire breaks out on the ground floor, Nathanael's "bold, active friends" are able to rescue his most valuable effects from his upper story room (201). At about the same time, the fiery Lothair and the fiery Nathanael contemplate a duel over Clara. She has refused to mirror for Nathanael precisely the self he wants mirrored: she does not like his dream-poem and asks him to throw it into the fire. In reply, he calls her a "damned lifeless automaton," provoking Lothair's anger (200). Nathanael feels disburdened when Clara prevents their fight, "as if by offering resistance to the dark power which possessed him, he had rescued his own self from the ruin which had threatened him" (201). Clara plays the part of a bold, active friend, rescuing his most precious psychological belongings. The fire at the university also mirrors the central pattern of his life. The fire begins in a ground floor chemist's shop, like his father's laboratory, and is parallel to the unconscious, that which should not be seen. Nathanael's upper story room, his conscious mind, contains his most precious belongings. Nathanael's precious relationship with his bright angel is threatened by the welling up of dark forces that demand recogniton in his poem. He wishes with the poem to "enkindle Clara's cold temperament" (199-200). Instead, her cold response enkindles him; he, in turn, enkindles Lothair. Clara rescues their precious relationship from this conflagration, but at the cost of silencing his unconscious.

What do these parallel events mean? Nathanael has nothing directly to do with the fire at the university, yet it is virtually simultaneous with a figurative fire in himself and in his relationships. This parallel could be simply coincidence, but Hoffman will not let it be. The literal fire places Nathanael in the position to see Olimpia. The figurative fire makes him want to see her, that is, to find the mirror that will reflect him as a whole by revealing the unseen. When Coppola as a seller of perspectives provides the instrument by which Nathanael actually sees Olimpia, the implied reader cannot help but wonder if there is an external plot against Nathanael. And if there is a plot, is it a natural plot, some perverse extension of Coppelius's tormenting young Nathanael? Or is there a supernatural plot, of which Coppelius is merely one instrument, along with Olimpia, Coppola, the fire at the university, the "magic" telescope, Spalanzani, and others?

We are suspended then between two readings of Nathanael's fate. Looking at more details in the story does nothing to resolve this suspension. Turning to the third-person narrator is also of little help, for he deliberately and openly sides with Clara. He says that though dreamers and visionaries found her gaze unbearably critical, "others, however, who had reached a clearer and deeper conception of life, were extremely fond of the intelligent, childlike, large-hearted girl" (197). He remains consistent in his choice; for example, he explicitly confirms Clara's judgment of Nathanael's later writing as tedious (199), and he affirms that when Nathanael hears such genius in Olimpia's speech, "it was his own heart's voice speaking to him" (209). But he undercuts the objectivity of his opinion when he reveals that he loves Clara. Has the narrator really reached a deeper and clearer (Clara) perception of life? Or has he made Clara his mirror just as Nathanael did with Olimpia? Ought the implied reader to view the narrator ironically?

Where does the implied reader emerge from this complexity? Nathanael, as tortured protagonist, needs sympathy and understanding. Clara is sympathetic, but not understanding. She is admirable, and the narrator values her for appropriate reasons, yet these very reasons—her sense of wholeness and balance in herself—prevent her from understanding Nathanael. Though the narrator is like Nathanael in his sense of having a mysterious soul and in his artistic ambition, he has a detachment denied Nathanael, a "firmness, fortified by cheerfulness" that Clara recommends to Nathanael (192). The view shared by Clara and the narrator that Nathanael is merely the victim of his dark fantasies, though powerful, is suspect. It is suspect, not only because of ambiguous details such as Coppelius's odd behavior and the coincidences of the literal and the figurative fire, but also because neither Clara nor the narrator understands Nathanael's problem as fully as the implied reader.

Hoffman, then, sustains the fantastic through the entire story. The implied reader is never able to gain a position from which to assert without reservation that Nathanael's problems are wholly psychological or that though they are psychological, they are deliberately exacerbated by an external supernatural agency. Such a reading experience ought to be profoundly disturbing, for it leaves the implied reader split or, at best, blurred. The implied reader becomes defined essentially as this hesitation between two incompatible interpretations of Nathanael's fate. And, as with the ambiguity in Brown's novels, a major effect of the pure fantastic here is to make the implied reader into a mirror image of the protagonist. Just as Nathanael is transfixed before and vibrating between the opposing aspects of his ego-ideal, so is the implied reader transfixed and vibrating between two versions of Nathanael's fate, and so the real reader is similarly situated in relation to the implied reader. Within this context of multileveled hesitation, the implied reader has also to contend with fairly powerful images of the repressed. Freud, for example, discusses a number of the "uncanny" images presented when Nathanael spies on Coppelius and his father (188-89). Suggested transgressions include patricide, incest, fear of dismemberment, but especially castration, and, implicitly, a desire to escape self-consciousness by returning to the infantile state. To understand Nathanael, the implied reader must deal with these suggestive images, but doing so does not yield a final understanding. This is quite an uncomfortable position for the implied reader. However, like Lovecraft, Hoffman has made some special arrangements to comfort the reader.

Though the fantastic is not resolved, the conflict between the two interpretations proves less disturbing than in other pure fantastic tales, because of the close relationship between the two interpretations. In both, Nathanael is psychologically disturbed, whether or not external supernatural agents cause and exacerbate Nathanael's troubles. The conflict is not so much over what is wrong with Nathanael as over what are the true causes of his troubles. The intensity of this conflict is further muted by the fact that no character in the story really experiences the conflict. Nathanael believes he is the victim of external agents. His friends and the narrator believe he is the victim of his own mind. The implied reader experiences a split of self analogous to but by no means the same as Nathanael's. The implied reader is left to choose whether to side with Nathanael or with virtually everyone else who has an opinion on the problem in the story. A fair decision is impossible, but the tale is so constructed that such a decision is not absolutely demanded of the implied reader. It is possible to complete the reading of the tale without making this decision.

Hoffman reduces the intensity of the problem and, therefore, the necessity of choosing by making such a decision relatively inconsequential: knowing the answer will not change Nathanael's fate. The death of the protagonist provides a fairly decisive form of conventional closure. Furthermore, in either interpretation Nathanael is pathetic; not only the nature of his problem, but also the emotional effect of his fate is the same in each case. Hoffman further strengthens closure by adding a conventional coda, an account of Clara's eventual happy marriage. One might also argue that the narrator's intrusion after his presentation of the opening exchange of letters between the friends helps to create a stable position for the implied reader by emphasizing the artificiality of the whole construct and preparing the reader both for the fantastic and for a kind of closure. Furthermore, just the use of a third-person narrator tends to distance the reader from too direct an identification with Nathanael. The end result is a highly disturbing tale that threatens, if only mildly, not to release the real reader from the reading experience. Maupassant's "The Horla" is similar to "The Sand-Man" in its effect, but makes use of a first-person narrator.

# III

Guy de Maupassant's "The Horla" (1887) creates an irresolvable ambiguity, leaving the implied reader suspended between two alternative explanations of the narrator's experience, but it, too, offers a kind of closure that reduces insistence upon this ambiguity and therefore allows the reader to escape the reading experience.

"The Horla" is the story of the transformation of the narrator into the Horla, an alien, invisible being. For this reason, it cannot easily be a retrospective narration. Instead, the story takes the form of a daily journal in which the gradual transformation is visible, even though it is not consciously presented by the narrator. Because the implied reader must deal with a document, there is a kind of built-in expectation of closure, an expectation that the document will have a limit. Furthermore, there is distance from the narrator's present condition, in contrast, for example, to *At the Mountains of Madness* or *Wieland* where the narrator's condition in the time present of the telling draws the implied reader into a close identification. This narrator has left a document in which time present coincides with the events narrated. The question that the story raises but never answers concerns whether this transformation is psychological or supernatural. Does the narrator go mad as he is taken over by an unknown aspect of himself, a second personality? Or, as he comes to believe, has a new sort of being made its appearance on the earth with an idea of conquest? Details in the story support both views.

All of the evidence for the supernatural interpretation has one inescapable flaw: it is reported by the narrator. The reliability of his reports depends upon his trustworthiness. This narrator does establish a fairly high degree of reliability by means of his own skepticism. Indeed, for most of the several months covered by his journal, he is convinced that he is hallucinating. He encourages the formation of a sympathetic implied reader who shares his love of the peaceful country life and whose mind moves with his in the examination of the unusual phenomena he begins to perceive. This parallel movement of minds is strengthened by the narrator's moving spontaneously to the kinds of explanations of his ambiguous experiences that their strangeness ought to provoke. He looks for natural causes and is incredulous of indications to the contrary. He is willing to grant that we do not understand all about the relations of our bodies and minds to the natural world. Though he is skeptical about a monk's belief in invisible spirits, he keeps his mind open. When the water disappears from his bottle at night, his first conclusion is that he has been sleepwalking. After his elaborate test of this possibility seems to prove the presence in his locked room of another being, he flees to Paris and society. The improvement of his condition there leads him to conclude that he must have been hallucinating and that solitude is bad for him. Though he is skeptical of the power of hypnotism and, then, momentarily convinced by a demonstration of its power, he returns to the openmindedness that he adopted in response to the monk at Saint-Michel. As the apparitions increase in power and as he comes to feel himself under the influence of the Horla, he continues to vacillate between the belief that he is mad and belief in the Horla. Only in the last month of the journal, when he feels possessed and gradually transformed, does he cease to assert that the Horla is a hallucination. The intended effect of this movement would seem to be to identify the narrator and the implied reader for as long as possible. Insofar as the narrator reacts plausibly to his situation, he seems reliable. The longer this reliability continues in a daily journal, the more fully the implied reader identifies with the writer.

The narrator's reliability is supported as well by third-party confirmations, reported by the narrator usually before he can appreciate their significance. His footman is haunted while the narrator is at Mont Saint-Michel. The servants report unusual events in the house. Dr. Parent seems to demonstrate the existence of some as yet unknown power when he shows that a hypnotized subject can use a card as a mirror to see what is behind her. A magazine reports an outbreak of supposedly hallucinatory illness in Brazil, connecting his experiences with the arrival of a Brazilian ship that was towed up the Seine past his house on the first day of his journal, the day before he first fell ill. These more or less verifiable external events add to the narrator's credibility. In fact, they make it almost impossible to prove that he hallucinates without either arbitrarily asserting that he dreams everything or refusing to take the story on its own terms. These confirmations work, of course, only as long as the implied reader continues to accept the convention that the journal was added to daily and not fabricated whole. A refusal to accept this convention opens up many possibilities—for example, that the journal is a hoax—but does not allow a verification of any of these new possibilities. Though we cannot prove he hallucinates, we can find ample evidence to *suggest* that he does.

For example, Brewster E. Fitz argues in his essay that the narrator's hallucinations may be explained psychoanalytically. He asserts that the narrator takes literally the paradox of the primary alienation necessary for the formation of self-consciousness in the mirror phase of development. This paradox is that the self must be both the perceiver and the perceived: "the 'I' must be thinking and thought at the same time, that is, it must be both subject and object, it must be where it is not" (960). Fitz helpfully works out various forms of mirror images and analogues to support this view. Another way of arguing this position, which seems to me a little more convincing, is to take note of the stages by which the transformation is achieved. From the beginning, the narrator has the feeling that something is trying to occupy his space. It sucks out his air in the night, leaving him in "low spirits" in the daytime. Then it shifts to drinking fluids belonging to him. It takes his place at home in his absence. It is near him in his home activities. It uses his chair and his book when he sleeps. Finally, it usurps his body and soul, taking his place in the mirror. This transformation, in which the exchange of bodily fluids associated with air, spirits, and blood seems crucial, goes through stages that are suggestive of a psychological origin.

When he first falls ill, he wishes for other organs that would make the invisible visible to him, as the card later does for his hypnotized cousin. Soon after this wish, he becomes more sensitive. He feels there is something near him that he ought to fear. Like the wishes of the characters in *Dracula*, his wish seems to begin coming true in a frightening manner. In his sleep, he is attacked by an invisible being of the air, which steals his air. When, on 2 June, he takes a walk to recover his *spirits*, he suddenly feels alone and afraid. This implied wish for companionship is immediately answered when he feels the presence of an invisible companion. These wishes, especially the first, seem to give form to all his subsequent experiences as he gains access to the invisible. As his desire is realized, he is terrified because the process of wishing becomes involuntary. In Paris, it is suggested that hypnotism "proves" the existence of an invisible power that humans might tap. Soon after he hears about this power and sees a demonstration of it, he feels himself to be under the same sort of power, as if to tap it were to submit to it. He sees it manifested in all sorts of mass behaviors, such as government holidays. His escape to Rouen takes him to the library where a book suggests that his apparition is no human invention. He then speculates that perhaps it is a conquering invader, a superior being from another planet. Once he has conceived this idea, it proceeds to become real. The journal story on Brazil then verifies his hypothesis, and on the same day the Horla uses the narrator to write its own thoughts in his journal. This, of course, is the equivalent of the card becoming a mirror that reflects the unseen; his journal has become a means of fulfilling his original wish. When the narrator realizes that the Horla has spoken through him, he exclaims, "He is within me, he is becoming my soul; I shall kill him" (268)! This incident is duplicated physically a few days later when he looks in the mirror and sees nothing at all. He has become invisible. He sees the Horla as having absorbed his reflection, his "I." In Lacanian terms, it is the subject who fails to appear in the mirror, for the Horla is the invisible subject that has no image except the "I." At this point, the narrator has lost his self and therefore can see nothing in the mirror. This perception leads eventually to the conclusion that the Horla can be destroyed by suicide.

That the narrator's perceptions of apparitions seem to grow directly out of prior wishes and that these apparitions seem generated by an initial wish to see the invisible make it difficult not to believe that the whole narration is an account of his efforts, unconsciously directed, to *see* his self as subject. We may even argue that this desire erupted out of the narcissistic calm of his extreme pleasure in occupying his point of origin in isolation. We learn in the 19 August entry that the Horla may have been attracted to his house because it, like the Brazilian ship, was white (blank). Perhaps this mirroring of the ship with the house of his birth draws the apparently involuntary pleasure and salute from the narrator on 8 May. This reflection, then, tempts him to examine his own reflection, to peer into the mirror of a journal page (also blank) in search of the reality behind the image, in search of the self that looks. To really see, he must undo the paradox that Fitz describes, but that paradox can only be undone by dying, figuratively in madness, or literally in suicide.

Does the narrator become the victim of some sort of alien being that attempts to usurp his body and produce a new species? Or does the narrator succumb to an unconscious wish to return to a state previous to self-consciousness? To affirm either possibility opens the implied reader to the critique of the other. The evidence in favor of each alternative is strong enough to explain by itself, but ever present is the evidence for the other alternative, which cannot be ignored. As in "The Sand-Man," the implied reader is split between two readings, and the real reader is subjected to the anxiety of aesthetic incompletion. Like Hoffman, Maupassant offers aid to both readers, though in this case primarily by means of a strong closure.

The narrator's conclusion that he must commit suicide is an acknowledgment of the completion of his transformation in either interpretation. His attempt to kill the Horla has only destroyed others, not the Horla. Whether the Horla is within as an alien being or as the alienated self, it now possesses him. The narrator's dilemma is at an end; his experience is closed. Since he is no longer the self who began the journal, his journal is also complete. Furthermore, the earlier stages of the transformation tend to gradually distance the implied reader from the narrator. It becomes impossible to continue moving with his mind when that mind is clearly taken over by some alien force, whether internal or external. The implied reader's investment in the narrator is reduced, the narrator's transformation is completed, and his experience and journal are closed off in the decision to die.

Though Maupassant provides a strong closure, the issue of whether his narrator is mad or victimized seems more urgent than in the case of Nathanael, partly because the elements of closure seem weaker than those of "The Sand-Man." The main reason for this is that the tale has no frame. Hoffman's third-person narration increases distance between the implied reader and the protagonist, in part by interposing a perspective between the implied reader and Nathanael. In "The Horla," the implied reader must deal directly with the narrator or, at least, with his document. Though the reader must pull away from the narrator as evidence of his transformation becomes stronger, he still must see that transformation from the terrifying "inside." It is also not clear that this narrator, like Nathanael, is from his earliest memory subject to his doom. He begins his journal a happy and healthy man, then alien experience suddenly intrudes upon his life. This sudden attack intensifies the implied reader's need to settle on an interpretation, to uncover the true causes of the narrator's destruction.

While Maupassant uses some of the same devices as Hoffman to help the reader deal with the anxiety his tale is likely to produce, he also intensifies that anxiety. "The Horla" presents a stronger threat not to allow a completion of its reading. In discussing "The Sand-Man," we said that the implied reader became defined as the hesitation between the two main interpretations of Nathanael's experience. Hoffman reduces the anxiety of this hesitation by means of distance within the work and closure. While the hesitation cannot be resolved, if its intensity is kept to a minimum, the effect will be an unusually disturbing tale of terror. The extra disturbance derives directly from the residue of irresolvability that must form part of the concretion of the whole work. Maupassant increases that disturbance, augmenting the intensity of the irresolvability of the two main interpretations of his narrator's experience. As a consequence, the split in the implied reader may produce a recognition of the difference between the implied and the real reader. The implied reader, like Lacan's "I" is after all a form of ego-ideal, implied in the language of a particular text. The real reader constructs this temporary "I" according to the rules of literary art to which he is accustomed. Maupassant's story threatens, more strongly than does "The Sand-Man," to make the implied reader into an alien being. Just as the narrator may be said to lose himself to an alien being of his own creation, so the real reader is threatened, at least mildly, with a similar relation to the implied reader. If the role will not end, the real reader cannot be rid of the implied reader; he will be "haunted" by the unresolved question for as long as he chooses to attend to the tale. Maupassant has so constructed his story that the role of implied reader has no end. Like Brown and Hoffman, he has intuited the possibility of enhancing the effect of a tale of terror by disturbing the expectations of aesthetic experience. In Maupassant's case, intuition may have been easier, because unlike Brown and Hoffman, Maupassant was able to read the first real master of this form of the tale of terror, Edgar Allan Poe.

# IV

In "The Black Cat" (1843) Poe achieves much the same effects Maupassant accomplishes in "The Horla," but uses more devices to entrap the reader. In her discussion of the tale, Brooke-Rose points out three central enigmas: (1) What is the black cat? (2) Is the narrator a mad hallucinator or the victim of supernatural force? (3) Why is the narrator to die the day after he tells his tale? She notes that though the story seems to focus upon and provide much information about the second enigma, in fact, it only repeats that question in various ways. Because the story never decides whether the narrator is a victim of self or others, the implied reader is never able to ascertain what the cat is or why the narrator must die. That the narrator is to be executed for murdering his wife does not explain why he murdered her. Indeed, that murder comes near the end of the central causal chain which is itself in need of explanation (116-22).

The narrator himself is involved in the central dilemma, though his perspective is somewhat different from the implied reader's. He begins his narrative with an implicit request: "For the most wild, yet most homely narrative which I am about to pen, I neither expect nor solicit belief. Mad indeed would I be to expect it, in a case where my very senses reject their own evidence. Yet, mad am I not—and very surely I do not dream. But to-morrow I die, and today I would unburthen my soul" (254). On one hand, the narrator's insistence upon his own sanity undercuts the reader's faith. On the other, he gives the appearance of sanity in his recognition that what he will say sounds mad and in his use of an elaborately balanced style. He sounds very little like the narrator of "The Tell-Tale Heart." As the narrator appears to be both sane and mad, so his tale is both "homely" and "wild." His tale proves to be as he describes it, both ordinary and unbelievable, both natural and fantastic. He reveals at the end of his first paragraph that he desires a natural explanation for his experience. He requests an implied reader who will transform his forthcoming wild tale into "nothing more than an ordinary succession of very natural causes and effects" (254).

From one point of view, the narrator's desire for a natural cause/effect explanation seems unnecessary. Though the events he relates are grisly and, perhaps, pathetic, there is little to make them seem unnatural. He explains that he became an alcoholic, and under the influence of alcohol, his genial personality changed. He abused his wife and his pets. Eventually he killed his beloved black cat, Pluto. On the night of this crime, his house burned down, leaving him poor and driving him deeper into alcoholism. After some time he obtained another black cat, which he grew to hate. The cat provoked his anger by its excessive affection for him, finally driving him into a rage of which his wife became the victim. Having ignorantly entrapped the cat with his wife's corpse behind a false wall in a cellar, he accidentally betrayed himself to the police by tapping his cane against that wall and causing the entombed cat to cry out. Of course, I have left out of this account all the appearances and suggestions that, though irrelevant to a natural cause/effect account, might suggest a supernatural agency. These appearances are important to the narrator, and they eventually lead to his conclusion that he is the victim of supernatural vengeance. These appearances aside, however, we have a clear natural account of how the narrator became a murderer, in which the major problem seems to be how the narrator was transformed from his original geniality into a cruel drunkard and murderer.

The narrator has a natural explanation: he theorizes that the human soul is double and that his drinking releases the spirit of perversity that, he says, inhabits every soul. If he accepts his own theory, then his actions are explained and his narrative loses its purpose of soliciting an explanation. Apparently, the narrator has reasons for being unable simply to accept this "natural" explanation, the main reason being his fairly strong conviction that he is a victim of the supernatural. He finds this natural explanation attractive, for it is the activity of the spirit of perversity that makes him into a victim of a force beyond his control. He can think of himself as innocent by reason of insanity. This attraction is increased by the fact that at the time of the telling, he is confident of his sanity. He looks back upon these terrible events in his life and sees a different person committing those crimes. He explains that he was temporarily possessed. On the other hand, he has seen other elements in his experience that suggest the involvement of an external force, which also offers an attractive explanation insofar as his sense of personal moral responsibility for his acts might be diminished.

The narrator's sense that the supernatural is involved increases after he kills Pluto. There is, first, the mysterious outline of the hanged Pluto imprinted on the remaining white wall of his burned home. The image on the wall becomes a phantasm in his fancy. Then, the phantasm becomes a reality in the advent of the second cat, which is in every way like Pluto except for the white mark on its breast. That mark seems gradually to take the form of a gallows, now without a hanged cat in the noose (see Ketterer 106-8). This succession of images suggests the revenge of the letter of the law; the narrator has hanged Pluto and so he must hang. In order for him to be hanged, he must kill a person. Therefore, the cat returns to insure the completion of the pattern. The cat provokes the narrator, takes advantage of the situation it creates to bring about the murder, and then betrays the murderer. If the cat is seen as a supernatural agent, then the coincidences become significant: the fire, the outline on the wall, the walling up of the cat, and the impulse to tap that wall. And once these coincidences become part of a causal chain that will end with the narrator's execution, we can push back further in time to see, perhaps, an even deeper plot than the narrator seems aware of. Was Pluto, as the narrator's wife suggests, a witch to begin with? Was the narrator's alcoholism also caused supernaturally? A supernatural causal chain suggests that there was a trap set in some obscure beginning to destroy the narrator. This is what he apparently concludes at the end of his narrative, that the cat has seduced him to his ruin.

Naturally, such an explanation would attract the narrator at least as strongly as the natural explanation based on the spirit of perversity. In either case, forces outside his control (demons, perversity) have forced him into criminal acts. This supernatural explanation also has a negative side: its pattern of retributive justice suggests his subjection to judgment whether or not he feels personal, moral responsibility. The narrator hesitates between these two explanations of his experience because both tend to exculpate the person he now conceives himself to be and because he has compelling evidence for each without a means of deciding between them.

There is a fairly natural explanation that can account for the supernatural occurrences as a combination of coincidence and hallucination. According to this interpretation, he hallucinates some, or even all, of the equivocal events, especially the shape of the white mark, and all the events involving the burial of the second cat. Whether or not there is really a second cat, that cat in particular becomes, for the narrator, an external manifestation of the genial self he has lost in his transformation. After his transformation, his abuse falls most heavily upon the three characters who show the most affection for him: the two cats and his wife. Until he is rid of all three, he is unable to sleep peacefully. The second cat is closely associated with his wife. She caresses it and it caresses him. As he comes to see them as mirrors of his old lost self, he comes to hate them and to wish them dead. Since his earliest childhood, he has been surrounded by such mirrors (his parents, his pets, his wife), and he has made himself in the image of what he has seen. As a result, he was in childhood the "jest of his companions." This peculiarity grew on him just as his later disease of alcohol grows on him. He has made himself into a mirror of the "unselfish and self-sacrificing love of a brute, which goes directly to the heart of him who has had frequent occasion to test the paltry friendship and gossamer fidelity of mere *Man*" (254). These observations suggest an unconscious motive, which could be the cause of his hallucinations.

The narrator wants to break the confining image out of which he has constructed his self. In alcohol, he finds the hint that such a transformation is possible. As he moves in that direction, he is irritated by the constant repetition of the image in "the mirror," which calls him, like an infinitely forgiving God (or superego), back to his old, good self. The pride that drives him is indicated by his response to the gallows mark on the second cat's breast: "And now I was indeed wretched beyond the wretchedness of mere Humanity. And *a brute beast*—whose fellow I had contemptuously destroyed—*a brute beast* to work out for *me*—for me a man, fashioned in the image of the High God—so much of insufferable wo!" (257-58). Much as he wants to be free of the old self, he cannot remove that self from within his soul. Destroying its externalizations gives him only temporary respite. Soon it returns in whatever means his final hallucination provides for exposing his crime to the police. When he reports this scene in the time present of his telling, he utters a revealing prayer: "But may God shield and deliver me from the fangs of the Arch-Fiend!" (259). Now the cat is associated with the evil self, the demon within. In the present of his telling, the narrator dissociates himself from the one who committed the terrible crimes. His confession is also a justification.

We now have a psychological reading that is, perhaps, more subtle than the narrator's own hypothesis about the spirit of perversity. In this psychological reading, the narrator is seen as unconsciously attempting to escape the confines of an oppressively narrow self by destroying his identity. He thus tries to externalize it onto the mirroring images of wife and cat, but this strategy fails. His hallucinations, then, result from his attempts at externalizing the tame self he wants to destroy and from the persistence within of that tame self that demands justice and compels his confession. We can see that in the time present in which he makes his confession, he has undergone another transformation. He is no longer the wild man who killed his wife and "involuntarily" confessed his crime. Now he is tame, more like his original self. He expresses shame and guilt. Now, instead of externalizing the good self, he externalizes the perverse self vigorously. He says "the fiend Intemperance" transformed his character and that the "disease" of alcohol grew upon him. He says of his removing Pluto's eye, "The fury of a demon instantly possessed me. I knew myself no longer. My original soul seemed, at once, to take its flight from my body; and a more than fiendish malevolence, gin-nurtured, thrilled every fibre of my frame" (255). He asserts that each of his crimes was committed while he was possessed by a demon. He even characterizes his perversity as a spirit, speaking of it as both internal and external. Though this experience of possession was thrilling when it took place, he rejects it in the account of his confession. Instead, he asserts, finally, that the crafty cat has "seduced" him to murder. The evil and criminal self is not himself, but some other. It is that other, separate from him-

self, who deserves punishment. We thus see the narrator splitting himself unconsciously, first to destroy his too repressive tame identity, then, after his crimes, to save his tame identity from the consequences of the crimes committed by his wild identity.

We now have three possible explanations of what has happened to the narrator. We have seen that he is caught between two explanations (perversity and demons), both of which he wishes to use for exculpation. Neither is clearly superior to the other. The third explanation suggests that, without being fully aware of it, he alternates between two personalities, one that enjoys the thrills of the forbidden and the other that does the forbidding. Does this third explanation effect a resolution of the first two? Does it comprise a superior point of view of the implied reader?

This psychological explanation is, essentially, an extension of the narrator's theory of perversity, which allows us to account "naturally" for the supernatural appearances. For the implied reader to accept this explanation as definitive, he must accept from the real reader the attitudes of our post-Freudian and secularist age.

Poe's original audience did not embrace our modern convictions that all macrophysical phenomena are rule-governed and that psychological explanations reach to first causes. Yet even if the implied reader does not impose modern attitudes on the tale and, so, remains within the enigmas as they are presented to the narrator, he is not completely cut off from psychological interpretations that are more complex than the narrator's. It would not have been beyond Poe's more sophisticated readers (e.g., Hawthorne, Melville, James, or Baudelaire) to extend the narrator's own psychological explanation in ways that could account for the appearances of the supernatural. How deep has the narrator's perversity gone? Is it reflected in his early peculiar love for animals? Do we see in the manner of his telling, in his careful style, the imp of the perverse obliquely displaying itself? Just as the theory of perversity is extendable over the narrator's whole life, so, too, is the narrator's supernatural explanation. We have seen that the supernatural explanation can account for the pattern of his life and can *justify* rather than merely explain his expression of paranoia, his final assertion that he has been attacked by forces beyond human comprehension. Just as our supernatural reading is a more elaborate extension of his own, so our psychological reading ultimately proves to be a more sophisticated extension of the narrator's theory of perversity. In this way, we come to see that "The Black Cat" suspends the implied reader between alternative explanations of the narrator's experience. Even though the implied reader may well formulate more complex readings than the narrator does, those readings are extensions of the narrator's theories.

This tale seems, then, to imply a reader who, though he may see depths in the narrator's account, is no more able than the narrator to move decisively toward one hypothesis or the other. Both the narrator and the implied reader hesitate between two explanations of the terrifying events of the tale. As in "The Sand-Man" and "The Horla," the experience of reading "The Black Cat" must continue after the completion of the perusal of the text. Because the story offers no resolution of this fundamental and foregrounded ambiguity, it threatens never to end. Like Maupassant, Poe seems deliberately to pull both ways with regard to closure. On one hand, he offers conventional patterns of closure, which stand in opposition to the openness of the pure fantastic. On the other, he intensifies the fantastic in several ways.

"The Black Cat" has a fairly strong illusion of closure. As a last confession and as an autobiography, the narrative is complete. Except for the central one, most of the enigmas are at least partly resolved. We can say that the second black cat is either an animal or a demon. We know he is to be executed for the murder of his wife. With some thought, it becomes clear how the narrator is attempting to unburden his soul by escaping responsibility for his acts; therefore, as a particular rhetorical action, the story also seems complete. In addition to these patterns of closure, Poe also establishes a moral distance between implied reader and narrator by making it clear that the narrator is trying to escape moral responsibility for his actions. This distance can reduce the intensity of the implied reader's need to determine whether the forces the narrator experiences are internal or external. While Poe imposes closure by completing these fairly strong patterns and may reduce the need for resolution of the fantastic by creating moral distance, he also works against closure by intensifying the need for resolution in other directions.

As we have noticed, the narrator begins by stating a problem. He specifically addresses his reader and asks for help. This opening draws the implied reader toward the narrator in two ways. First, the request to engage in problem-solving is immediately attractive in itself. The real reader responds by imagining the construction of the implied reader who can solve this mystery, much as one identifies with the detective in crime fiction. Second, the implied reader is cast in the role of sympathetic listener, an interested party in this individual's case. The implied reader begins with a challenge and a promise, to solve the mystery and satisfy the speaker. This sort of involvement of the reader is quite different from that in "The Sand-Man" and "The Horla." In those stories, the fantastic emerges out of the ordinary, gradually becoming a problem. There is psychological distance between the protagonist and the implied reader. Poe works from the beginning to minimize this psychological distance, to make the narrator's problem the implied reader's as well and to specify that problem as having to deal with fantastic hesitation.

# V

Of the three pure fantastic tales of terror we have examined in this chapter, "The Black Cat" is the most disturbing. It may be that Poe so effectively enmeshes the implied reader in the tale that some readers do not escape it, even though he has provided means of closure and at least one way of backing away from the narrator. In our examination of the three tales, we can see a movement toward fuller exploitation of the tendency of the pure fantastic to prevent closure. Hoffman seems the most cautious, for he provides several protections from the pure fantastic's desire to subvert fictional form. Maupassant is more willing to entrap and terrify his readers. Poe seems most willing to harrow the reader; in fact, we shall see that in "Ligeia" and "The Fall of the House of Usher," he had written significantly more terrifying tales before "The Black Cat." In exploiting the tendency of the pure fantastic to disturb closure, these writers have developed a form of horror story that differs significantly from those we have examined in previous chapters. In uncanny tales of terror and in horror thrillers of various kinds, if the real reader is really terrified, it is by accident. Those tales desire an audience susceptible enough to the images they present to be thrilled, but not so susceptible as to be unprotected by the strategies of distance and closure they employ. These pure fantastic tales reach out directly toward the real reader and, in the group we have examined, tend progressively to strip away the protective devices between the terrors of the tale and the real reader and approach the limits of the possible in the horror thriller. Once the line is deliberately crossed between maintaining and destroying Bullough's antinomy of aesthetic distance, we arrive at a radically different though clearly related form of the tale of terror that I call terror fantasy. The pure fantastic tales of terror we have just examined stand on the border between the horror thriller and the terror fantasy, maximizing the thriller's potential, but coming so close to entrapping their real readers in real terror that many readers may well experience real terror in these stories. These pure fantastic horror thrillers suggest that the terror fantasies we are about to examine may represent an "ideal form" toward which all tales of terror point, a form that seems designed not to provide safe thrills, but to actually terrify the real reader. We see in these "borderland" stories an impulse to experiment toward the elimination of aesthetic distance in the tale of terror.

Before turning to detailed examinations of those masterpieces of terror fiction, it may be useful to observe some of the common thematic patterns in the tales examined thus far. The plots are similar: the protagonist discovers and is attracted by an alternative identity; against his conscious will he is transformed into that identity with the result that he brings about his own death. When Todorov examines the themes of the fantastic, he finds a division between the themes of the self and the themes of the other. The themes of the self, associated with the world of the infant, the world before language, when desire is for the self or for what is perceived as self, which is the whole world (145-46), seem more relevant to the texts we have examined so far. Rosemary Jackson assimilates these themes to Lacan's description of the mirror phase. She finds fantasy most subversive when it uses its power "to interrogate the category of character—that definition of the self as a coherent, indivisible and continuous whole which has dominated Western thought for centuries and is celebrated in classic theatre and 'realistic' art alike" (82-83). This interrogation takes place when texts represent protagonists being torn between "an original, primary narcissism and an ideal ego, which frustrates their natural desire" (89). Fundamental to this thinking is an acceptance of the basic idea of psychoanalysis as it is elaborated by Lacan. We are split into subject, the point of consciousness, and "I," the series of choices we have made about who we will be. We are self-conscious only in relation to the "I." In a sense the subject is "imaginary," invisible. Mentally, we are visible to ourselves only by means of representations or symbols. We look in mirrors. We perceive the evaluations of others in discourse. We write ourselves on paper, in language. What we see of the subject is its edges, where we exceed or miss the mark. The subject is visible only as a deficiency in the "I." Jackson sees subversive fantasy—for her, some fantasies are not subversive—as in one way or another expressing the desire to escape the judgment of the "I," to return to what we imagine or "remember" the state of pure subject to be, the state of infancy. In this state, there is no self-consciousness.

These ideas shed light on the plots of our three pure fantastic tales. The predicaments of the three protagonists present to the reader images of his own desire, which is both attractive and frightening in the consequences of its realization. To return in reality to that stage in which alternative selves are equally powerful leads to the end of self-consciousness, to madness and/or death. To go there and return with articulable memories of the experience is as impossible as it was for the narrator of "The Pit and the Pendulum" to return from sleep with his memories intact. These stories promise to allow the reader to contemplate such a return within the boundaries of a protective aesthetic

structure, but then weaken, perhaps even subvert, the protective structure. *Dracula* entertains a monster symbolic of human desires to transgress boundaries. The monster is turned loose for a limited time and
then repressed, allowing the reader the pleasure of reenacting the formation of the self. These stories, too, turn loose the monster, but do
not reenact repression: the monster is left on the loose. Closure is at
best equivocal. Equally disturbing is that the monster is no longer in
the text, but both there and not there, for the question of the hesitation
of the pure fantastic concerns precisely the location of the monster.
Whereas the monster is objectively present in most tales of terror em-
ploying the marvelous, in tales of the pure fantastic, it is never certainly
present. Fantastic hesitation becomes a means of placing the reader off
center. The splitting in two of the implied reader threatens the real
reader with transformation into the implied reader, with becoming
conscious of his dividedness with consequences similar to those that
have befallen the protagonists. This threat of transformation, if it is
strong enough, can dissolve the aesthetic relationship between the real
reader and the work.

There is a consistency, then, between the themes of the self and the
structures of these pure fantastic tales of terror. Only the sensation
stories seem minimally concerned with such themes. The tales that
offer as part of their pleasure the reenactment of repression tend to
produce images of terror that suggest the original repression in which
self-consciousness is born. They allow a momentary entertainment or
contemplation of the always desired, but forbidden imaginary state of
infancy, that is, the adult's "conception" of what infancy must have
been like. The pure fantastic tales point in rather a different direction,
even though they make use of the same thematic material. By exploiting
the pure fantastic, they make possible at least a momentary experience
analogous to the imaginary state of infancy. Insofar as the real reader
experiences with intensity the split of the implied reader and the threat
of being absorbed and, hence, split in himself, he approaches not an
image of transgression, but the actual experience of transgression, a
brush with madness itself. We may well ask what pleasure there can
be in this experience. It is easier to answer this question when we have
looked closely at the three great masterpieces of terror fantasy.

## CHAPTER SEVEN

# Anticlosure: Poe's "Ligeia"

Though "Ligeia" (1838, 1845) is similar to "The Black Cat" in several ways, there are two key differences between the tales: the handling of the fantastic and the focus of the narration. Each story is told by a narrator whose self-command is less than complete. Both narrators suffer losses and make substitutions for those losses. In both cases the substitutes seem chosen, in part, by powers independent of the narrators, and both substitutes undergo terrifying transformations.

The main difference between "Ligeia" and "The Black Cat," in their presentation of the fantastic, is that "Ligeia" withholds the full development of the fantastic enigma until virtually its last sentence. When the revivified corpse of Rowena is apparently transformed into Ligeia, all of the preceding narrative becomes new. This is the central device of "anticlosure" by which Poe makes this one of his most terrifying tales. The "surprise" ending, as one would expect, transforms the import of the entire narrative, but in a terrifying way, for it makes the narrative into a trap: the surprise leads to questions, and the questions lead to the terrifying entrapment of the real reader in the role of the implied reader.

The other major difference is that the narrators focus their tales in different ways. The narrator of "The Black Cat" conceives of himself as writing a confession/justification. He claims to want to talk about himself. The narrator of "Ligeia" does not offer a reason for what he writes, but centers his story on a particular group of experiences, his memories of Ligeia. Though he inevitably reveals much about himself, his apparent purpose is to talk about his lost beloved.

These two major differences lead to radically different effects in these similarly shaped narrations. The announcement of a confession and the presentation of several enigmas in the first paragraph of "The Black Cat" set up the minimal requirements of the horror thriller, a character about whom we can care who has had some possibly fantastic experience. "Ligeia" begins with a less suspenseful enigma and with no implicit promise of fantastic adventure. The main question raised by the long first paragraph of "Ligeia" is, why is he talking about her? For the first one-fourth of the tale the narrator pursues, in a scholarly fashion, the mystery of Ligeia, the secret of her strangeness that made her beauty perfect. In the process he raises a number of questions that involve the implied reader in his somewhat pedantic pursuit.

In the first paragraph the narrator reveals himself as a pathetic widower. His memory is feeble through much suffering, and therefore he cannot recall the circumstantial details of his first acquaintance with Ligeia. He feels that her gradual progress in the possession of his heart may also have obscured his memory of the beginnings of their relationship. He is now retired from the world: "Buried in studies of a nature more than all else adapted to deaden impressions of the outward world, it is by that sweet word alone—by Ligeia—that I bring before mine eyes in fancy the image of her who is no more" (79). He appears to be a scholar, not mainly for the sake of learning, but to cultivate the image of Ligeia in his fancy. His present narrative is the result of this cultivation, his memorial to Ligeia. As he continues, however, Ligeia becomes an enigma. His lapses of memory and the peculiar gaps in his knowledge hide her origins. Because he can tell nothing about where she has come from, the ways in which she came to be so beautiful, so learned, and so eloquent loom large before the reader, achieving a disproportionate importance because the narrator unconsciously underlines their absence: "I have *never known* the paternal name of ... the wife of my bosom." Why not? "I have utterly forgotten the circumstances" (79). Unless he should have another flash of recollection, such as the not very promising one that revealed his never having known her last name, the reader will never know Ligeia's origins. The first paragraph concludes with the assertion that his marriage with Ligeia was ill-omened. This sentence implies the promise of a romance, a story of lost love, but the paragraph as a whole raises other mysteries.

This opening is clearly more subtle than that of "The Black Cat." The reader is offered two major questions: Who is Ligeia? Why is the narrator writing about her? The first is accentuated by the initial lack of one kind of information. The second receives a partial answer. She is his lost beloved, and he seems obsessed with her, hiding himself away from the world to study, and he also seems to use a significant portion of his time contemplating her image in his imagination. There is no promise of thrills and only the slightest hint of the possibility of the supernatural in her mysterious background. We are promised a pathetic story. This promise and that her origin and her end remain mysterious draw the reader into the tale.

The next major division of the tale begins as a physical description, which turns out to be an attempt to define precisely the element of strangeness that made Ligeia's beauty perfect. Throughout, the narrator provokes more questions about himself and about Ligeia while apparently elaborating answers to the questions about Ligeia's identity and his purpose in writing.

His analysis of her beauty and strangeness emphasizes his obsession with her image. He says, "Ligeia's beauty passed into my spirit, there dwelling as in a shrine"; he affirms that after that moment he found in the material world objects that aroused the same sentiment that her eyes once aroused in him (80). To this sentiment he has traced the strangeness of her beauty. Only after years of reflection has he been able to articulate some idea of this sentiment. It is associated with the much analyzed epigraph to the tale, attributed to Joseph Glanvill: "And the will therein lieth, which dieth not. Who knoweth the mysteries of the will, with its vigor? For God is but a great will pervading all things by nature of its intentness. Man doth not yield himself to the angels, nor unto death utterly, save only through the weakness of his feeble will" (79, 81). The narrator remembers in Ligeia's eyes "the tumultuous vultures of stern passion" (81). He sees this passion also as an intensity (like the intentness of the great will), a gigantic volition, a fierce energy that seemed to underlie all her actions. This gigantic volition never revealed itself to him directly during their marriage, but he has since come to believe in its presence and to understand it as the strangeness behind her beauty.

The articulation of this passion in Ligeia reveals a division in her that complicates one's understanding of the narrator. Ligeia is split in a way parallel to the split of the narrator of "The Black Cat." The outwardly calm, "ever placid" Ligeia contains a storm of passion. An awareness of this split pervades the narrator's physical description of her. One of its indices is the word *wild*. She is described as a divinity, radiating holy light. She is majestic. When her eyes expand, she partakes fully of "the beauty of beings either above or apart from the earth" (80). When, after her death, he is able to articulate more fully his response to the expansion of her eyes, he says it "at once so delighted and appalled me" (81). But when he knew her, he found her "wildly divine." She habitually uttered wild words in her low, musical voice. As he gives the history of their marriage and her death, he refers to her wild eyes, her wild desire for life, the wild meanings of her words, and, by implication, her wild love for him, her "more than womanly abandonment to love" (82). It is apparently this wildness that perfects Ligeia's beauty for the narrator and that inspires his idolatry of her in life and his obsession with her in death.

In this first one-fourth of the narration, little has happened. The narrator has intimated mysteries about Ligeia and himself. By the point at which he completes his analysis of her beauty, she has become more mysterious, and their relationship has become problematic. It is clear that he has been entranced by her for as long as he can remember. The essential quality by which she holds him is at least equivocal, underlining a challenge to the reader to fill her in, to make sense of her. Whereas *At the Mountains of Madness* promises an explanation of its warning, which it then delivers, and whereas "The Black Cat" promises some resolution of its enigmas, but offers, instead, a restatement of the main ones, "Ligeia" begins as a sad love story, but quickly becomes a mystery. It invites the reader to read, to fill in the increasing number of gaps it creates as it moves in an unclearly defined direction. The story asks the reader to define the mysteries and to seek out solutions. The narrator mulls over key experiences in his life, pursuing his own questions about his lost beloved. Out of these questions, the implied reader constructs himself as a reader/detective trying to understand what the narrator is talking about. The underlined absence of details about Ligeia's past invites curiosity. The narrator's worship, which seems to extend into the present of his writing, heightens the mystery and raises further questions. The text creates the reader as detective and invites him to see into these mysteries, but the story does not openly declare itself as a mystery nor does it promise solutions.

The next part of the story includes the narrator's account of his marriage and of Ligeia's death. He begins by explaining that he has only recently realized that Ligeia's tremendous knowledge was apparently perfect, that he never found her learning at fault in any way. Like her volition and her beauty, her acquisitions were gigantic: "yet I was sufficiently aware of her infinite supremacy to resign myself, with a child-like confidence, to her guidance" (82). Nearly all he reveals about their marriage is that she taught him, led him down paths of knowledge that were untrodden and gorgeous toward a wisdom that is split, "too divinely precious not to be forbidden" (82). This increases her mystery. What forbidden knowledge does she have (if her knowledge is perfect), and why does she want to teach it to him? They were studying transcendentalism, he explains. What is forbidden about that? Again, the implied reader is invited to fill in, to construct himself out of the story's gaps and commit himself to explanations. While the relation of Ligeia and the narrator becomes more problematic as the reader wonders about what she teaches him and why, one aspect of the relationship is reaffirmed. He is a submissive mourner, a submissive lover, and, also, a submissive pupil/son. He, too, is one of her acquisitions. And when she dies, he is a child benighted without her illuminating radiance.

As she dies, the narrator makes two surprising discoveries about Ligeia, one of which was probably a key step in his eventual conclusion that the strangeness of her beauty derived from her gigantic volition. Although he thought that what he had seen of her stern nature indicated that she would accept death easily, he finds that she resists death fiercely. Indeed, his instincts are to comfort and reason with her, but her desire for life overwhelms him. The tension of contrast between her voice and her utterance enthralls him: "My brain reeled as I hearkened entranced, to a melody more than mortal—to assumptions and aspirations which mortality had never before known" (82). Another surprise is the degree of her love. He says he never doubted it, but in her death she reveals her love for him as idolatry. He feels in this revelation a painful paradox, for he has no understanding of how he could have merited from her the kind of worship he has bestowed upon her. This paradox is painful because it tortures him with the loss he is about to suffer. Strange as this love seems, he accepts its sincerity because it accounts for the first surprise, that is, her unwillingness to die. He reads her as a mirror of himself, as unwilling to lose one whom she worships.

These surprises and the subsequent account of her death cast the first serious doubt upon the narrator's perceptions. The implied reader sees possibly quite significant implications in the narrative, which the narrator appears not to see. This brings up the extremely vexed question of the narrator's reliability.

In this tale much depends upon whether one judges the narrator reliable or unreliable. Years of critical debate and the resulting passions may lead some readers of criticism to doubt the possibility of rational discourse on the topic. I would like to propose a principle for dealing with the problem of a narrator's reliability: that, in cases such as this, the appropriate reading is the probable first reading. This principle derives in part from Tzvetan Todorov's observation of the difficulty of rereading fantastic fictions. Once one has read an uncanny/fantastic or a marvelous/fantastic fiction and knows the sort of resolution it has, rereading becomes difficult. Where there was hesitation upon the first reading, certainty governs the second. For this reason, tales of sustained ambiguity, like "Ligeia," may be more powerfully terrifying than those tales that resolve their ambiguity even partially. With "Ligeia," the problem is more complex, because the fantastic hesitation will not be resolved by the story. However, insofar as a reader believes he has resolved it, he will *reread* the story in the light of that resolution. Therefore, to reread successfully, as every critic must to be accurate and persuasive, one must attempt to "recapture" the original reading. One way of doing this is to attempt the construction of the implied reader. On first reading, one can only "discover" the degree of the narrator's reliability. This discovery can only take place when the narrator's reliability becomes crucial to understanding the tale. For example, we could decide that the narrator's failure to see the depths the implied reader may see in Ligeia's suddenly expressed, idolatrous love renders him unreliable, not only as an interpreter of Ligeia's motives, but also as an observer of "objective" events. In that case, we move inevitably toward the readings we will notice hereafter, in which the narrator is a mad hallucinator. However, if we take what seems to me the more natural path of noticing that there may be more to Ligeia as a character than the narrator has yet seen, then the story deepens in interest at this particular point in the "first" reading by revealing simultaneously a limitation in the narrator and another surprising mystery in Ligeia. I would argue not only that this is the kind of reading the text requests here, but also that, in fact, the text does not require the reader to question the narrator's reliability in the reporting of external events until he sees the fantastic, the impossible. Up to the point when he describes Ligeia's last appearance, every limitation on his perceptions has a plausible explanation and none of the limitations seems crucial to understanding the story. The text seems to want a reader who judges what the narrator says without seriously questioning its accuracy throughout the first perusal of the text. At the end of the text, however, when he does claim to see the fantastic, the various limitations on the narrator's reliability take on a new significance, as we shall see.

We see at this point in the text, however, that there *are* limitations on the narrator. The mysteries about Ligeia and about his relationship with her, both stated and implied, do not seem fully visible to the narrator. The structure of his presentation underlines mysteries about her that make her difficult to see whole, yet the narrator seems unaware that he places barriers before the reader. His relationship with Ligeia is peculiar, at the least, and perhaps obsessive. In her surprising resistance to death and in the sudden appearance of her idolatrous love is a suggestion—hard to ignore—that she has purposes beyond his ken and ours. This suggestion is consistent with the mystery of why she is teaching him forbidden knowledge.

He is first impressed with her desire for life and then by her "more than womanly abandonment to love." Neither of these wild desires is quite consistent with his previous view of her, but he uses the latter desire to account for the former. However, the reiterated emphasis on her desire "but for life" and her double repetition of the epigraph on the last day of her life suggest that she offers him a pretense of wild love as an excuse for the more primary desire for life. The subordination that he constructs—life to love—may, in reality, be reversed. Love is an excuse for the passion she cannot conceal. This suggestion *seems* to be there for the original encounter with the text, underlined by the narrator's greater emphasis on her expressions of desire for life and by his sense of a reversal of their relationship in his receiving unmerited worship. If it is not there on first reading, not much is lost, for after the last words pass into the reader's consciousness, this suggestion must come to life. If it is there on first reading, then the reader is drawn still more deeply into the mystery of Ligeia. Why was she teaching him? Why does she worship him on her death bed? What have these acts to do with the desire for life, which seems to have been the controlling passion of her being, the essence of her beauty, the gigantic volition itself?

While it remains unclear what she wants with the narrator, Ligeia's death does clarify what she wants in general. When she quotes Glanvill, she omits the sentence about God as a great will pervading all things. It seems clear that she wishes to place herself in that gap, to rise above humanity by achieving the immortality of her individual gigantic volition. The continuation of the narrative pretends to cut off further inquiry in either of these directions. With her death, she disappears from view, though her desire hovers over what follows like the other shoe as yet undropped.

Out of sight is neither out of mind nor out of the story. The narrator has stated earlier that there was a period in his life, apparently between Ligeia's death and some later, unspecified date, when her *beauty* passed into his spirit. The section of the story that follows the account of her death may cover this period of his life. In this penultimate part the narrator acquires substitutes for her. His new home is decorated in a mixture of wildness and majesty, an unsatisfying substitute for her beauty. He becomes a "bounden slave in the trammels of opium" (84), an unsatisfying attempt to recapture her radiance, which was "the radiance of an opium dream" (80). Furthermore, his slavelike addiction mocks his devotion to Ligeia. And he marries Rowena, an unsatisfying substitute for Ligeia's companionship. The main result of the failure of these substitutions is that the narrator is transformed by the intensity of his desire for the missing Ligeia into her double: "Now, then, did

my spirit fully and freely burn with more than all the fires of her own
. . . I would call aloud upon her name . . . as if, through the wild
eagerness, the solemn passion, the consuming ardor of my longing for
the departed, I could restore her to the pathways she had abandoned—
ah, *could* it be forever?—upon the earth" (85). He has joined his will
to hers or, perhaps, she has attached the power of his will to her own.
Her beauty, with its strangeness, may occupy his spirit in a more sinister way than he has yet perceived.

I do not wish to strain this part of the text, especially since doing so
depends on the previous strain of doubting Ligeia's motive for declaring
her worship of the narrator. Whether Poe intends the reader to see so
far beyond the narrator *at this point* is by no means clear to me. It is
clear that at this time in the narrator's life, he is out of control. He
wanders aimlessly, he gives way to childish impulses, he sees incipient
madness in himself, and he indulges in opium. Even within the present
of the narration, he uses nearly half of his account of this period between Ligeia's death and Rowena's death to describe the new bridal
chamber. His primary act in this part of the story seems to be a surrender of his will, yet the result is a firing up of his will that Ligeia
live. Ligeia may well seem to be somehow actively involved in his
actions. Insofar as she does, the fantastic hints at its presence. Again,
it is not crucial to understanding the story for the implied reader to
pick up this clue and incorporate it immediately into his attempt to
penetrate the mystery of Ligeia. The end of the story will force him
back to this point. Still, this suspicion seems there to be found on the
initial encounter with the text, and, if one does encounter it, the mystery
of Ligeia looms larger and more ominous.

The rest of the narrative tells of Rowena's death, of her apparent
revivification during the night the narrator watches with her, and, finally, of her apparent transformation into Ligeia. This final one-third
of the text reads much more like a horror thriller. Rowena and the
narrator feel an alien presence among them. She grows more and more
ill. The narrator has visions of an angelic form and of the ruby drops
that fall into Rowena's medicinal wine. He gives detailed attention to
his experiences with the body during the night of the transformation.
This experience is compounded of his longing for Ligeia and his dutiful
and grisly attempts to assist in what appears to be Rowena's recovery.
But until the last lines of the story, all of this is a mystery. Gripping
as it is in itself, what is its connection with the rest of the narrative?
What is the meaning of this terrible experience?

The answer to these questions, presumably, *is* the transformation.
As the narrator tells it, this change is another surprise. Though it is
what he longs for, it is not what he expected. He details his amazement

and shock as he is gradually forced to recognize that the woman who rises from Rowena's death bed and who shrinks from his touch is Ligeia. However, this final scene is no final answer. The narrative seems to break off at the crucial moment. This ending launches the implied reader back into the tale in search of an explanation of how this utterly unexpected event came about. Like "The Black Cat," but unlike *At the Mountains of Madness*, "Ligeia" does not end with its last word. "Ligeia" is, however, even more extreme than "The Black Cat" in its failure to close, for it offers an *anticlosure*. It presents at the end a shocking mystery for which the implied reader is largely unprepared. This does not mean that the implied reader has no information to apply to the solution of this problem, but rather that he is not prepared to anticipate this problem. As a result, his reading must be done again. As Frederick Garber observes, "Much of the horror of the story lies in our pondering of these spaces between the ending and the beginning, our wonder at what could have filled them" (239). The implied reader must rearrange his interpretation of the narrative to be able to include Ligeia's transformation within it. This is the point at which much of the critical writing on this tale has struck sand. In what way is the implied reader to rearrange his interpretation to achieve a proper and desired closure for this tale?

Poe seems to heighten the reader's desire for closure from the beginning of the tale, when the reader is invited to play detective. The reader is challenged to piece together an understanding of the mysterious woman and of the true relationship between her and the narrator. Every new mystery in the tale has contributed in its way to complicate and to heighten these major mysteries. The implied reader has been challenged to answer these questions, but he has not been given answers, only the material out of which answers might be constructed. Such material is, after all, what detectives (and readers) want. But at the end of the tale is another astounding clue, not a final illumination or a detective to explain all. The desire to answer these questions contributes strongly to the anticlosure of this tale. Of course, the intrusion of the impossible in the last sentence can only intensify the desire for answers, but at the same time the appearance of the fantastic impossibly complicates achieving closure.

Reflection on personal attempts at solving these mysteries and on the range of published attempts leads me to generalize three modes of approaching this problem. In the next chapter, I will deal with more of the critical material, specifically with attempts to deal with the situation that develops out of these modes of response. The three modes make a nice progression, so nice, in fact, that one might easily assume that a good reader would move through them progressively. I will argue, however, that whether one at first takes the story to be marvelous or uncanny, one inevitably arrives at a mode of ambiguity in which the possibilities of the marvelous and the uncanny become poles between which the implied reader vibrates until he invents a new way of seeing the problem. Even if the reader performs his role in such a way as to immediately perceive the ambiguity, his experience will be hesitation between the marvelous and the uncanny explanations of these events.

How are we to account for Ligeia's resurrection if we take the story as the narrator apparently intends to present it? If we accept the accuracy of his perceptions but suspect his interpretations, we come to see that Ligeia's intention was not to die. When her body died, her will survived. She bound the narrator to her on her death bed, completing the subordination of his will to her own. After her death, he becomes her unwitting agent. Her will inhabits him, without his full awareness, and uses him to acquire Rowena and to create the occultly decorated room in which the combined wills of the narrator and Ligeia can effect the destruction of Rowena and the re-creation of Ligeia. As Joel Salzberg has argued, Ligeia *becomes* the Conqueror Worm of her poem (113). This transformation is terribly ironic, for her stated desire was to conquer the conqueror, to become like the great will that pervades all things. However, she remains a limited will, pervading only a few things. In her fierce passion not to surrender to the angels and to death, she becomes a mirror of her foe rather than of God. She attains the immortality of death rather than of a creator. Unable to create out of nothing, she must first destroy and then re-create. Though his conclusions differ from mine, Lawrence Stahlberg supports this view of Ligeia in his argument that the epigraph is significantly ambiguous. While the narrator believes that the quotation attributes human mortality to a feeble will, the somewhat slippery grammar may mean that it is only feebleness of the human will that resists death. Were human will perfect, it would embrace death and yield to the angels (206). I would argue that Ligeia reads the quotation in the same way as the narrator does, and that this is a grave error.

In its initial appearance, Ligeia's resurrection is a miracle that forces the detective/reader to ask, "How?" If the implied reader turns first to the supernatural interpretation, Ligeia emerges as monstrous. The more one ponders her monstrousness, the more horrible she becomes. Her acquisitions are gigantic. She has acquired Rowena and the narrator. Before these additions, she had wealth and knowledge beyond all mortals. Furthermore, her origins are unknown. As these important imponderables leap into significance, they produce the suggestion that Ligeia has acquired her many possessions by continual repetition of the act just narrated. Perhaps this is not the first time she has recon-structed her body out of the energies of others. Her mode of vampirism extends backward into time and becomes still more like that of the Conqueror Worm. She has achieved her satanic immortality by feeding spiritually and physically upon the rest of mankind, dominating their feeble wills with her great will.

The horror of her acts increases and begins to move toward the possibility of terror when the reader thinks about her motives. Why would she do such horrible things? Her motive is clear: she desires life so strongly that all other human values become no more than tools for its pursuit. From a human perspective, her desire is normal and understandable, perhaps even tragic. It is a desire like our own. But she lives in a universe, also like our own, in which the monomaniac pursuit of that desire procures its opposite. Either one is a mortal or one is mortality. Either one dies or one kills. Insofar as the implied reader moves toward such a perception of the implication of Ligeia's failure, one may feel rather deeply the fundamental terror of entrap-ment in this mortal coil.

If the implied reader accepts the marvelous at the end of the tale and rearranges his experience of the tale to account for it, he encounters Ligeia as a monster and her world as a horror. These effects, together with the pressure of the shock of the impossible, are likely to push the reader toward an alternate arrangement, an uncanny reading of the story. The alert detective knows that the narrator's opium addiction, his psychological instability, and his longing for Ligeia may well have led to a hallucination. Perhaps the main pressure impelling the reader toward entertaining an alternate explanation, however, is another gap, which is difficult to ignore. At the end of the tale, Ligeia is back. Yet at the beginning of the tale, years after the end, there is no Ligeia. Of course, Poe intimates in a 21 September 1839 letter to Philip Cooke that he should have made "the will" fail in the perfection of its in-tention so that Ligeia would have faded back into the dead Rowena (Ostrum, ed., 1: 118). However, when Poe added "The Conquerer Worm" to the tale in 1845, he did not add this revision. Years after Ligeia's death, the narrator hides away in his study, dreaming of her. Perhaps it was all a dream. Unfortunately, those who would argue that hallucination is the only possible explanation of these events are faced with the perfectly plausible explanation that Ligeia has gone elsewhere. Her shrinking from the narrator in the last paragraph sug-gests that her interest in him has cooled. Still, the uncanny hypothesis is attractive. The gap of her unexplained absence in the time of the telling demands that one explore the possibility that the narrator only imagined her return. The horrors of the supernatural interpretation encourage the implied reader to split, to seek a more comfortable explanation. The supernaturalism of the transformation may stimulate skepticism, and the narrator's prominent limitations, which now seem very significant, grant a license for such an attempt. What results from this arrangement?

The published criticism of "Ligeia" shows that the main problem is a lack of information. One gap leads to another. As Joel Porte implies, the whole story, every word, may be a lie or a hallucination (69-74). Critics who stop short of such a blanket assertion find it difficult to separate the factual from the hallucinated. For James Gargano, Ligeia is a vision from the very first, but Rowena is real. For Roy Basler, both women are real, but the transformation is a hallucinattion (Regan; see bibliographic note at the end of this chapter). If the narrator hallucinates only part of what he tells, why? Does his love for Ligeia drive him to murder Rowena as Brian Barbour argues? Is it his will to live rather than hers that is frustrated by her death as Basler thinks? Is the narrator attempting to regain a lost experience of the ideal as Gargano believes? Perhaps Porte and Salzberg are correct to see the narrator as a sort of ruthless idealist who almost knows what he is doing when he murders Rowena. The main problem with most attempts to sort out hallucination from actual external event is that there is too little information to establish any one possible reading as authoritative. The more one tries, the more one is driven toward positions like Porte's, toward the conclusion that the entire narrative is the construction of a madman and that none of it is reliable.

Thinking through the implications of the possibility that the narrator hallucinates is not comforting. One is driven toward the conclusion that nothing the narrator says can be accepted as descriptive of the world. If all that he says is about himself, what sort of self does he describe? He pictures a self who dreams a world in which the events he narrates take place. Dreamed or real, that world is equally horrifying. To the horrors we have already seen in that world must be added the horror of realizing that a desire of his has led him into hallucination in search of something that his world fails to provide. In the marvelous reading, the narrator is the unwitting victim of his beloved, of his desire. She becomes a terrifying and indifferent will who dominates and uses him. In the uncanny reading, he imagines a universe presumably the answer to his desire, and that universe is precisely the one the reader encounters in the marvelous reading. If, as is suggested by his attention to the epigraph, by his studies with Ligeia, and by the fate he imagines for her, his desire is for immortality, then what a mockery of his hopes is his imagination! All he can imagine is a universe in which human immortality is monstrous. The narrator becomes a man whose universe failed him and who, then, tried and failed to imagine a satisfactory remedy. He is doubly the prisoner of a hostile cosmos and of his own mind, which cannot escape mirroring his world.

The narrator's obsession with Ligeia may be a dream or the product of his extraordinary waking experiences. The text pushes the implied reader in both directions and does not allow either to dominate. Whichever the reader chooses, he encounters terror and the gap. If Ligeia really came back, where is she now? If the narrator only dreamed her, how did he do it and why? The incompleteness of each of these major directions of interpretation leads the reader back to the other in a continual vibration. To describe this vibration, the hesitation of the pure fantastic, is to describe the third of the modes of response to this tale.

G. R. Thompson indicates something of what I understand the nature of this experience to be when he discusses Poe's dark romantic irony in *Poe's Fiction.* He says that "Ligeia" leads the reader "first, into the world of supernatural horror, and then out of that world into a world of mental horror, and then, out of that purely mental world into a limbo region of ambiguity where we cannot be sure what did or did not take place" (104). I argue that this region of ambiguity is, in this tale, terrifying to the real reader.

Whether the narrator has experienced Ligeia or dreamed her, he has *been* her. She has inhabited him, worn him, and tossed him aside like an old coat. Now he is unable to cast her aside. He says he continues to call her image before his eyes, though she is no more. His mental necrophilia is obsessive and finally appears as his primary motive for writing. The story is a memorial to her, but it does not end his mourning. He cannot exorcise her. Whether dead or merely absent, she lives inside him. As he is positioned in relation to Ligeia, so is the implied reader positioned in relation to the tale. For the reader encoded in the text, the tale has no end. The role of implied reader is suspended between two modes of arranging the story, between two unsatisfactory and mutually exclusive concretions. The implied reader's desire is for resolution, to be whole, for it is less than comfortable to remain in vacillation in a "region of ambiguity where we cannot be sure what did or did not take place," especially when the role has been partially defined as a detective and when there is nothing pleasant and much that is horrifying about the poles between which we vacillate. The story has put on, inhabited, and abandoned the implied reader. But the role continues, like an obsession, and for the real reader there is no conventional way out of it. The relation of the real reader to the implied reader mirrors the relation of the implied reader to the tale, which, in turn, mirrors the relation of the narrator to Ligeia. The real reader has been trapped in the role of implied reader. The tale is a trap.

This entrapment is the third mode of response to the anticlosure of this particular tale. It means, quite literally, that the text has provided for a reading that the text itself will not bring to an end. The burden of constructing closure falls upon the reader. This is not utterly unique, for many works require considerable effort on the part of the implied reader to achieve closure. Perhaps a major feature of Ernest Hemingway's short stories is the requirement that the implied reader continue "reading" for a noticeable period after the perusal of the text to pull the elements of the story together into an appropriate unity. Any story with a surprise ending requires a rearrangement of its elements in memory to make them consistent with the ending. But those works still contain their closure; they offer signals to indicate when the reading is complete. They allow for their own successful concretization so that readers are regularly able to reach a fairly high level of agreement about how these stories are to be understood. Though practiced real readers are used to assuming the burden of constructing closure by making complex inferences, they may have few, if any, strategies for ending a reading that *refuses* to end itself. Those strategies for creating closure, which all of us command to some extent, come more from our dealings with life than with art. They are the means by which we seek to impose patterns upon our life experiences that infuse those experiences with meaning. Therefore, it is no accident that there is, as Todorov suggests, a strong tendency to read fantasies as allegory. Terror fantasy, of course, places an added pressure on the reader to allegorize the story, to place it within a frame of ideas that has its own wholeness; Kafka, among other modern writers, has trained us well in the necessary techniques. The sense of entrapment that "Ligeia" creates may derive in part from its refusal to accept the imposition of any of the patterns that it suggests for itself. This tale is less passive, perhaps, than the world is.

"Ligeia" asks us to play detective. It then deploys the material of a mystery in such a way as to prevent its solution. It turns the screw of our desire for solution by means of horror and of the supernatural; it becomes an example of the pure fantastic. The real reader enters the role of implied reader in good faith and plays the role as instructed, only to find at the end of the text that the role demands eternal elaboration, that it will not let go. It seems rare in our experience of life that we so commit ourselves to some point of view as to be entrapped by it. My discussion in later chapters suggests that this subjective sense of freedom from role playing is largely an illusion; still, we may not often *feel* so entrapped in life as we do in fiction. Yet it is only a fiction!

Surely, if it refuses closure, that is all we need to say. We can go on to the next story and forget this one.

This story has haunted me for years. I do not think I am alone, for it seems also to haunt others. The collection of critical literature mirrors my personal entrapment and is an index of the entrapment of real readers in the role of the implied reader of "Ligeia." To read most of the critical pieces on "Ligeia" is to go around and around, from one pole to the other on a kind of circle of interpretations, none of which seems to reveal the secret that will allow the tale to end satisfactorily. And the problem is not that interpretations vary, that there are disagreements over details or even over the meanings of major portions of the text. The problem is that the marvelous and the uncanny are mutually exclusive; they present an either/or to which there is no final answer within the context of the question.

Norman Holland discusses an interesting analogue of this experience in *The I.* Some optical illusions leave the brain unable to decide which pattern to impose on the presented lines. This is the case, for example, in the figure that is either a vase or two profiles facing each other. Holland says that the brain "restlessly tosses back and forth between inconsistent hypotheses about those objects" (111). Caught between this either/or, the brain cannot rest. For most people, this fluctuation continues for as long as they attend to the representation. One reason for this vacillation is that we organize our perceptions at the highest possible level of completeness. Since vase and faces are at the same level of completeness as presented by the illusion, we are unable to decide between them. Holland implies that when we are unable to complete such perceptions at the first level we try, we then fall back to lower levels. In other words, we do with objects, such as an optical illusion, what we have just done with "Ligeia." When the object fails to be single and complete, we go back over it, reexamining the details, or the constituent parts, in search of a new unifying hypothesis. Perhaps most interesting for the inquiry here, Holland points out that most people can "beat" the vase/faces illusion by means of imagination. We can imagine a higher order of unity, "two people pressing their noses up against a vase" (111). If we again look at the presented lines with this hypothesis in mind, we can see both vase and faces simultaneously. The problem of "seeing" an optical illusion may be solved by creating a new perspective on the object.

When the real reader becomes entrapped in the role of implied reader, the character of his experience of the fiction changes radically. The real reader has, in effect, come upon a literary work that is similar in character to the vase/faces optical illusion. While he was more or less innocently doing what fictions usually ask one to do, the tale reached out its claws and grabbed him. As soon as the reader feels so clutched, his relation to the fiction ceases to be that of an aesthetic attitude, which Ingarden says is necessary to the concretization of the work as a work of art. By reserving until the end the shock of the pure fantastic, Poe has pointedly, almost violently, refused closure. Virtually nothing is finished in the tale. The text has ended, and a vision is revealed, but the vision is a terrifying image of the pure fantastic. As a result, the tale becomes a threat, a kind of obsession, that makes the implied reader into a double of the narrator. In effect, the real reader, as he struggles to find a way out of the role he has accepted, becomes a mirror image of the narrator who is struggling to extricate himself from his beloved. We shall see that the history of the criticism of this and other terror fantasies illustrates the attempts of critics to find a perspective from which escape is possible.

Poe has devised a kind of anticlosure for this tale. The potential for this radical denial of closure is inherent in the pure fantastic. We can see a similar, perhaps less successful, anticlosure in Poe's *The Narrative of Arthur Gordon Pym*. There, too, a narrator undergoes a series of horrifying adventures, most of them perfectly appropriate to a sensation story or the uncanny tale of terror. The only hints of the marvelous in his narrative are subdued until the end of his telling. The reader may notice repetitive patterns in Pym's adventures. Once he voyages below the Antarctic Circle, his adventures become exotic, but not marvelous. Only the final image of the gigantic white figure strongly suggests the marvelous in his narrative. However, his telling is framed by an editor who at the end attempts to draw the entire story into the marvelous. He notices that the patterns Pym traces in chasms on Antarctic islands are recognizable as writing and seem to contain messages from a divinity. One result is a shock of the pure fantastic, which is similar to that of "Ligeia," but much less powerful. Though this novel has attracted critical attention similar to that of "Ligeia," the intensity of the fantastic in the novel is dissipated by the split between Pym who does not, as far as the reader can tell, actually experience the marvelous or the fantastic and the editor who asserts the marvelous. Though Poe uses a similar device at the end of this tale, he does not seem to have intended the same effect as is produced in "Ligeia." It is more likely that Poe was working toward an effect such as that described by John Carlos Rowe, an intellectual demonstration of the limits of language in coinciding with the reality it attempts to represent. If Rowe is correct, then *Pym* may join *The Castle* and *The Crying of Lot 49* as an example of an intellectually frightening apologue. However, in "The Fall of the House of Usher," Poe again exploits the possibilities of anticlosure in the pure fantastic to entrap the implied and real reader.

*Bibliographic Note*

Many important essays on Poe's fiction have been reprinted in various collections of criticism. When I refer to such pieces here and in subsequent chapters, I give the editor's name with the citation to indicate the volume in which the article appears.

## CHAPTER EIGHT

# The Entrapped Critic: Poe's "The Fall of the House of Usher"

In this chapter we explore a second example of terror fantasy and look at the rich variety of critical response to "The Fall of the House of Usher" as a means of examining how real readers attempt to deal with the unique effects of a terror fantasy. "Ligeia" terrifies the real reader by entrapping him in the role of implied reader and splitting that reader. That tale refuses the closure it has made the implied reader desire, and so adds to the tension generated by the pure fantastic, the hesitation between a natural and a supernatural explanation of unusual events. The implied reader splits between two readings and eventually enters a third mode of response, a suspension between the readings. Because the tale heightens rather than resolves this split, the reading must be ended by the reader alone, without the assistance that most fictions provide. The discussion of "Ligeia" was intended, in part, to describe this situation. The following consideration of "The Fall of the House of Usher" starts with how Poe creates the same situation with this tale. Then, we will look at critical responses to the tale to see how real readers have attempted to end their readings. What routes of escape are available once one is entrapped within the role of reading a terror fantasy?

# I

The opening paragraph of "The Fall of the House of Usher" introduces the problem of the fantastic in a subdued and subtle way. The narrator recounts an experience for which he cannot account by rational means, but for which he insists there is a natural explanation. Opposed to his insistence is the repetition of the experience. He looks at the House of Usher, and "a sense of insufferable gloom" pervades his spirit. He distinguishes this feeling from his experience of the sublime, which contains in its terror some poetic sentiment. Unable to deal with or account for his response, he is forced "to fall back upon the unsatisfactory conclusion, that while, beyond doubt, there *are* combinations of very simple natural objects which have the power of thus affecting us, still the analysis of this power lies among considerations beyond our depth" (88). To prove to himself that simple combinations of natural objects can influence feelings, he experiments by changing his point of view. But the reflection of the house in the tarn produces "a shudder even more thrilling than before" (88). When he returns to his perusal of the house after explaining the reasons for his visit, this conflict between the reports of his senses and his interpretations of these reports persists. As he gazes at the reflection his sense of an occult presence grows, but there is a natural law to account for that, too. Being conscious that one is giving way to superstition accelerates the speed at which one gives way. This is "the paradoxical law of all sentiments having terror as a basis" (89). When he looks again at the house and sees hanging over it—and over the whole area—a peculiar atmosphere that is actually palpable as an odorous vapor, he characterizes this apparent perception as "a ridiculous fancy" that has grown in his mind.

The narrator has entered a part of the world that pointedly contradicts his previous experience, which had taught him that the mind interacts with and, on the whole, dominates the world. While he acknowledges that on occasion part of the world can give shape to the mind, he also believes, first, that the world is plural in its essense and, therefore, cannot radiate gloom exclusively and, second, that by changing his point of view, by actively using his mind, he can exercise a sort of freedom of vision. Like Emily in *The Mysteries of Udolpho*, he expects to be able to turn from the terror of a threatening object to the sublime vista of some surrounding landscape and, thereby, to transcend the immediate terror. But the landscape in which he finds himself seems to have an opposing force, a sentient will that imposes itself upon him. There is no plurality in the reflected image of the house, but rather an increased intensity of monochromatic gloom. If the world, properly seen, radiates only gloom, then it becomes irrelevant that one has the power to vary the direction of his gaze. One is entrapped.

The opening of this tale, then, sets up an opposition between the narrator's experience of a force that may be supernatural and his insistent interpretation of this experience as explainable according to obscure psychological laws or else illusory, the mere product of "nerves." He is made to hesitate between the natural and the supernatural despite his displayed preference for the natural. The implied reader can only enter into this dilemma. Parallel to this conflict is a subtle opposition that will grow increasingly important as the story progresses.

Like "Ligeia" and unlike both *At the Mountains of Madness* and "The Black Cat," "The Fall of the House of Usher" provides no opening statement of the narrator's purpose in telling this story. The focus of this tale is also apparently on objects other than the narrator: the Usher family and the physical house. Yet the opening paragraph reveals as much about the narrator as about the house. In fact, they are placed in opposition to each other as antagonists, as representatives of two differing views of the world. Also, even though the narrator is never explicit about why he tells this story, he reveals his reasons indirectly from the very beginning. Unlike the narrator of "Ligeia," who is explicitly *writing* his tale, this narrator speaks. His tone is conversational, punctuated with such phrases as: "I know not how it was . . . I say insufferable . . . which I compare to" (88). Though the narrator of "Ligeia" also uses such phrases, he does so less frequently and usually makes a reference to writing when he does. This narrator has or imagines a listener. Indeed, he seems to encode the implied reader as a listener who pretends to be dramatically present at the telling of the tale. One effect of this implied close contact between speaker and listener is a corresponding distance between the narrator in the time present and his experiences in the past. This is a distance upon which the narrator insists, not only by judging his past experience as either illusory or ultimately explicable, but also by a rhetorical device—regularly reminding the reader of their current location. This distance is in opposition to the primary feeling of entrapment conveyed in the first paragraph. The narrator describes the physical oppression of the weather in an opening sentence, which also conveys through its diction, sound, and rhythm a corresponding psychological oppression: "During the whole of a dull, dark, and soundless day in the autumn of the year, when the clouds hung oppressively low in the heavens, I had been passing alone, on horseback, through a singularly dreary tract of country, and at length found myself, as the shades of evening drew on, within view of the melancholy House of Usher" (88). The paragraph ends with an image of psychological entrapment when he fails to change his response to the setting by changing his point of view. The main implication of this fairly subtle opposition is that the narrator is reluctant to tell this story, that in the very telling, he resists the oppressive memory of these events.

The narrator mildly resists his own story, trying rhetorically to dissociate himself from it. The frequency of his assertions of the present tense increases at crucial points in his narrative: when he recounts his perception of the atmosphere (89), when he discusses Usher's artistic productions (92-93), and, especially, when he reports Usher's belief in the sentience of all things (93-94). However, such assertions virtually disappear after the death of Madeline. The narrator also resists the House of Usher. In fact, though the story is ostensibly about the House of Usher, the opening paragraph sets up an opposition between the narrator and the house, which proves to be the primary action of the tale.

It bodes ill for the narrator to discover that Usher and his house mirror each other. The physical similarities are the clearest; they suggest that both man and house are living corpses, for though they look dead, they remain whole or animated. They are also alike in their manner of being, both showing a "wild inconsistency" between order and disorder, between life and death. Both are afflicted with constitutional ills that enhance their isolation, the house's atmosphere and Usher's morbid acuteness of the senses. Each appears on the verge of collapse. When Usher acknowledges these resemblances by asserting that the *"physique"* of the house affects the *"morale"* of his existence, he indicates that at the center of his malady is a growing dominance of the material world over his spirit, a world that includes both his house and his body. Usher seems to feel imprisoned in his body and in his house; as his body has come to resemble his house, so he fears a peculiar advance of mortality as his failing spirit comes to resemble his decaying body. The narrator has been called to Usher to relieve this situation. His purpose is to resist the progress of Usher's illness by the cheerfulness of his society. Once he has seen Usher's condition, it seems clear that any resistance is futile. Usher's condition is the condition of his world; its cause is in the nature of things. When Usher hesitantly admits "a more natural and far more palpable origin" of much of his gloom in Madeline's fatal illness, he implies that the narrator might comfort him, but this possibility is negated when Madeline herself passes through "a remote portion of the apartment" without noticing the narrator's presence. By this appearance, the narrator is, again unaccountably, oppressed and, turning expectantly to Usher, he finds that he has *buried* his face in his hands. Images of burial abound on all sides. The narrator is clearly helpless; he can do nothing.

The middle of the story consists of a succession of images of Usher's imprisonment in his world and of the narrator's attempts to resist the oppressive feelings that attack him. The narrator reports no direct actions of his own upon Usher until the last night of Usher's life; he apparently does not try to change Usher's point of view. Instead, he reveals only his own efforts to resist becoming "ushered," efforts that fail, at least in the short run. Although the struggle of the narrator to resist becoming another image of Usher continues through the middle of the story, the narrative focuses on the image of Usher. What is the content of that image?

This question has provoked so much controversy among the critics that I can hardly hope to claim for my account greater validity than any of a dozen other accounts of what happens to Usher. I have said that the root of Usher's problem is a fear of transformation. This view does not differ greatly from many other interpretations of Usher's character and malady. Where I differ is in my attempt to avoid inferences from the facts Usher gives or reveals that require validation from a theoretical construct imported from outside the story. I try to stay as close to the story as possible, to follow my principle of attempting to construct a first reading. As a result, I explain relatively little about Usher. He and Madeline remain essentially mysterious. As Patrick Quinn says, the story makes no direct exploration of the internal causes of Usher's "disease"; rather it presents Usher to the narrator and to the reader as an impenetrable mystery (Woodson 84-88). Instead of explaining *why* Usher is as he is, I want to explain the effect Usher has on the narrator.

The root of Usher's problem, as he states it, is the fear that he will be transformed, that he will go mad. His body has come to mirror his cadaverous house and he believes his soul is being forced into a similar shape. The wild inconsistency between order and disorder in the appearance of the house is reflected in the death-in-life of Usher's body and in the state of Usher's soul, in his alternation between the vivacious and the sullen. Thus, it appears to Usher that the house is transforming him body and soul into a mirror of itself. Usher's morbid acuteness of the senses may be both cause and effect of this strain on his spirit. The combined strain and sensitivity place Usher on the brink of dissolution, awaiting the shock that will push him over the edge. Behind all is the house as cause.

In Usher's mind, the sentient house wills this transformation. Indeed, it wills that all things in it mirror it. Madeline's passing briefly through the apartment where the men first visit seems symbolically suggestive on several levels, one of which is the passage of the old preferred order out of the house. On another level, it suggests the brief progress of the human soul through this vale of tears and through a door from which there is supposedly no return, for the narrator will not see her again until her burial. Her passing, then, parallels all of the losses Usher fears: of Madeline herself, of his physical integrity, of his composure, his sanity, and his life.

While Madeline is dying, Usher entertains the narrator with works of art that reflect the polarities of his mental state, even though the narrator sees these works as products of the manic rather than of the depressive state. The narrator says they are "the result of that intense mental collectedness and concentration to which I have previously alluded as observable only in particular moments of the highest artificial excitement" (93). This observation may recall an image from the story's opening, which has been gaining in significance at least since the description of Usher's symptoms. The narrator compares his experience of "utter depression of soul" to "the after-dream of the reveller upon opium—the bitter lapse into every-day life—the hideous dropping off of the veil" (88). The feelings that accompany this image, "an iciness, a sinking, a sickening of the heart—an unredeemed dreariness of thought which no goading of the imagination could torture into aught of the sublime" (88), constitute an accurate description of the effect of Usher's art. At his most ecstatic, Usher produces feelings of intolerable awe; his works partake of a "highly distracted ideality" that throws "a sulphurous lustre over all" (92). His works compel the narrator's spirit to awed contemplation. This experience might be termed "the satanic sublime," an inversion of the heavenly sublime as seen in Ann Radcliffe. Usher's art draws the narrator's attention to a universe in which the heavenly sublime is impossible, an illusion of those observers whose imperfect senses lend color to the charnel house. Usher's painting most vividly produces this effect, for as a product of Usher's visionary mood, it portrays the confinement of vision: the light in the exitless tunnel, the soul imprisoned in the coffins of the body, of the house, and of the cosmos itself. A depiction of Usher's universe, the painting suggests what a man of morbidly acute senses may "see" when his sharp eyes pierce the veil of "every-day life." Usher's vision derives from ecstasy, not from the after-dream of opium. Ecstasy for Usher is the extension of his reason to the utmost reach of his senses. At this limit, he discovers a blank wall that turns him back into his dark and gloomy prison.

"The Haunted Palace" continues a logical pattern suggested by the painting. In an allegory based upon key images and ideas in the story, the poem expresses Usher's sense of the inevitability of the spirit's madness within its bodily prison, the unavoidable surrender of the individual self to disintegration. It is no wonder that Usher believes the material world to be alive since its vitality seems to overcome his spirit. Usher's books reflect a similar sense of imprisonment and of desire for escape, alternating as they do between treatments of the ideal and contemplations of mortality. Usher, despite his acute sensitivity, is entrapped in the prison house of his senses. All objects in his world exhale gloom: every object he makes radiates this same gloom; and he himself has come to radiate gloom. His experience tends to prove the sentience of the material universe. His power to pursue the ecstatic pole seems to depend on the existence of Madeline, for when she dies, his searches cease.

As he reports Usher's behavior and their activities, the narrator's rhetorical reminders of his presence increase and become more desperate in tone. He describes their artistic pursuits: "I shall ever bear about me a memory of the many solemn hours I thus spent alone with the master of the House of Usher. . . . His long improvised dirges will ring forever in my ears. Among other things, I hold painfully in mind. . . . (vivid as their images now are before me) . . . I have just spoken of that morbid condition of the auditory nerve. . . . that intense mental collectedness and concentration to which I have previously alluded. . . . The words of one of these rhapsodies I have easily remembered" (92-93). These signals of the narrator's presence in the present tend to emphasize an irony that pervades this telling. His experience is inescapable. It repeatedly overtakes him. Usher's images of himself are oppressively persistent. The narrator's very efforts to escape into the present of the narration betray him, for what he wishes to escape in the past awaits him in the future, "will ring forever in my ears." Within the drama of the *telling*, the narrator's most desperate moment seems to be just before Madeline's death, when he returns to the subject of the sentience of the house.

The narrator begins the first paragraph after his recitation *from memory* of Usher's poem, this way: "I well remember that suggestions arising from this ballad led us into a train of thought wherein there became manifest an opinion of Usher's which I mention not so much on account of its novelty . . . as on account of the pertinacity with which he maintained it" (93). The narrator reports that he started at Usher's mention of the atmosphere enclosing the grounds. Usher builds his case out of the hauntingly inexplicable experiences that the narrator himself has had in his approach to the house. Under this pressure to believe, the narrator flees vigorously into the rhetorical present: "Such opinions need no comment, and I will make none" (94). Of course, he has already called such opinions ridiculous superstitions (89, 91). However, his experience at Usher has so far tended *to confirm* the reality of the impressions he wants to insist are illusory and *to confirm* the main effect that follows from these impressions, belief in some inimical occult power. Such opinions, in fact, need a great deal of comment. They demand of the narrator his tale.

It would be rather difficult at this point for the implied reader to see himself other than as the object of the narrator's rhetoric. What the narrator asks for now is agreement with his judgment of the situation. Whatever the causes of Usher's decay, they cannot be willed upon him by an external force such as a house. The implied reader is also pressured to resist the narrator's rhetoric, for appearances are against the narrator, and he has no alternative explanation. The narrator appears to be telling his story to deny the significance upon which his story insists. As he resists his story, so his story resists him, refusing to take the shape he desires for it. His story mirrors the House of Usher, which seems to utter rather than to be uttered by Usher. The narrator thus reveals his obsession. In the final one-third of the story, we shall see that the narrator is ushered and uttered. He becomes the voice of Usher speaking to the implied reader, trying not to speak what he must speak, trying not to mirror Usher, but mirroring him just the same. Could he convince his listener that what he has experienced is illusion, he might perhaps convince himself and so exorcise the story. Somewhat like the Ancient Mariner, he is compelled to tell his tale, but compelled by inner necessity to be free of the tale, to save himself. Infected (the word is the narrator's, 95) by Usher, he proceeds to spread the disorder, his dis-ease, far and wide in the effort to be cured. After the account of Madeline's burial, the narrator's efforts at identifying with his listener are less frequent and less desperate. The death of Madeline is followed by the disappearance of all light from Usher's eyes and by rhetorical hopelessness in the narrator. Usher roams without object from chamber to chamber and gazes "upon vacancy for long hours," as if listening (95). Soon the narrator is doing the same. This ushering of the narrator precedes a series of three visions that the House of Usher offers the narrator as final evidence of its view of the world.

First, Usher comes to the narrator's room in a mockery of the narrator's mission to cheer up Usher. His "mad hilarity" appalls the narrator, but since anything is better than being alone, the narrator welcomes his presence. Usher has come to show him something, the peculiar storm outside, which the narrator at first thinks sublimely beautiful. Upon further observation, he concludes that Usher *must not* look at it. He reaches this concluson when he notices that the seemingly living whirlwind appears imprisoned within "the unnatural light of a faintly luminous and distinctly visible gaseous exhalation which hung about and enshrouded the mansion" (96). For the first time, the narrator reports direct resistance to Usher's perception and a direct attempt to explain it away as "merely electrical phenomena not uncommon" or as the result of the miasma of the tarn. As a diversion, he suggests reading.

The second vision is much more complexly presented. Indeed, in its complexity it threatens to become ludicrous. While the narrator attempts to entertain Usher with a hopeful sounding story, Usher is not diverted except by the irony that he alone perceives. As Usher's arrival in the narrator's room mocks the narrator's earlier arrival at Usher, and as the revelation of the storm emphatically affirms Usher's world view, so Madeline's escape from the tomb mocks "The Mad Trist," and her appearance turns the screw of the horror of Usher's world view.

"The Mad Trist," while it may, as the narrator asserts, lack imagination, speaks rather directly to Usher's despair. The story, in the portion the narrator tells, is of the reconquest of a palace of gold, which had been reduced by a dragon into a hermit's hut, a hut with most of the characteristics of the haunted palace of Usher's poem. Ethelred's progress, then, suggests the possibility, the hope, that King Thought might retake his lost kingdom and don again the purple for which he was born. However, in the background is the opposite horror, the echoing series of events leading up to the destruction of the metaphorical king, Usher, and his palace. Madeline's escape from her tomb is a mockery of the recovery of reason.

Because Madeline has been associated with Usher's hope that the universe is unbounded and because she has been the main source of comfort in his life, placing her alive in the tomb is the most horrifying image of the human condition in Usher's world. The image of living burial, echoed by all the images of enclosure in the tale, even by the idea of mirrored images, expresses the fear that Usher cannot bear to face. Upon her burial, Usher looked most like a corpse, and she looked most alive, for it appears characteristic of their diseases to wear aspects the opposite of their actual states. But though they appear opposite, their appearances are different facets of the same meaning: life, the spirit, is entombed in this alien world. Essentially, death and life are indistinguishable; the siblings are both dead and alive. Madeline's reappearance after her "death" suggests that death is not final, that it is not an exit from the prison house of life, but rather, a kind of reentrance. Madeline's defining motion in the tale is to pass through doors, all of which are within the House of Usher: the apartment where the narrator first sees her, the lid of her coffin, the door of her temporary tomb, and the door of the narrator's room. Each time she passes through a door, she finds herself in another space that mirrors the condition of Usher. Her universe is Usher's universe, the exitless tunnel unnaturally lit from within. She, Usher, and the narrator have been placed alive in the tomb. For them, this is the human condition.

From this view of the universe, the narrator attempts to flee, but in his flight he encounters the third terrifying vision. In the immediate face of this revelation, he tries feebly to deny, but he cannot deny what he *sees*. Surrounded by mirrorings—the twins, the reelings, the usherings, the collapses, the doublings of storm and house—enclosed on every side by images of his containment, the narrator flees: "From that chamber and from that mansion, I fled aghast" (98). But as the irony of his rhetoric has already revealed, he cannot escape. He is infected. The House of Usher utters him with its last breath, and he is expelled into a space identical in meaning with those he has left. Were the narrator speaking rather than being spoken, he might seize his last opportunity to assert that with the destruction of the house and the appearance of the natural light of the moon, Usher's disease disappears from the earth. But it is clear from the manner of his telling as well as from his vision of the moon that the narrator has not yet accomplished this exorcism. The moon insists upon being unnatural, "a wild light . . . a gleam so unusual . . . the full, setting, and blood-red moon," which bursts upon his sight (98). Usher is dead and yet, in the narrator, Usher lives on. The universe is a coffin unnaturally lit from within.

The narrator's terror is multileveled. He has received a vision of the universe as a claustrophobic entrapment deliberately imposed by an alien sentience with the apparent goals of destroying the unity of the individual and of transforming the self into a part of the inimical universe. This universe is a devourer, and the human soul is its food. This vision has proven irresistible. It has become the narrator's vision. Turn where he might, he sees only Usher. In the effort to throw off this burden, he tells his story, asking his implied listener to confirm his fruitless assertions that his experience was illusory, but in the very act of telling, he is again caught up in the compelling vision of Madeline's return and the doubled collapse of the house. How is the implied reader to dissociate himself from this narrator? What sort of closure does this tale offer?

The implied reader, as the recipient of a failed act of persuasion, has been deeply implicated in the narrator's terror. Implicit in his attempts at persuasion has been the promise that the tale would come to an end, that his unaccountable experiences would be explained. The story ends in dreamlike visions, the full return in memory of what the narrator would gladly alter or forget. The final image of the tarn's waters closing over the fragments of the house violates probability, and the narrator offers no explanation for it. If the opposition between the narrator's rational explanations and his unaccountable experiences is to be resolved, the implied reader must do so without the help of the narrator, and the immediately available alternatives are not satisfactory. On the one hand, there are no unequivocally supernatural events in this story. On the other, much of what the narrator has experienced has been strange and has tended to confirm that the narrator has been convinced of Usher's world view against his will and despite his continuing resistance.

The evidence for Usher's interpretation of events is circumstantial. Atmospheres can appear naturally. Unconscious people can appear to be dead and then regain consciousness. To a panicked, fleeing observer, a house collapsing in a storm may appear to fall wholly into a nearby pool. These events are improbable rather than impossible. They affect the narrator so powerfully because they occur so close together in time and space, because Usher has a persuasive theory to account for the conjunction of such coincidences, and because the narrator has personally felt the apparently malignant force that Usher says is responsible for such events. As long as the implied reader accepts the role the narrator offers, that of sympathetic listener, there is no evading the narrator's quandary. Because puzzlement is permanent, closure is cut off in this direction: the implied reader must share the narrator's obsession.

One alternative for escaping this uncomfortable position is to turn against the narrator. Taking the hints of the dreamlike experience of the last night, the implied reader may enter into a judgmental role. Perhaps the narrator is mad. Indeed, he must be mad to believe that his world is an alien intelligence bent on his destruction. That is paranoia. If by rereading the reader can find a new set of instructions for constructing the implied reader and can rearrange the story in such a way as to explain the narrator's paranoia, then he may be able to explain away the world that the narrator fears. Here we run into a lack of information about the narrator. To confirm any hypothesis about what is wrong with him beyond his being a rather prosaic and thoughtful fellow who has had an extraordinary experience, the implied reader must treat his narration as a dream to analyze.

A significant portion of the criticism of the tale has considered the narrator as a mad dreamer and has attempted to work out the meaning of his dreams. Most such interpretations are, of course, psychological allegories, though some extend into Poe's metaphysics and aesthetics. We will look at these interpretations more carefully in the next part of the chapter. At this point, the significant fact is their variety. Several critics see the tale as a metaphysical dream-allegory in which the narrator is confronted by an opportunity to achieve transcendental union with the universe. In this case, the narrator fails to understand that what he is offered is visionary blessedness rather than terror. Prominent proponents of this view include E. W. Carlson in the introduction to his casebook on the tale and Richard Wilbur in "The House of Poe," which is reprinted in the same casebook (see bibliographic note at the end of chapter 7). Other critics see the tale more as a psychological dream-allegory in which various characters stand for different components of the personality. Such readings tend to agree that the tale shows the disintegration of a mind, either Usher's or the narrator's. That disintegration may result from the hypertrophy of one faculty at the expense of others as Edward H. Davidson argues (Woodson). Or one can go with the Jungians: Colin Martindale says that Usher is unable to achieve individuation by transforming the terrible mother into the anima, David R. Saliba that Roderick as a symbol of the narrator's conscious mind fails to dominate Madeline as a symbol of his unconscious. In addition to these readings are those that treat the tale as an allegory in which the narrator is comparatively unimportant. All of the psychological readings of this type can easily be translated into interpretations of the narrator as dreamer along the lines followed by William Bysshe Stein (Carlson 1971) and K. A. Spaulding (Carlson 1971). One result of such readings is the kind of disorientation we discovered when we considered the possibility that the narrator in "Ligeia" hallucinates. If we follow the strong critical precedent for considering the whole tale as a dream, we need not concern ourselves too seriously with sorting out internal and external events. But to assume that all the reported events are internal to the narrator is to have to face an account with so many gaps in it, with so much abstraction already present, as to invite allegorical readings that can multiply almost endlessly. The narrator's dream can mean many things; therefore, it cannot be shown to mean any one thing. Furthermore, the major division among these readings is between those who argue that the narrator has failed to achieve unity in this life and those who argue that he has failed to see Usher's true blessedness, the "psychal" vision of divine eternity which Usher supposedly offers. Should real readers who are not Poe scholars achieve the latter reading, they would encounter, again, a pull of contrary poles that makes this tale unreadable.

When one attempts to judge the narrator, he encounters a stubborn indeterminacy. This indeterminacy is just as strong if one does not assume the narrator to be a dreamer and still judges him as mistaken. Suppose he is an ordinary person come to help Usher. Does he fail because of his own rationalism as Bruce Olson argues (Carlson 1971: 97-99)? Because his own mind is diseased as Clark Griffith says (Veler 24)? Because, as Robert Crossley argues, he does not understand his role (226-27)? Because, as David Ketterer believes, the opposition is too strong (195-97)? Or because Usher is too weak, as the narrator might conclude? Behind the implied reader's attempts to judge the narrator is a desire to escape the terror of identification with the narrator. This desire is fruitless, for in the attempt to judge, the implied reader occupies the position the narrator attempts to occupy in relation to Usher. In his discovery of indeterminacy, the implied reader fails to master the narrator, mirroring the narrator's failure to master Usher.

"The Fall of the House of Usher" will not be mastered. Like "Ligeia," it leaves the reader suspended between two views of the narrator, neither of which is satisfactory. Ketterer calls this effect "the arabesque." The tale can be interpreted in a variety of ways, but there are not levels of meaning: "A complete intepretation involves the ability to maintain these varying approaches and possibilities in a state of omnidimensional fusion" (181). Ketterer believes that this is the effect Poe desired as a means of teaching readers to beware of "conventional reality," the illusions of closure that we impose upon the world: "Poe made it his life's work to destroy this fabric of deception . . . and if possible to see into that actuality beyond three-dimensional existence" (26). I believe Ketterer is correct about this tale, though the complexity of the means by which Poe accomplishes that end has yet to be revealed. Human beings are not generally made to be comfortable maintaining multiple viewpoints in omnidimensional fusion, nor, I suspect, are we capable of really seeing beyond this world. Nevertheless, we are capable of knowing the limitations of our intellectual instruments. This tale seems to force us to a state of perception in which we cannot, in good faith, *impose* a closure upon the tale. The role of implied reader is incomplete, yet the discomfort of that anticlosure makes the real reader desire to escape the role. What can real readers do to exorcise the ghost of an implied reader who will not go away? To begin to answer that question, I will examine some major features of the criticism that this tale has stimulated.

# II

There are many reasons why a work of art attracts to itself volumes of criticism many times its length. In the cases of Shakespeare and Faulkner, richness and complexity may be primarily responsible. In the more specific case of *Hamlet*, it may be that a deeply felt sense of mystery about the power of the work draws critics to it repeatedly. In the cases of "Ligeia" and "The Fall of the House of Usher" (and *The Turn of the Screw* as well), these factors are important, but the deliberate withholding of closure is a crucial cause of the extended debate over these stories. Some critics argue that the narrators are mad. Others vehemently respond that these are simply horror thrillers and the narrators merely vehicles for the tales. Others, like Ketterer and G. R. Thompson, search out a middle ground upon which the suspension between these two poles is consistent with Poe's metaphysics and literary theory. Helpful and suggestive as such middle positions are, they leave the stories unmastered, unread, and, therefore, haunting. I believe that these stories do produce closure, but of a kind radically different from that of most other fictions we encounter. In a step toward explaining how that closure comes about, I will examine the history of the *imposition* of closure upon "The Fall of the House of Usher."

The imposition of closure is mastery of terror in bad faith, the assertion of victory without the substance of victory. I use the language of war because, as Stephen Mooney has accurately observed, these stories make the reader feel as if he is involved in a war (Carlson 1966: 295). Reader and work become adversaries when the work makes the reader desire closure and then refuses to grant it. I do not mean to suggest that the critics I discuss have written in bad faith about the tale. They have done what all of us critics are trained to do: they have looked at the text, the author, and his culture and have attempted to make sense out of all three by balancing them against each other. In that process, they have *indirectly* provided models for escape from a terrifying work, but those models are ultimately unsatisfying, even when they succeed.

To be entrapped is intolerable. The reader and the text become adversaries, and there is no internal mechanism of release from the text. The "natural" closure of the last word is made to fail, and other forms that might provide a sense of an ending are absent, for example, the tying up of loose ends, projections of futures for the characters, a distribution of rewards and punishments, some sense that a significant event is more or less complete. The real reader cannot rest in this situation, but must find some way to end his experience, to disengage from a text that refuses to release him. The history of criticism of "The Fall of the House of Usher" is especially useful for examining the effects of placing readers in such an intolerable state, for much of that history records the efforts of readers to "fix" the tale, to relocate it outside of themselves and leave it behind. To be entrapped in a tale, to see oneself in the tale becoming the double of an afflicted narrator, to dissolve into multiple voices—these processes are to some degree terrifying, threatening to the real reader's integrity of self. One can deal with such threats through various forms of denial, such as repression, naturalizing the story, or trivializing it. One can deal with the story through what may be more sophisticated forms of denial, such as masking the terror by focusing on allegorical meanings. Or one can deal with the terror by accepting it, making it an acknowledged part of oneself.

The simplest form of denying the tale's terror is to actively forget the story, to push it away. Trivializing and naturalizing the terror are more sophisticated forms of denial. Todorov suggests that tales of the fantastic tend to resolve themselves when they end, either into the marvelous or into the uncanny. In the marvelous, the reader discovers the world of the tale not to be the real world of material causes that he occupies, but rather a world of pan-determinism and pan-signification where supernatural events are normal. In the uncanny, the reader learns the probable material causes of the apparently supernatural events. In the marvelous, supernatural events may be trivialized by being taken out of the "real" world; in the uncanny, they may be naturalized, shown to be natural events that only appeared supernatural. Poe's narrator is committed, even in the narrative present, to natural explanations of events, but his hesitation between natural and supernatural emerges in the urgency of his telling and of his attempts to naturalize the inexplicable. From Todorov's point of view, it would be natural for the reader to deal with a terrifying tale in the fantastic genre by completing the resolution that Poe does not provide. Such a solution amounts to fixing upon one of the first two of our three modes of response to anticlosure. J. O. Baily offers a typical example of trivialization toward the marvelous in his attempt to make the tale a literal vampire story, and John Hill offers a typical example of naturalization in his argument that Madeline's reappearance is an infectious hallucination resulting from Usher's insanity (Carlson 1971).

Interpretations that emphasize abstract patterns in the story can be used as more sophisticated forms of denial. While one cannot assert with confidence that any particular critic is attempting to escape the tale's terror by retreating into abstractions, such interpretations offer the reader avenues of escape. That there are several persuasive allegorical readings is less likely to cause discomfort to the reader than do other indeterminacies of the reading experience. Sophisticated readers can comfortably accommodate many allegorical readings, for competent allegorical readings are nearly always plausible. However, they tend to focus on abstract patterns at the expense of the concrete experience of the story; they offer the reader an escape analogous to that of the subjects in Stanley Milgram's famous obedience experiments, an opportunity to ignore the suffering of the victim by concentrating on the technical aspects of the task of torture. The purpose of the story becomes the communication of a pattern, and the terror at the center of the reader's experience is pushed into the background.

The most convincing of the allegorical interpretations draw their patterns directly from the careful study of Poe's thought and practice. For example, Maurice Beebe has offered a highly satisfying reading of the tale based on Poe's ideas of the structure and processes of the universe as expressed primarily in his cosmological meditation, "Eureka": "Roderick Usher is not depicted as a person in the universe; he is himself his universe. The power to create is the power to destroy, and his most triumphant creation is the obliteration of his suffering, diffusèd self in a return to the oneness which is nothingness" (Regan 133). This reading brings the tale into the pattern of creation in which the universe expands from its center to some limit of diffuseness only to collapse in upon itself again. Of course, this collapse may still be terrifying to the narrator and the reader. It may be argued that there is no guaranteed finality to Usher's dissolution, since the universe repeats its pattern of expansion and retraction; triumph is not certain. The main point here is that if the reader is not rigorous about dealing with his experience, he may accept this way out of the terror. Several of Poe's best-known critics have taken positions similar to this one. Carlson is perhaps the most insistent and, hence, the least convincing, in arguing that Poe wrote no tales of terror at all, but only pleasant allegories of vision; the end of this tale, according to Carlson, shows Usher and the narrator "undergoing a psychal vision," which hints "that the psychic and the transcendent are finally related" (Veler 18-19; see also Carlson 1973). While one must grant that there is a relationship, it seems difficult to characterize that relationship as positive or liberating. Wilbur, like Carlson, takes this sort of interpretation to the extreme point at which terror is no longer a noticeable element in the tale.

Wilbur argues in "The House of Poe" that the tale is an allegory of the narrator's journey into himself to recover the visionary soul symbolized by the ideal original state of the Haunted Palace, but which has now fallen into the ruin symbolized by Usher and his house: "When the House of Usher disintegrates or dematerializes at the close of the story, it does so because Roderick Usher has finally become all soul. *The Fall of the House of Usher*, then, is not really a horror story; it is a triumphant report by the narrator that it *is* possible for the poetic soul to shake off this temporal, rational, physical world and escape, if only for a moment, to a realm of unfettered vision" (Carlson 1971: 94). Such an interpretation is a wrenching denial of Usher's and of the narrator's characterizations of their own experiences. It is available to the real reader only if he insistently, indeed doggedly, reads the tale as a chapter in "Eureka" rather than as it is traditionally read by thousands of people. Perhaps one of the most troubling aspects of recent Poe criticism is the trend, exemplified by Wilbur but visible in many other critical pieces, of forcing every Poe text into too simple a conformity with "Eureka." I am not prepared to deny that there may be a consistency between "Eureka" and "The Fall of the House of Usher," but I am inclined to see that consistency as more subtle than it appears in Wilbur's argument. For Wilbur, the reality of the experience of Usher, the narrator, the implied reader, and the real reader is absorbed into an intellectual abstraction, an attempt to neutralize if not actually reverse the polarity of that experience. One of the paradoxes of Wilbur's reading is that in arguing that the narrator recovers an imagination that was oppressed by the intellect, Wilbur asserts the intellect's power of abstraction over the imaginative power of sympathy that binds the narrator and the implied reader together in terror. In Wilbur's reading, the reader divides himself and casts away concrete experience for the security of an intellectual sanctuary.

Though I think such readings wrong-headed, they remain highly effective escapes from the terror of entrapment in the tale. However, the especially sophisticated reader who moves to this level of reading continues to mirror the narrator. He continues to attempt to explain away the feelings the story has created, to talk himself out of this trap. Such an escape may work, just as repression, trivialization, and naturalization may work. The human mind is nothing if not versatile. But the critical intelligence cannot, in good faith, accept such escapes and continue to admire its own integrity. For this reason, if the real reader turns to criticism in search of help to bring an end to his reading, he is bound to be more attracted to readings such as those offered by Thompson, Ketterer, and Katrina Bachinger, readings that, in one way or another, affirm the ambiguity of the tale and acknowledge the hesitation/tension in which the implied reader is trapped. At least these critics do not drain the tale of the real terror that has reached out toward the real reader. Yet Ketterer and Thompson, as we have seen, leave the reader in the "limbo" of ambiguity. They assert, correctly, that Poe meant to put us there, and they imply that we can only stay put. If the real reader does not find a satisfactory exit from the tale, he will eventually take a "bad faith" exit, most likely some form of passive repression, such as allowing the story to fade from conscious memory. Among Poe's critics, one of the most interesting from this point of view is Joseph Garrison, Jr., who argues that the experience of terror in Poe's Gothic tales may be reconciled with Poe's desire to move his readers toward transcendence.

Because terror fantasy reaches out toward the reader with a psychological threat, the normal human response is to use his own psychological powers against the terrors. Denial is one form of this exercise, but ultimately it is less satisfying than some form of facing the terror squarely, of holding it in the consciousness, recognizing it for what it is, and being able to say, "I have in myself the resources for contemplating this terror. Even if the universe I experience as I read this story is the real universe, I can live in it." Georges Poulet says of

Poe: "If for him, man is buried alive, then man's mission is to explore the interior surface of the dwelling" (Woodson 105). While D. H. Lawrence falls into the trap of Usher and never really escapes, his evaluation of Poe's tales of terror seems profound on this point: "Man must be stripped even of himself. And it is a painful, sometimes a ghastly process. . . . For the human soul must suffer its own disintegration, *consciously*, if ever it is to survive" (Carlson 1971: 35). But how is it possible to escape from the trap of the tale in a satisfactory way? Garrison argues:

> In Poe's writings, the protagonists who fail to discover Existence as a stairway to Essence document the tragedy of the human struggle, as Poe understands it; but they also affirm Truth, in an indirect way, in that they demonstrate the inadequacy of finitude and actuality as a foundation for total experience, and in so doing, suggest the possibility of another kind of resolution. (143)

> One cannot be horrified by Prospero's demise or the fall of the house of Usher, for example, without implicitly affirming principles which are antithetic to the world views to which these protagonist submit. (146)

> Horror and terror are legitimate effects when they are calculated to compel the reader to turn his attention and affections from a debilitating and terrifying analysis of the human condition to an alternative—an ideal—in Poe's case, "the sentiment of Intellectual Happiness here, and the Hope of a higher Intellectual Happiness hereafter." (148)

This argument seems precisely to describe one way of meeting the terror of the tale. One asks oneself how Poe accepted it and looks at Poe's other writings to find out. One does not deny the terror, but discovers instead one of several ways of coming to terms with it, by accepting Poe's entire vision. Garrison points out that in "The Premature Burial," one sees a protagonist whose terrifying dreams strengthen his soul. The narrator says:

> My soul acquired tone—acquired temper . . . I became a new man, and lived a man's life. . . .
> There are moments when, even to the sober eye of Reason, the world of our sad Humanity may assume the semblance of a Hell—but the imagination of man is no Carathis, to explore with impunity its every cavern. Alas! the grim legion of sepulchral terrors cannot be regarded as altogether fanciful—but, like the Demons in whose company Afrasiab made his voyage down the Oxus, they must sleep, or they will devour us—they must be suffered to slumber, or we perish. (316)

This narrator implies that by facing terror, one is strengthened to live with it, without necessarily falling into the obsessions of Usher or his friend. Garrison also points out that further reading of Poe leads to the resolution of terror in Poe's "religious" ideas, in the ideal of intellectual happiness, and in Poe's faith in the ultimate goodness of creation.

Garrison's solution seems particularly satisfying because it shows how the tale of terror itself may be a part of Poe's entire artistic program. He does not force a premature closing of the tale, which would amount to a discomforting denial of its central quality, the terror it arouses by entrapping the real reader. Still, Garrison's solution is problematic. Consistent as his idea may be with Poe's theory and practice, Garrison's solution is not an aesthetic, but a moral one: it conceives of the effect of the tale as a particularly convincing proposition about the world. One's terror amounts to an affirmation of principles, a rejection of finite actuality; this leads to a search in Poe for some articulation of these principles, an articulation to be found, perhaps, in "Eureka." One difficulty with this solution is that several principles might just as easily be invoked in opposition to the world view expressed in the stories, for example, any of several religious systems and even a nonreligious system such as that suggested by the "grace under pressure" of several Hemingway heroes. As a moral effect, the terror of this tale would seem to be rather "hit or miss." The reader's response to the terror here seems to be an intellectual response, a lining up of principles on each side to balance some form of faith or of value judgment against a view of the world that robs faith and value of external support. In other words, Garrison's solution, attractive as it is and true as it may be to what Poe thought he was doing, seems finally another highly sophisticated allegorizing of the tale. Although the narrator of "The Premature Burial" shows an improvement in his psychic health as a result of his terror, there is little in what he says to suggest that this improvement is the result of adopting or reaffirming his faith or his values. We shall have to look further if we are to understand the nature of an aesthetic response to this tale of terror.

All of the critical responses I have discussed share the feeling that the tale lacks an internal mechanism of closure. Most interpretations of "The Fall of the House of Usher" and of "Ligeia" are attempts to find closure. To borrow Frank Kermode's borrowed description of the simplest form of plot, these tales say "Tick," then leave the reader in the interval before "Tock." By refusing to say "Tock," they force the reader to find a way of saying it for himself. For most of the critics, even those as insightful as Garrison, the great temptation is to formulate "Tock" as an intellectual affirmation of a moral content against the perceived moral content of the terror of the tales. The variety of attempts to close these tales demonstrates the power they have to make the reader desire closure. "Ligeia" and "The Fall of the House of Usher" entrap the real reader in the role of implied reader by opening rather than closing at the ends of their texts. Each compels the real reader to seek revisions of the implied reader by rescanning the text in search of resolutions. By refusing to provide resolutions, by refusing to be read, the tale makes the role of implied reader obsessive and intolerable. The role has no end, no last word. It holds the reader within it, reading him. Just as the narrator compulsively repeats his tale to some listener to regain his previous comfortable state and to escape the nightmare in which he finds himself, so the implied reader and the real reader retell their experiences to each other in what threatens to be an eternal colloquy, mind-splitting and transforming. It is little wonder that critics reflect some desperation to assert closure and yet are unable to articulate a convincing version. Even Garrison leaves the terror untamed in itself. In chapter 10 I shall argue that the aesthetic response to these tales makes such relief virtually unnecessary, that it, in effect, blesses the monsters and makes them beautiful. The need for that blessing will be more acute after we have seen how the greatest masterpiece of terror fantasy turns the screw of the reader's desire for escape by implicating him in unspeakable crimes.

## CHAPTER NINE

# The Master's Trap: Henry James's *The Turn of the Screw*

Henry James's *The Turn of the Screw* has a deceptively simple plot. Douglas presents to the narrator a first-person account by a now dead governess of the strange events of her first job. The governess tells the story of how she took care of two young children, Miles and Flora, during one summer and autumn and discovered that they were haunted by vicious ghosts, Quint and Jessel, who were attempting to "get" the children. She tells of her efforts to combat the ghosts and of her "success" in separating the ghosts from the children, though this success consists of rather equivocal facts, the death of Miles and the illness of Flora. No one familiar with the critical history of this tale would argue that this plot is anything like simple, for it, too, has generated many times its length in passionate critical controversy. The center of the conflict has been between Freudians and anti-Freudians and mirrors the conflicts over the narrators of the Poe tales. Is the governess what she says she is, a good young woman doing her best in a battle against evil, later confessing that her best was not good enough? Or is she a sexually repressed neurotic, who hallucinates ghostly projections of her repressions and harms the children in working out her internal psychodrama? Around these poles of interpretation, many ingenious but secondary interpretations have gathered, prompting minds of the caliber of Wayne Booth to throw up their ghostly hands in despair (284-301). Brenda Murphy has argued that interpretations of this tale provide a model of the inescapableness of the hermeneutical circle, and Booth has attempted to reduce the number of necessary stopping points on that circle, yet the ambiguity of the tale persists in obsessing its real readers.

Clearly, then, the effect of *The Turn of the Screw* on real readers is similar to the effects of "Ligeia" and "The Fall of the House of Usher." It leaves readers desiring closure, yet unable to find it within the tale. The refusal of closure arises from doubts about the governess.

Like "Ligeia" and "The Fall of the House of Usher," this tale offers three modes of response: acceptance of the narrator's account; doubt about that account accompanied by the construction of possible explanations of what she reports; and, finally, a suspension between these first two modes of response. The general intention of the text seems to be for the reader to move through these modes in this order, but it is perfectly possible for a reader to actualize on first reading the various signals of the narrator's uncertainty in the present of the telling, including the weaknesses she reports of herself. Should this implied reader develop on first reading, the order of development would be different from that which I shall present, but the final effect of suspension remains inevitable.

By means of the opening frame, which presents the origin of the governess's narrative, James establishes the governess as an admirable character. Douglas has known her and loved her. He affirms that she was agreeable, clever, and nice, worthy of any position of trust with children. She shared her narrative with him in part because she liked him. His sharing it with his friends may be because he likes them, but deeper reasons are hinted. He has held back, but apparently this particular holiday (perhaps the ghost story he had just heard) has "broken the ice," which seems connected with his sympathy for the governess. He acts as if he has loved her, as if he has felt deeply the "general uncanny ugliness and horror and pain" that *she* has suffered (2). The special understanding that appears between Douglas and the frame narrator makes it appear that the frame narrator is Douglas's specific intended audience for his repetition of the governess's tale. Indeed, the final passing of that narrative in its original handwritten form to the frame narrator at Douglas's death seems to define a role for the implied reader. The frame asks for a sympathetic and concerned auditor, who will listen for the throbs of love in the tale, not the delicious morsels of holiday horrors around a country house hearth. The governess's narrative offers considerable support for continuing the co-creation of this sympathetic implied reader, though before the tale can be read, this sympathy must rise to a higher level. The governess's text draws the implied reader close to her on first reading by emphasizing her admirable intellectual and emotional powers, by making the children special, and by stressing the degree and the effects of her isolation in her troubles.

The governess is unlike any narrator at whom we have looked so far in that her mental powers appear to be at least equal to the reader's. If we assume, as we must in this part of the argument, the accuracy of her perceptions, she makes extraordinarily complex inferences. She is not always correct, but she is rarely far off the mark. She believes after Quint's second appearance that she can protect the children, but after Miss Jessel's first appearance, she sees that she cannot protect, only try to defend. She believes that Flora, when confronted with evidence of her communication with Jessel, will confess and that Miles, if he confesses, will be saved. These are, perhaps, her most serious errors, and it is not perfectly clear that they are errors. Most of her mistakes are less serious, and she rather easily takes them in stride. She is also very perceptive. She successfully sees into Mrs. Grose, the housekeeper, feeling with accuracy how much relevant information she can provide. She usually reads the children's behavior well enough to predict their reactions. Given what she believes she is doing, she is also extraordinarily courageous to face such terrors on behalf of a stranger's children. Of course, the stranger and the children are special, and she loves them on sight.

The children are gifted orphans who charm the sensitive and intelligent governess with their goodness, beauty, intelligence, and manners. They are the sources of the richest experience of her young life. The emergence of a suspected dark underside to their Edenic life is horrifying, for it appears to the implied reader, who is closely identified with the troubled narrator, that something is eating away at their bliss. Holes appear in it, first, in the form of a letter announcing Miles's explusion from school, hinting at an unknown and unnamed dimension of Miles. Then, figures appear who have no place in the home. These apparitions are associated with the unknown and unnamed sides of the children's lives and with an unspecified and illicit sexual relationship between a "lady" and a "servant." These manifestations of a world beyond or outside of Victorian reality seem to the governess—and to the implied reader—to center on the children. The implied reader is expected to move with the governess in sympathetic horror through this thriller plot. Each manifestation leads to a discovery; each discovery escalates the danger to the children and the urgency that the governess act in an effective way.

The extraordinary limits imposed by the governess's isolation further enhance the implied reader's closeness to her. Not only is she forbidden to "bother" the master by his own command, but also she is forbidden to appeal to authority higher than her own by the peculiar circumstances of her situation. Any major action to bring in experts must pass the guardian who wants to hear nothing. She is distinguished from most Gothic heroines by Providence's lack of interest in her as well; no God or thought of God comes to her aid. Her social and intellectual milieu prevents her from communicating her concerns either to the children or to outsiders. She can confide only in Mrs. Grose. She cannot frankly ask the children about Quint and Jessel, and since, for whatever reason, the children avoid mention of the infamous pair, her hands are tied. No one, not even the local clergyman is going to believe that preadolescent children are haunted by ghosts. If no one in authority is disposed to believe such a tale, no one will forgive her if she herself exposes the children to these superstitions, to ideas of evil and, perhaps, of sex from which it is her duty to shield them. The governess believes that the forbidden is becoming manifest, but she is forbidden to speak of it. As the urgency for action increases, the demand that she violate the silence of taboo also increases. The implied reader's sympathy for the plight of the governess and the children demands that the governess act. When she does act, when she breaks her silence, the consequences are so terrible and equivocal that they send the reader back to the governess's perceptions and reasoning to discover what it means.

The two final confrontations, first with Flora and then with Miles, threaten to undermine the implied reader's confidence in the governess. It is a severe blow to read her account of the discovery of Flora by the lake. The governess sees Jessel's apparition across the water, big as a blazing fire. In her mistaken relief that she is finally less alone in her position and that now she may be able to settle part of what has haunted her, the governess assumes too much. Certain that Mrs. Grose will back her, she deepens her own defeat. Mrs. Grose cannot see, and Flora insists when she is confronted that she also does not see. As the governess recalls how she felt her position crumble in the past, the implied reader may feel the pressure of a split in which his position also crumbles or least vibrates ominously. Mrs. Grose images this split. She has stood "shoulder to shoulder" with the governess, but now the denying little girl suffers, and there is nothing visible. Mrs. Grose's loyalties are divided, and the implied reader is temporarily cut loose. The vertigo is temporary, for next morning she and Mrs. Grose are again shoulder to shoulder. Mrs. Grose has seen such a transformation in Flora as to be convinced that Flora has been influenced by an unseen force that she can only associate with Quint and Jessel. The implied reader may, but need not, abandon the governess at this point. The final scene of the story induces a more permanent disturbance in the relations between the governess and the implied reader.

In the final scene Miles confesses that he stole the governess's recent letter to his uncle and that he said "things" to those he liked at school, which were repeated from friend to friend until they came to the masters. And he seems to confess that he has seen the ghosts of Jessel and Quint. According to the governess, this confession frees him finally from the ghosts, blinding him to their presence. When he discovers that though Quint is present, he is invisible, Miles dies. This event is extraordinary, for it demands the turnabout in how this narrative is to be taken of which the confrontation with Flora gave warning.

How can Miles be saved if he is dead? How does the governess *know* if he is saved? These questions are hard to avoid. Once they are asked, the whole tale reopens, and just at the point where the reader expects closure. The readings to which this anticlosure points are *prodigious*. I use that word with care, for the discovery forced upon the reader by Miles's death is parallel to several discoveries made by characters in the tale. Quint's second appearance drops the governess beneath the surface of the quotidian at Bly, pointing at something hidden, perhaps the same thing at which the headmaster's mysterious letter expelling Miles points. Douglas's hearing of this narrative freezes him into a forty-year silence, and his release of the story points to depths in him. Each of these characters has passed on something heard from someone he or she liked to someone else he or she likes. From whom has this message originally come? For whom is it destined? The reader enters deeply into these questions when the governess again shows a hidden side of herself, becoming also the bearer of something hidden. What is perhaps most remarkable about the governess, of all the levels upon which this "message" is expressed, is her self-awareness. When one goes back over her narrative in search of that hidden side of her, one discovers that the governess has already been there.

Why does the governess write the narrative? This question is unlikely to insist upon itself on the first reading. The frame, of course, has implied as a motive that this was a terrible experience and that she recorded it because of its interest. This implication and the questions it might well raise are obscured in the frame, however, by the more explicit appeal to the reader's expectations for a horror thriller. The frame narrator and the eager ladies at the country house anticipate a thriller from Douglas; they are not inclined to look deeply at the governess. It is hard to avoid appreciating the tale, at first, as a sophisticated thriller. Being forced back over the tale by the revelation of an underside of the narrative brings to the fore the governess's personal motives for telling her story. The implied reader can no longer settle for the cozy pretense that the governess exists only to convey this chilling tale to a reader who seeks thrills. The governess is implicated. What she desires is suddenly crucial to understanding.

But what does the governess desire? In telling her tale to Douglas, she seems to want the confirmation that she has done the right thing. Upon rereading, the implied reader is likely to be struck by the degree to which her narration is a *re*telling, a search for the meaning of her experience. The cleverness and the niceness of the governess receive a new turn when they are shown to operate in her narration as well as in her handling of affairs at Bly. Her telling amounts to a "nice" moral review of her actions. A leading characteristic of her manner of telling is her maintenance of a certain objectivity toward her past experiences. She does not tell her story in the mode of a flashback in which the past is made present. The past does not overwhelm her as it does Poe's narrators in "Ligeia" and "The Fall of the House of Usher." Her procedure is more rational, more meditative. She repeatedly refers to her present obligations to remember precisely, to be clear, to use appropriate language, and to judge herself. From her first sentence, she promises to try to give a complete account starting with the whole beginning. She meticulously recounts her past judgments and past errors, judging them again in the present of her telling. When the reader moves back to judge the governess, he finds his role again defined by her actions, for the tale has been, in part, her attempt to reach a judgment of her acts and perceptions.

The final pair of confrontations—with Flora at the pond and with Miles in the house—emphasizes the duality of the implied reader's role. On the one hand, these two manifestations are nearly overwhelming. The governess tells them more in the mode of flashback with relatively little commentary, but when she thinks about them, her judgments are nice. She thinks it strange that her first feeling upon seeing Miss Jessel in the company of Flora and Mrs. Grose was the joy that she was no longer to be thought cruel or mad now that others see (71). In the final confrontation with Miles, she judges her actions more harshly: "I ought to have left it there. But I was infatuated—I was blind with victory" (87). The governess, though she believes she has acted in the best way she could conceive, nevertheless remains concerned about her own motives, just as she is not perfectly sure what she has done. This uncertainty is reflected throughout her narrative. She comments on the oddness that her fear began with "an instinct of sparing" Mrs. Grose (18). She is acutely and continuously aware of the "queerness" of her position as the only one who admits seeing the ghosts (e.g., 25, 52). She is aware that, unawares, she came close to madness and was "saved" by the second appearance of Jessel (28). She knows that all her perceptions of hidden depths in the children can be questioned

(50). She emphasizes often how trapped she was by social injunctions against speaking of the return of the dead with the children and against speaking about the children's predicament with any authority. To do either is to lose her chance to save them. She is aware that her moral position is extremely vulnerable. For example, to allow Flora to convince the master that the governess is depraved will not only ruin the governess professionally, but it will result in the moral ruin of the children. Flora makes this clear to the governess in her choice of Miss Jessel over the governess at the pond. We can see how this uncertainty comes to tell on the governess in the way she addresses Douglas.

The governess implicitly promises to tell Douglas the whole story as accurately as she can remember it. In the present, she judges her past predicament. This promise and this judgment are part of her request for Douglas's sympathetic understanding of the importance of this telling to her. Her request is not an easy one; her telling comes at a cost: "I find that I really hang back; but I must take my horrid plunge. In going on with the record of what was hideous at Bly I not only challenge the most liberal faith—for which I little care; but (and this is another matter) I renew what I myself suffered, I again push my dreadful way through it to the end" (40). And as she enters into the heart of the matter, Flora's predawn watching from her window while Quint walks the stairs, she turns directly to Douglas with an appeal. At that manifestation the governess first felt the longing to "break out at" Flora, to speak frankly: "This solicitation dropped, alas, as it came: if I could immediately have succumbed to it, I might have spared myself—well, you'll see what" (42-43). A few sentences later, she again asks directly for Douglas's sympathy: "You may imagine the general complexion, from that moment, of my nights" (43). The governess seems to be unsure of her actions, and she seems to want Douglas to evaluate them sympathetically.

This desire is not surprising in the context of her character, but it is easily ignored. This desire repeats a pattern that is crucial to the governess's original acts. She wishes to speak to the master. As Christine Brooke-Rose points out, one simple way of understanding the structure of the tale is as a violation of an injunction (175-87). In the frame is revealed the master's injunction never to contact him about the children. Within her narrative is a specific instance of this injunction, the letter from the master that contains the unread letter from the headmaster. This instance is double and contradictory. The two messages, in effect, cancel each other, for while the master commands her to deal with the headmaster's letter, the governess cannot deal with Miles's dismissal from school without calling upon the master to find a new school. Since she cannot deal with the headmaster without bothering the master, she decides to do neither, to obey by disobeying. She obeys the command not to bother the master, but she "represses" the headmaster to do so: she ignores his message. As Brooke-Rose notes the governess is gradually forced to attend to the headmaster's message and to break the original injunction by sending Flora to town to her uncle and by presiding over the death of Miles. The text ends with this violation, but information in the frame indicates that there are two main consequences of her transgression. First, she goes on working as a governess, which seems to mean that she is not held responsible for events at Bly. Second, she tells her story to Douglas, reliving her pain, which suggests that she continues to *feel* responsible.

The governess's desire to speak to a master appears on two levels in the tale. As soon as she receives the letter from the headmaster, she needs to speak to the uncle. In her narration she seeks a substitute for the master, someone to confirm the view of herself that she wishes to establish. This desire to speak to a master does not belong only to her. The "things" that Miles said at school seem designed to attract the masters'—the teachers'—interest. At any rate, they do attract such interest and eventuate in a letter to *the* master, his uncle. At Bly, both children, along with the governess, dream of the return of their uncle and pretend to write him letters, that is, they write letters to him that they never send. Douglas provides another example of the desire to communicate across some barrier that must be broken, the ice of his years of silence, with some authority, the frame narrator whom he believes will bring to the story special understanding. It is significant that nearly every attempt to communicate with authority in this tale is blocked and that intermediaries are nearly always necessary. Even Mrs. Grose must have someone else write for her.

Noticing this pattern supports the idea that what the governess wished for in the first place was to be loved. She says as much in her account of the moments preceding Quint's first appearance. She was proud of her work and wanted the master's approval. Instead, as it turns out, she must submit to the gaze of the master's dark double, which judges her without apparent sympathy, which challenges with increasing insistence her confidence that she has managed well. The final elaboration of this challenge in Miles's death leads to a second wish, the desire for *a* master who will remove her doubts and, she hopes, restore to her that image of herself she treasured before Quint appeared. Quint's appearance takes her back to the letter from the headmaster, that assertion of something hidden which she has ignored, but which indicates that her mastery of the situation has been, from the beginning, illusory.

The governess desires mastery so that she may be loved. When the ghosts remind her that her mastery is incomplete and when they threaten to master her by winning the children, she struggles against the ghosts to "regain" control. In this situation, she longs to have the assistance of the master, but she more than once refuses to call him down. Indeed, she refuses to involve him until the crisis of Flora's illness. She states fairly clearly her reasons for these refusals. First, there is the injunction. Though she wishes his assistance, he has forbidden her to ask for it. To love the master and to be loved by him, she must obey. Second, she is not in control. To love and be loved, she must obey the command to be master in place of the master, to deal with the situation without disturbing him. Third, she loves the children. She thinks that to go to the master when the situation is out of hand will destroy the children. Because she is the only one who sees into the situation, she is vulnerable. The uncle will not believe the chilren are haunted. Instead, he will believe the governess is mad and that she has concocted all this fantasy to attract his attention. The ghosts will be left to their own devices with the children.

The governess longs to speak at Bly, but is hedged about by prohibitions. She cannot speak frankly with anyone except Mrs. Grose, and, as Brooke-Rose points out, Mrs. Grose is usually a mirror, reflecting the governess rather than advising her with authority (176-79). Later Douglas appears, a reflection of both Miles and the master in his position and disposition. From him she may receive what she has never received before, confirmation of her final mastery of Bly. If she conscientiously gives him her whole story, he may act as her master mirror, telling her at last whether she has seen it all, or if her "blindness" of victory has, as she fears, obscured her vision, covering up her failure. Her doubt centers in Miles's death. She turns to Douglas, who loves her and who will judge her out of his love. She asks him whether she mastered her situation and, by doing so, freezes him into decades of silence. He cannot say. After those decades, he passes her story on, with the injunction to his listeners that the governess is unquestionably worthy of his love, but also with his doubt, his sense of "general uncanny ugliness and horror and pain," still intact (2). Judging from Douglas's reaction, there would seem to be no master of this situation and, therefore, no mastery.

In her narrative, then, the governess asks for Douglas's judgment. She needs someone to tell her unequivocally that she has done well or badly. There is a strong temptation to reconstruct the implied reader, after seeing Miles's death, in such a way as to deny this request. At least, many readers have done so. As Brooke-Rose shows, the more closely one examines the governess's language, the more one sees subtle but telling weaknesses in her character: "Thus the first chapter gives us, over and above what the narrator consciously tells us, information about her: she is impressionable, highly strung, dualistic, has a tendency to dramatise and to exteriorize, has a narrator's talent, hidden desire for love, power, and possession, she is imaginative or at least fanciful" (193). The most attentive reader will most fully incorporate such indications into a new view of the governess after seeing Miles's death and may utterly abandon her. To see that the governess may have completely misread the ghosts in some way and, therefore, that she may be an unconscious murderess can lead to a strong revulsion against her. The real reader may reverse the identification between implied reader and narrator by constructing a new implied reader who rejects the narrator. James has attempted to head off such a reaction in several ways.

We have seen two of his ways. When one attends to the governess's indirectly expressed motives for her confession, one discovers her self-doubt and her request for loving judgment. That she has seen most of her own weaknesses makes it difficult to judge her as more blind than the implied reader. That she, too, sees into the moral enormity of the possibility that she has misread her situation makes it difficult to accuse her either of simplicity or negligence. That she has tried to act out of her love for the children and their uncle makes it difficult to wholly reject her good intentions. Furthermore, that she asks for loving judgment reveals her need, which must be acknowledged if one is to be fair. When the governess longed for the master to see her and love her during the idyll before the ghosts appeared, she wanted him to see an illusion, to ignore her failure to deal with the headmaster's letter. When she writes her narrative to Douglas, she wants to be loved as a whole person, as one who has a secret, unseen side. This desire, of course, is unspoken. She seems unconscious of asking for loving judgment, but behind her entire performance is the implied message to Douglas: "To love me, you must also love my secret." Were there really a master who could explain fully whether she succeeded at Bly, then, of course, she would have no secret. Perhaps that would be better. Perhaps it would not. In any case, there is no one living who can know that secret.

James gives plenty of latitude for doubting the governess. There is almost no end to her human weaknesses and flaws. Yet James exerts inexorable pressure on the implied reader to identify with her and to love her even though a major gap in her interpretation of events at Bly opens with Miles's death. On the one hand, that gap pushes into the foreground other gaps of which Brooke-Rose provides rather a full catalog (chapters 7 and 8). On the other hand, are the governess's love, her need, her moral concern, and her awareness of personal weakness. The governess's self-doubt encourages the construction of alternate readings of Bly. If she is mistaken, then what else *might* have happened? Before turning to the possible answers to this question, it will be useful to make explicit a pattern that has implicitly informed much of our discussion up to this point, that of the secret message.

From one point of view, *The Turn of the Screw* is about a secret message. We have seen that there is a secret message implicit in the governess's narration—that to love her, we must love her secret. In her overt text, there is a covert message, just as in the letter from the master is an unopened letter from the headmaster, which fails to specify why Miles is being expelled. This pattern pervades the tale. We can trace the secret message back from the reader, the last to receive it, toward its origin: reader to frame narrator to Douglas to governess. From whom does the governess have it? She has her letters with their suggestion of an infinite regression of secret content. The letter from the headmaster withholds some presumably wicked secret about Miles. If it is reasonable to see this letter as the message that is elaborated in events at Bly, events that the governess then claims to read, what is its source? It comes from the headmaster who had it from the masters who had it from their friends who had it from Miles. He said "things" to those he liked. What things? Where did Miles hear them? Where did Flora learn the words that shock Mrs. Grose? The governess and Mrs. Grose believe that these things came from the dead, from Quint and Jessel.

What would the dead have to say to these children? What might they not say? This Jamesian question gains force when one considers how the pattern of messages from the dead pervades *The Turn of the Screw*. The tale opens with the summary of a story of visitation, a message so vivid that the child passes it to the parent, and both see. Miles and Flora are more acquainted with the dead than with the living. In their short lives, they have lost parents and grandparents. Though their substitute father has let them love him, he is conspicuous by his absence. In his place he has left his substitute, Quint, and Jessel. They, too, die. Finally, the children are left with their absent guardian and the new governess, their latest parent figures. More than any other characters, the children have the dead from whom to receive messages. This pattern is repeated for the implied reader, whose message also comes from the dead. Only the frame narrator remains in life, so far as can be known. The chain of communication from Quint through Douglas is made up only of the dead. This progression suggests that the message's destination as well as its origin is outside the human world, for it never comes to rest. The message is never finally read. The governess is a great reader, and she senses that she has failed. Douglas remains at a loss to explain it; he only passes it on. As Shoshana Felman and Brooke-Rose argue, critics also repeat the story, showing in their contentions our inability to *read* the story, not because we lack reading ability, but because the message refuses to be read. The letter from the headmaster is addressed to the master, but he declines to read it. As a substitute for the master, Douglas cannot say what he has read. He can only repeat the message. What Miles said comes around to the masters and finally to the headmaster, but it is not (cannot be?) specified. The message seems to be *for* the master *from* the dead.

But there is no real master; no one can successfully read the covert meaning of the message. The governess is told to be the master, and she tries with equivocal results. Her problem elaborates the problems of all who would be master. What, precisely, is the message? What do the dead want to say to the master? This second question offers one way of generating the kinds of answers that criticism, in its attempts to master this secret, has given to fill the gap on which the story insists. As Felman argues, the defining characteristic of the message is its silence. It appears in indicating figures that reveal its presence—ghosts, play, letters, pranks, and confessions—but in itself, it remains unspoken (161-77). One of the main labors of the criticism of this tale has been the effort to speak *for* that silence, to speak with the voice of the dead.

What are the consequences if the implied reader attempts to discover alternative readings of events at Bly? This reader is not so anxious to escape identification with the governess that he will ignore her depth of self-knowledge as it is revealed to Douglas. Rather, the implied reader is trying to *be* her Douglas, to look where she has not seen, to see what she cannot see. The reader strives to grant the governess her request. He gives her her goodness and asks what other meanings there might have been in what she saw at Bly.

The governess may have been right: the ghosts could be spirits of evil persons, now deceased, who desire, for their own perverse reasons, to have more company in their torment. On the other hand, she may be entirely wrong. According to Mrs. Grose, Quint and Jessel were in love. They separated and they died. At Bly they had been together, and so they return. Perhaps their spirits haunt Bly as ghosts traditionally haunt the places where the crucial events—usually the sins, but sometimes the injustices—of their lives took place. Perhaps, therefore, the children are never really in danger. This possibility is not very strong because there are so many circumstances to suggest that the ghosts are somehow connected to the children, but it is quite possible that they communicate with the children without intending harm.

It is also possible that the children use the ghosts. When Miles dies in the presence of the governess, apparently as the direct result of learning that he has lost contact with Quint and Jessel, how are we to understand this event? Perhaps it is not the case that the ghosts try to get the children, but that the children try to get, or keep, the ghosts. Thrice orphaned, the children cling to their most recent pair of parents. Quint and Jessel may haunt the house because the children will not let them be dead. Why might the children doom Quint and Jessel to haunt Bly? There are several possible, related reasons. Quint is a double of the master. Jessel is a lady. Quint and Jessel are lovers, and the children are, to some degree, aware of that. These dead are manipulable. The children can see them when they will. But it must be a secret, for when parents are living in the world, they are out of control. They disappear. This hypothesis is not the only one of this kind available, but all those I can think of work in about the same way, for example, the ghosts are the children's parents but appear to the governess as Quint and Jessel. In any case, such an hypothesis accounts fairly completely for the strange behavior of the children. They are so good for at least two reasons. First, their goodness is a strategy for insulating them from the living world; it reduces interference with their fantasy. Second, their goodness to the governess makes her love them, binds her to them, for it seems fairly clear that they prefer living parents, though they fear they cannot depend upon them. When the subject of the return of the dead hangs in the air, they dream of the return of the master. If they can pair the governess and the master into living parents, the reversed doubles of Quint and Jessel, perhaps they can give up the dead parents who, after all, are not particularly comforting. It may even be that the disturbances they create are *their* "fine machinery" for bringing down the master. Finally, then, Flora, forced to choose between the dead and the living mother, chooses the dead. To her the living mother appears cruel in her attempt to displace Miss Jessel. Miles, when he is forced to choose, is so divided that he cannot live. His love for his dead parents and for the governess kills him.

That the children construct the ghosts or call them forth for their own use is at least as strong an interpretation as the one the governess constructs. This interpretation may also be wrong, for the ghosts may be working out their own unconnected problems or there may be no ghosts at all. That the ghosts' actions are unrelated to the children is suggested in the first paragraph of the frame. Why does the governess not consider any other possibilities mentioned so far? Why is she so certain that the ghosts rather than the children are the agents at Bly? First, she shares her culture's assumption of the innocence of children, and second, to her the ghosts appear evil. Considering these alternative readings pushes us back to the governess's reading, making it look more like an invention, to which she and her culture may contribute. The governess, of course, has feared from the beginning of her supernatural experiences that she was inventing, though she has never been able to see what she might have invented. That is why she needs Douglas: to look at her and tell what he sees.

To read the governess's interpretation of the ghosts as her invention, we must return to her love for the master. She loves him, but is forbidden to speak to him. She longs for him to see her devotion to him, but can only show it by her silence and her care for the children. The children easily replace him as the substitute objects of her devotion. Miles, especially, fits into the mold. He is called the young master. He is connected via his "pretty waistcoats" (54) with Quint and the master. The metaphor of the honeymoon turns up on his final evening with the governess. Critics have pointed out many other elements suggesting that the governess unconsciously looks upon Miles as a lover. This love for the children undergoes a split because she cannot possess them as she wishes to possess the master. She cannot tell them of her adult love. I am not being prudish by avoiding the word *sex* in this description, for as Felman says, love here includes more than mere coitus (99-113). The governess's desire to possess the master has more content than the mere desire to have sexual intercourse with him. Her desire for him is connected with her desire for mastery and her repression of the ghosts, but may not be the reduced meaning of those manifestations. None of this desire to possess may be spoken of to the children, for they too, by means of social convention, command silence. To speak of her desire to them would be to corrupt them. The ghosts, then, are inventions of her repressed desire to speak the unspeakable. They are evil because they do, whenever she is absent, what she longs to do but cannot. To her consciousness, this longing takes the form of wishing to speak to the children about the dead. From her unconscious, this longing appears as the dead returned, the ghosts themselves, who speak to the children. The message these ghosts carry from her unconscious is *for* the master, but, diabolically, they speak it to the master's substitute, the children.

Whatever the status of the ghosts in reality, the governess may have unconsciously appropriated them for her own use. She seizes upon these dead as just the ghosts she needs: illicit lovers, violators of boundaries such as class, and corrupters of children. She makes the ghosts into externalizations of her secret desire to possess the master. She then struggles with them for the children. This struggle for the children figures forth an internal struggle over who will possess the governess, over who is to be her master. She eventually tells her story to Douglas because he is the next master she encounters and loves. Even more important, he loves her, so to him she can pass the whole message with its holes, with its underside exposed, as it were. Her secret is that she may have cruelly hurt Flora, and she may somehow have caused Miles's death. That he has died challenges her overt interpretation. He ought to have been saved, but dead, he keeps his secret.

In her experience of the ghosts and in her telling of that experience, her unconscious seems to present itself as "the discourse of the Other," as coming from the outside, as the uncanny. She comes to her listener as to an analyst because she remains unable as yet to see that what the Other says belongs to her. From this point of view, the governess may look quite evil in herself. This appearance would put the implied reader in the awkward position of having to condemn the character in whom he has invested so much. If Douglas felt this tension, his forty years of silence becomes explicable, but his conclusion that she was worthy of any position would remain mysterious. Working through the implications of the governess's reading leads to an understanding of Douglas's final praise.

Felman provides a way into the implications of the possibility that the governess invented her reading of the ghosts. Her invention would arise from her need for mastery, the need to regain the illusory sense of control she had before the ghosts appeared. The governess is insistent about her reading because she needs urgently to master the crumbling situation. Therefore, to the governess, Flora's manipulation of two pieces of wood in the presence of Miss Jessel *must* mean something. If it seems to mean that the children and the ghosts communicate, possibly about sex, then the governess insists on that meaning—in self-defense. The urgency of regaining control, for all the good reasons she can give, pushes her toward investing the situation with the unknown content of her unconscious, whether or not that situation springs from her unconscious in the first place. The governess's insistence on this meaning is a form of self-defense in two senses. First, it externalizes her own desires, keeping them repressed. Second, it asserts that it is not the governess, seeing ghosts, who is mad, but the children, talking with ghosts, who are mad. Her struggle to be pure and sane condemns the children to corruption and madness. In her effort to close an open structure, she excludes the children's point of view. To get hold of this situation is to lose it. As she imposes her will on Miles, he grows more distant until, finally, she grasps him, and he is gone (Felman 161–77).

Such an act would be depraved were it consciously done. Those critics who are hardest on the governess tend to forget that what is unconscious is truly unknown. We cannot condemn the governess for a death that was not consciously intended. But perhaps she should have known better. Surely someone should have known better. The mad ought not to be hired to care for small children. They certainly ought not to continue in the profession. If the governess is mad, what is the cause of her madness?

Brooke-Rose argues that the governess has not moved through the three phases of Lacan's mirror stage and so has not arrived at an identity. Specifically, she has not moved from the recognition of the other to the recognition of the other as self. Therefore, she cannot move through the third phase of recognizing the other as self but other (161ff.). In more common terminology, the governess's restricted life before this first job has kept her unaware of her own conscious/unconscious split. Therefore, she is not prepared to deal with the experience of the unconscious as her own experience. She is unable to integrate her experiences. When the repressed appears under the pressure of the sudden expansion of her life at Bly, with its promises and limits of pleasure and power, she can only externalize the repressed desire, seeing it as belonging to the other, *her* ghosts. In this view, the need for mastery is generated entirely from within the governess. In her correction of the standard hallucination reading, Brooke-Rose unsurprisingly concludes that from this point of view, the governess eventually abandons the children in order to save herself (178). However, even in this hallucination interpretation, this is not necessarily the case, for the governess always connects the children's salvation to her own. If they are saved, then she is. While putting it this way, as the governess does, may seem to imply that her own salvation is more important, it also says directly that the governess must concentrate her efforts on saving the children. They come first in time, and there is plenty of evidence to suggest that they come first in her heart, even if only as substitutes for the master. Brooke-Rose also hints at the explanation of self-defense, which I want to develop further here, when she points out that "hysteria is both a personal and a socially produced illness" (158).

While the need for mastery arises from within the governess, that need itself is produced by her society. Why does the governess come to Bly without her identity intact, if that is her problem? How is it that a person of her intelligence, sensitivity, and education needs to use the dead? Clearly, it is because, in her society, the dead are not taken seriously enough, at least openly. Her culture insists that the dead do not exist and ridicules the dead in its Christmas tales by the fireside. But this insistence masks doubt; it is a prohibition rather than a scientific statement. Secretly this society fears the dead. It absolutely forbids that one talk seriously of the supernatural with innocent and impressionable children. The governess's society mirrors her split, revealing itself to be the source of her split. To see ghosts is to be mad; to pretend to see them is great fun. To believe in ghosts is childish, but no child should be allowed to believe. To talk seriously of the supernatural is forbidden. Indeed, the "deliciousness" of Douglas's tale may spring directly from his implied intention to violate this prohibition. The governess's society refuses even to recognize the Other (the dead) much less to see it as a reflection of itself. This refusal in real Victorian society can be seen in contemporary reviews of the tale, just as the protest against this refusal can be seen in that same society's literary and scientific preoccupation with the paranormal. This preoccupation is reflected not only in the quantity of fantasy written in the late nineteenth century, but also in James's other stories of the supernatural. Within the text, this refusal to give the dead their due is reflected in all of the responses to the message from the dead, except for those of the children and the governess. The master will not read it. Only those who truly love each other will try to read it or at least to communicate it faithfully. In their spiritual isolation, hedged about by commands of silence from all sides, these three seem at least to look upon and commune with what appears to be outside normality. It is very difficult to determine whether any of them move beyond recognition of the Other to identification with it as self *and* other.

Bly offers the governess a chance to grow, to move beyond the childishness imposed upon her by her society. She does remarkably well, from *any* point of view, for a twenty-year-old woman in a society that commands her both to remain a child and to preserve the childhood of others. Her attempts to save the children amount to attempts to exchange places with them, to see for herself, and so to learn to be an adult, while preserving for the children the childhood that belongs to them as literal children. The reversal she sees has been imposed upon them by the structure of society (the definition of the forbidden) and by the structure of the empire (the deaths of parents in India). This reversal—in which the children are old and she is young—is evil, she thinks. Both she and the children have been treated badly. As she sees into this situation, she becomes determined to correct it, but in doing so, she is hampered by the structures that have so far held her back. Her freedom is largely illusory as long as she is forbidden to speak either to the master or to the children. She must maneuver in an extremely narrow space. There is much more arrayed against her than even she is likely to be able to discover. In her attempt, however, the governess rises above her narrow society, achieving a stronger identity than it would allow her. If she is clumsy, even wrong, in her reading of the ghosts, even if she misappropriates them for her own uses, she at least looks upon them and struggles with them courageously. For this reason, Douglas can love and admire her despite her secret, despite her inability to know (an ignorance he shares) what she

really has done. Though he cannot resolve the question of her responsibility, he cannot fail to see her as heroic.

This tragic dimension of the governess's predicament makes it difficult to condemn her. The more deeply one looks into the possibility
that she has radically misread the events at Bly, the more she appears
to be a comparatively innocent victim of power beyond her control.
In this view she becomes a violated child. As her society totalizes its
world view and excludes the dead, so she totalizes her view of the
ghosts and excludes the children—or so it would appear. Their exclu-
sion mirrors her own. If the implied reader's identification with the
governess is shaken by the death of Miles, it is eventually steadied
upon reconstructing the tale as the governess's confession of doubts
and as a secret confession of failure. The implied reader can be realized
as identifying with the governess who saved Miles by bringing about
his death, or he can be realized as identifying with the governess who,
as an instrument of powers beyond her control, murdered Miles. The
governess hopes she was the former, which is bad enough, and unconsciously fears she was the latter, which is terrifying. Felman says,
"The reader of *The Turn of the Screw* can either choose to *believe* the
governess, and thus to behave like Mrs. Grose, or *not to believe the
governess*, and thus to behave precisely *like the governess*" (190). I would
argue that whether we believe or disbelieve, we act like the governess
and like Douglas. In short, the implied reader is entrapped within a
dilemma that mirrors the entrapment of the governess and of Douglas.
Of course, Felman means something different; she means that the governess's action in the past was to close her situation by insisting upon
her reading, whether right or wrong, of the ghosts: not to believe the
governess is to perform the same operation upon her. If the real reader
insists upon a single reading of the governess, if he denies the ambiguity of her situation, he duplicates her equivocal act. Furthermore, he
duplicates that act without provocation equal to her own, for his situation is much less desperate than hers was. By accusing the governess,
one violates her. By exonerating her of all serious error, he also violates
her, ignoring her secret message, the very doubt and concern that led
her to tell her story.

The tale demands that the implied reader love the governess. It
challenges that love in its last events, but reconstructing the implied
reader as a doubter leads again to love. The attempt to fill in the
unspoken in the governess's narrative leads the implied reader back
to pity for her sufferings. To love the governess means accepting ambiguity and, therefore, accepting terror—the terror of not knowing what
she has done, the terror that apparently haunts her to her deathbed.
She passes this terror to Douglas, who is haunted in his turn. And

finally it comes to the reader. The governess cannot know whether she saved Miles or murdered him, whether his death was worthwhile. Neither can any implied reader. When the governess and the reader come again to the end of her narrative, it is love for the children and for the master that keeps her doubt alive, that tortures her with the possibility that she has failed, and that drives her to seek some master for her narrative. And it is the implied reader's love for the governess that preserves the ambiguity of the tale. The reader desires to know the truth *and* to love the governess. As long as one loves the governess, the truth cannot be known. The implied reader, therefore, must share the governess's obsession, and the tale must continue to seek its master.

Such a trap is trap enough, but James is more diabolical than Poe. Like Poe, he suspends the reader between two modes of response. Neither the natural nor the supernatural explanation of events is alone satisfactory. The implied reader is left in vibration between these two uncomfortable readings and is provided with no escape. The role of implied reader is without an ending, and the tale haunts its readers. James is more diabolical in the way he closes off conventional escapes.

It ought to strike any reader familiar with the criticism of *The Turn of the Screw* that I have been rather tender with the governess. I have emphasized the degree to which the tale requires the implied reader to love the governess, asserting that this love is a crucial element in James's trap. Felman and Brooke-Rose demonstrate persuasively that criticism of this tale has been much more aggressive, much more psychologically violent (Felman 94-102; Brooke-Rose ch. 6). I return to this point because it is proof of James's mastery of terror fantasy. By demanding love from the implied reader, James has attempted to close off the kind of escape we saw critics suggesting for "The Fall of the House of Usher." James has discouraged allegorical readings by tying the appearance of the fantastic to psychological realities, such as sexual desire and the loss of parents, as well as by giving a high degree of verisimilitude to character and event. He has discouraged naturalizing and trivializing the tale by increasing the discomfort of such attempts.

Attempts to escape finally center in the Freudian/anti-Freudian debate that Felman and Brooke-Rose examine so carefully. Generally, the Freudians have been naturalizers. In their insistence upon making the ghosts into hallucinations, they condemn the governess to madness. Felman explains how this comes to be the case in Edmund Wilson's reading:

> Thus, for the governess to be in *possession* of her *senses*, the *children* must be *possessed* and *mad*. The governess's very *sense*, in other words, is founded on the children's *madness*. Similarly, but conversely, the story's very *sense*, as outlined by Wilson, by the *logic* of his reading, is also, paradoxically,

> based on madness—but this time on the madness of the *governess*. Wilson,
> in other words, treats the governess in exactly the same manner as the
> governess treats the children. It is the governess's madness, that is, the
> exclusion of her point of view, which enables Wilson's reading to function
> as a *whole*, as a system at once *integral* and *coherent*—just as it is the
> *children's* madness, the exclusion of *their* point of view, which permits
> the governess's reading and its functioning as a totalitarian system. (195)

Such a position is not comfortable. Wilson's own discomfort with it is
suggested by his subsequent vacillation (see Willen 115-53). This vacillation, in turn, is uncomfortable because it violates not only the manifest ambiguity of the tale, which Wilson set out to affirm in his original
essay, but also because it violates the demand that the implied reader
love the governess. Poe's terror fantasies depend upon ambiguity to
restrain the reader from making bad-faith escapes. James depends upon
ambiguity and upon love.

Love also restrains attempts to trivialize the tale. As the existence of
the debate shows, one cannot easily deny that there *are* ambiguities.
Though it is perhaps illogical that the burden of proof should fall on
those who are willing to give the governess the justification she desires,
still these readers must struggle against the "naturalizers" to make
their arguments count (Felman 94-102). It is important to keep in mind
that neither the trivializers nor the naturalizers are necessarily acting
with bad intentions. For example, Robert Heilman in "A Note on the
Freudian Reading of *The Turn of the Screw*" certainly does not mean
to trivialize the tale when he eloquently defends the governess. Still,
the point of view he argues tends to eliminate the most disturbing
ambiguity from the tale by trivializing the fantastic. This point of view
also fails to love the governess by failing to listen to her *whole* message,
the secret, hidden side as well as the open, conscious side of it. To
affirm the governess's innocence is to deny her own consciousness that
she went too far, used too much psychological violence. It is to be less
true to her than she is to herself. As a friendly betrayal, it parallels the
acts of Miles's friends, who passed his remarks toward the masters
who read them as evil and had him expelled. Any form of mastering
another in this tale seems to be a failure of love.

It is a masterstroke, then, to make the governess worthy of the implied reader's love, for doing so cuts off conventional paths of escape
from the terror of entrapment in the role of the implied reader. In this
way James surpasses Poe in realizing the potentials of terror fantasy,
tightening the screw on his reader's already well-secured thumb. To
remain in the role of the implied reader is to identify ever more closely
with the haunted governess. This entrapment and the threat of transformation it entails may tempt the reader to escape by fixing the gov-

erness as either mad or innocent, but James has made traps of these escape routes as well. Each tends to make the reader conscious of acting in bad faith in his attempt to detach the implied reader from his identification with the governess. The ambiguity of *The Turn of the Screw* is not resolvable, the tale not readable in the way most fiction of "the great tradition" is readable. As Felman says: "James's trap is then the simplest and the most sophisticated in the world: the trap is but a text, that is, an invitation to the reader, a simple invitation to undertake its reading. But in the case of *The Turn of the Screw*, the invitation to undertake a reading of the text is perforce an invitation to *repeat* the text, to enter into its labyrinth of mirrors, from which it is henceforth impossible to escape" (190).

Felman's analysis raises in a radical fashion the difficulty of responding to this tale and, by implication, to all tales of terror fantasy. She seems sometimes to imply that all literature is terror fantasy, but I understand her to mean that all literary language, as Lacan argues, carries with it a fundamental split between conscious and unconscious. That this is so does not make *Anna Karenina* or *Pride and Prejudice* unreadable in the same way as is *The Turn of the Screw*. Those novels offer acceptable illusions of closure and do not call attention to the ways in which they are unclosed; terror fantasy refuses closure. The terror fantasies we have examined pretend at first to play the usual literary game with the reader, but when the moment of closure arrives, they pointedly refuse to play the usual game, leaving the reader in a limbo that requires a new reading strategy. James has, indeed, set a trap for the reader, and the reader's fundamental problem is to escape. The critical histories of all three of our terror fantasies testify not only, as Felman says, to the tales' power to make their readers repeat texts in several senses of *repeat*, but also to their power to make readers desire escape.

Felman argues that though there is no escape from the terror of the tale, still it is possible to read the unreadable (143, 200). She means that while the story encloses the implied reader in its "labyrinth of mirrors," there is still some perspective outside the labyrinth from which it may be viewed. To remain in the labyrinth is to be driven mad; outside the labyrinth is James, the master of his own tale. His mastery, she says, consists of escape: "It is because James's mastery consists in knowing that mastery as such is but a *fiction*, that James's law as master . . . is a law of flight and of escape" (206). There is no master. Mastery is a fiction. To fix a meaning upon the governess, to master her, is to lose her, just as her mastery of Miles may have lost him. What does it mean to say that mastery is a fiction, if not to affirm that the self that attempts mastery is a fiction? The attempt at mastery is, after all, the attempt to assert the self's dominance over the ghosts (if they are real) or over the Other (if the ghosts spring from the unconscious). The search for a master is a search for the gaze in which one is whole, the master of one's self; it is the search for the gaze of love. Such a gaze is imaginary; it is constructed by the desiring self. Likewise, the critical mastery of *The Turn of the Screw* is imaginary, a construction of an expert reader desiring closure. The name we have given to that construction is *the implied reader*. The implied reader refuses to give up its independent life; it will not be closed, will not be possessed. As a result, the real reader becomes possessed. The perspective of escape from this possession, in which mastery is seen to be a fiction, must be outside that constructed self, the implied reader. The elaboration of this idea generates an aesthetics of terror fantasy.

## CHAPTER TEN

# Escape: An Aesthetics of Terror Fantasy

## I

And philosophers agreed, like a kinetic gas, that the universe could be known only as motion of mind, and therefore as unity. One could only know it as oneself; it was psychology. . . . To his mind, the . . . [soul] took at once the form of a bicycle-rider, mechanically balancing himself by inhibiting all his inferior personalities, and sure to fall into the sub-conscious chaos below, if one of his inferior personalities got on top. The only absolute truth was the sub-conscious chaos below, which everyone could feel when he sought it. (Henry Adams 432-33)

How does terror fantasy work?

Why do we value it?

We have examined several tales of terror that realize the potentials of the pure fantastic as defined by Tzvetan Todorov. Each tale sustains the hesitation of the implied reader over how to interpret ambiguous events through the end of the story. Such events may be interpreted as supernatural or natural, as marvelous or uncanny. "Ligeia," "The Fall of the House of Usher," and *The Turn of the Screw* distinguish themselves in that they first create and then destroy aesthetic distance. They *violate* Edward Bullough's antinomy of aesthetic distance: "What is, therefore, both in appreciation and production most desirable is the *utmost decrease of distance without its disappearance*" (758). Those works that I call horror thrillers, such as *At the Mountains of Madness* and *Dracula*, are careful to *preserve* the antinomy, for their effects depend upon safe brushes with the forbidden that will generate the desired safe thrills. The simpler forms of the pure fantastic tales of terror are located between horror thrillers and terror fantasies. Tales such as "The Black Cat" and "The Horla" threaten to entrap the implied reader, but they stop short of the radical step of anticlosure. We have seen such a trap sprung three times in what I call terror fantasies.

Like all literary works, a terror fantasy invites the reader to use the signals of the text to construct an implied reader and to establish thereby an aesthetic relation to the text. Unlike most literary works, a terror fantasy offers at least two simultaneously valid but opposed readings, each of which illuminates the strengths of the other and betrays its own weaknesses. This splitting of the role of implied reader precludes the ending of that role. As a result, the terror fantasy produces anticlosure; it pointedly refuses to end.

Anticlosure is not merely a failure to resolve thematic complications, nor is it a thematic assertion of the openness of reality. It is not at all like the story with its last page removed nor the "slice of life" in which it is presumed that life goes on after the arbitrary ending of the history. Anticlosure results from the tale's turning back on itself to form a closed loop. It is not the text that fails to end, but the reading, the activity of concretizing the work. This activity cannot stop because each of its possible resting places is disturbed by the presence of another.

In these tales, then, the role of implied reader becomes a snare. And the trap by itself produces anxiety. In *Mystery and Its Fictions*, David Grossvogel demonstrates how unclosed, metaphysical mystery fictions, such as Kafka's *The Trial*, arouse anxiety. Terror fantasy exploits this same anxiety by means of the threat of transformation. When the role of implied reader splits, its doubleness becomes a third role, an entrapped, vibrating suspension between the alternative readers—and readings. This heightened hesitation mirrors the narrator's terrified hesitation. The more desperately the implied reader tries to complete the reading, the more he becomes like the narrator who attempts to complete the telling, which in each case is also a reading. As the narrator obsessively strives to complete the reading of the world, the implied reader obsessively strives to complete a reading of the tale. The catch is that so long as the implied reader is engaged in the reading, the real reader, who constructed this implied reader, cannot be free: the real reader is also ensnared.

Insofar as the real reader feels the anxiety of entrapment and the threat of transformation, the antinomy of aesthetic distance is violated. For as long as it takes to read the tale after completing the text, the real reader is haunted; he labors under the pressure of literary terror to complete a reading, and the tale resists him, pushing back with exactly the force that he exerts on it. As Henry James says, the texture of the work stiffens as one challenges the character's interpretation of his or her experience (*Theory of Fiction* 113). When the antinomy of aesthetic distance is violated, the real reader's relation to the work of art is transformed. The implied reader has been constructed as one (but not always the only) intermediary between the real reader and the work. That implied reader is one element of aesthetic or psychical distance. But when the implied reader's role becomes a trap, when by it the work reaches out a claw toward the real reader, then the relationship between real reader and work ceases to be disinterested. I mean *disinterested* in the special sense implied by Bullough's definition of psychical distance as the separation "of the object and its appeal from one's own self by putting it out of gear with practical ends and needs" (756). The real reader becomes personally interested in this work, which has taken hold of him in an unexpected way and from which he cannot disengage in the way he has learned from traditional fictions.

Included in this fall from the grace of an aesthetic attitude is a deep nostalgia for the lost state. The drive to complete the reading comes from several directions. First, the aesthetic relation to the work is much more comfortable than a personal relation. To complete the reading requires reentry into an aesthetic relation. Furthermore, for many if not most readers, a literary work is not supposed to behave this way; it offends their sense of propriety. This observation points toward deeper needs of humans to complete patterns and to experience wholeness. The strength of this drive is seen everywhere, but most notably for our purposes in the unprecedented conflicts of interpretation that surround these particular texts. It is little wonder that Wayne Booth should discuss criticism of *The Turn of the Screw* in *Critical Understanding*, a book centrally concerned with totalitarian conflict in literary criticism. The strength of this drive to closure has its foundation in the ego's inherent need for mastery, which these tales frustrate in a way perhaps calculated to teach the ego about the limits of mastery.

How, then, can this drive be dealt with in this situation that stimulates and frustrates simultaneously? How do we read the unreadable? Shoshana Felman suggests that the unreadability of *The Turn of the Screw* can end in madness or escape (206). For her madness is a continuing, obsessive relation to the work, either by continued reading or by fixing the governess in one interpretation or the other. Escape then becomes the surrender of mastery: "James's very mastery consists in the denial and in the deconstruction of his own mastery" (205). This, of course, is the author's response to his act of creation. James consciously makes this denial in his refusal, in his prefaces and notes, either to affirm the objective reality of the ghosts, to validate the characters' interpretations of them, or to specify the "values" of the ghosts (*Theory of Fiction* 111-14, 173-74). How can the reader successfully imitate this escape? How does the reader escape madness? To come to this question in a manageable way, it is useful to look briefly at the real terror that some people experience in their real lives.

# II

William F. Fischer, in "Towards a Phenomenology of Anxiety," contrasts the generalized state of anxiety with the state of fear: fear is essentially physical, a response to potential physical danger, while anxiety is a response to psychological danger. When he speaks of anxiety, he refers to what I call terror:

> My world, my relations, my situation no longer speak to me in the familiar language. I am no longer at home. The situation seems dissonant, inappropriate, even meaningless. Nothing offers support as I frantically run from object to object seeking support.
>
> . . . The situation is collapsing and I am caught in the here-and-now of its destruction. The future recedes into vaguery and I can neither clarify nor recapture it. Who, where, and what I am are no longer clear. My wants mingle in confusion. The past seems uncertain as it ceases to support the present and it surrounds me without revealing avenues of escape.
>
> . . . If and when anxiety appears in reflection, then the anxious individual finds that his standing and competence as a human being . . . is vulnerable, under attack, in danger of dissolution. He is threatened as a psychological creature. . . . That totality, that matrix of meanings which made all objects and relations significant in the first place, is slipping through his fingers. He continues to will the totality to be so, but the world is more resistive and he becomes still more uncomfortable. . . .
>
> Temporally, the individual experiencing anxiety flees from the disquieting, dissonant, anticipated future into the here-and-now of a meaningless present. . . . There are no places to run, nowhere to hide or to recover the feeling of familiarity. That which threatens in anxiety cannot be avoided by movement. It is so close that it is oppressive and it stifles one's breath, and yet it is nowhere. (110-11)

Fischer's description of anxiety touches precisely on those central elements of the narrator's terror in the tales we have discussed. The narrator loses a familiar and relatively secure world, finds him- or herself isolated in an eternal present without connections in any direction in time or space. Identity begins to dissolve, and that into which he or she is changing is the terrifying other that seems to approach from all directions. This experience is most completely the "Usher" narrator's, but the "Ligeia" narrator and the governess share many of its elements.

We can shed more light upon terror as a subjective state by looking at anxiety dreams or nightmares.

In *Nightmares and Human Conflict*, John E. Mack defines the nightmare as "a type of severe anxiety dream in which the level of anxiety reaches overwhelming proportions" (209). He argues that nightmares normally are not, as some have thought, discharges of aggressive or sexual libido, but rather responses to more or less immediate conflicts in the dreamer's life, often some insecurity over an impending or presently occurring life change. In sleep and dreaming, there is a tendency for the ego to regress toward earlier stages of development, drifting backward through other critical life changes. The dream tends to weld together the anxieties associated with any or all of these developmental stages. In this state, the "I" of the dreamer becomes more childlike, losing certain adult ego functions. The dream-ego loses the ability to sample and limit anxiety through repression and intellectualization. It loses the faculty of reality-testing, the ability to distinguish frightening thoughts from "real," external threats. Mack distinguishes nine forms of anxiety in developmental order, that is, in the order in which humans normally experience them when moving through the life cycle. The following is a paraphrase of Mack's list:

1. Stranger anxiety, fear of a strange face;
2. Separation anxiety, fear of the absence of parent;
3. Fear of loss of love of the caretaking person;
4. Fear of loss of a valued part of body;
5. Fear of disapproval by the superego, of internal self-judgment (a major element of this fear, which often appears in nightmares, is fear of one's hostility toward others);
6. Fear of masochistic surrender;
7. Fear of risks of adult responsibility, e.g., marriage, parenthood, career change, fear of failure;
8. Fear of death;
9. Fear of loss of bodily functions in old age (210).

These fears, which are sources of anxiety in nightmares, are related to the major features of conscious anxiety as described by Fischer and to the terrors of the narrators in our tales. To lose the familiar world and find oneself in an alien, unfamiliar world is like the experience of having differentiated one's mother as essential to one's well-being and then seeing her replaced by a strange face. To be threatened by powers in the world is like being threatened by any of fears numbered three through nine. Furthermore, the regressive process of any nightmare is reflected in waking anxiety and in the narrators' experiences. One is confronted by some fear that originates "in the world" and that pushes one back toward the loss of that world and finally toward the loss of one's identity, when the naked, defenseless ego stands before some overwhelming transforming power. A useful illustration of this sort of dream appears in Nathaniel Hawthorne's *The House of the Seven Gables.*

In the eighteenth chapter of *The House of the Seven Gables,* Hawthorne attempts to entrap the reader momentarily in an anxiety dream to evoke a deeper sympathy for the suffering of his protagonists, Clifford and Hepzibah, and to make the reader feel more deeply the humanity and secret suffering of the proud Judge Pyncheon. Examining this chapter briefly reveals the degree to which Hawthorne and his contemporaries, Edgar Allan Poe and Henry James, could have understood the nature of anxiety and how to produce it in readers. Furthermore, the examination helps us move toward a conception of the characteristics of the reader's anxiety in a terror fantasy.

The chapter begins in a tone of mockery as narrator and reader play the game of pretending that the judge is alive, though he has just died in his chair, to judge him for his sins and to twit him for his inability to act out his greedy ambitions. But, as we mock the judge, time passes. The twilight comes "glooming upwards out of the corners of the room" (240). *We* are left in utter, deathlike darkness: "An infinite, inscrutable blackness has annihilated sight! Where is our universe? All crumbled away from us; and we, adrift in chaos, may harken to the gusts of homeless wind, that go sighing and murmuring about, in quest of what was once a world!" (241). We have been captured in our game, and the mockery has turned back upon us. Evil as he was, the judge is not to be judged finally by us. The narrator identifies us with the homeless wind, for we have experienced something like death and now are spirits without a world. While time is no longer of importance to the judge (so we agreed when we mocked him), now we experience it as unendurable duration: "Would that we were not an attendant spirit here! It is too awful! This clamor of wind through the lonely house; the judge's quietude as he sits invisible; and that pertenacious ticking of his watch!" (242). When the moon restores some light, the narrator lightens the tone by mentioning the ghost legends of the house. However, we again are caught by his efforts to make "a little sport" with the legends. His vision assumes a life of its own and reveals more than we can know, that the judge's heir is also dead. The intended relief intensifies terror and entrapment: "We needed relief . . . from our too long and exclusive contemplation of that figure in the chair . . . yonder leaden Judge sits immovably upon our soul. Will he never stir again? We shall go mad unless he stirs!" (245). Several distancing factors, including a certain playfulness in the narrative voice, prevent the dissolution of aesthetic distance in this chapter. Still, it is clear that Hawthorne seriously intends to give his readers a taste of terror by compelling them to imagine death, to undergo entrapment in an alien world, confrontation with a threatening other, and the threat of transformation into that other.

Because Hawthorne is fairly transparent about his end and means, we can see with some clarity what threats he believes are most terrifying: the loss of a familiar world, the fears that powers in that world will harm one, and ultimately that one's personality will disintegrate. The terrors of the narrators in our terror fantasies are the terrors of waking anxiety. These are parallel to the terrors of the nightmare, except that the narrators are unable to awaken. Their anxiety is "real." To the degree that the stories are effective in their drive to threaten the real reader, entrapped in the role of implied reader, with transformation into the narrator's double and with consequent loss of identity, the reader's experience is also of "real" anxiety.

Mary K. Rothbart's flow chart of "Affective Responses to Sudden, Intense, or Discrepant Stimulation" also sheds light on the response to anxiety (figure 2). The narrator, the implied reader, and the real reader all find themselves in intense and discrepant situations: there is an insistent division between the "reality" of present experience and either the expected or the desired. Rothbart constructed her chart to illustrate how such incongruous experiences might be made to end in laughter, but the chart has two infinite loops in which the release of laughter cannot be reached. When the experience of intense discrepancy is high or medium, when danger is not present, and when the stimulus challenges existing schemas (i.e., fundamental patterns of organizing personal experience), then the reader engages in problem-solving to resolve the discrepancy. As long as the problem-solving is unsuccessful, there is no exit from that loop. Of course, if the stimulation goes away and if its memory can be repressed, one can escape conscious awareness of the feeling of obsession, but one cannot really escape the experience. As in the case of natural anxiety, escape, if it is not a cure, is an illusion. In the case of nightmares, if the cause really is essentially external, the stimulus may go away. Terror fantasy is more like natural anxiety; it must be repressed or cured. Repression is the most likely response if the work seems too dangerous, if "danger is present." This response probably occurs only in a few readers of terror fantasy. In this case, the stimulus still cannot be permanently removed by flight, aggression, or seeking shelter. As a psychological threat, the terror fantasy stays with the reader. If he feels it as a danger, the level of stimulation is stepped up, and attempts at avoidance become obsessive. Terror fantasy is so constructed that neither problem-solving nor avoidance produces closure. Still, there are important dif-

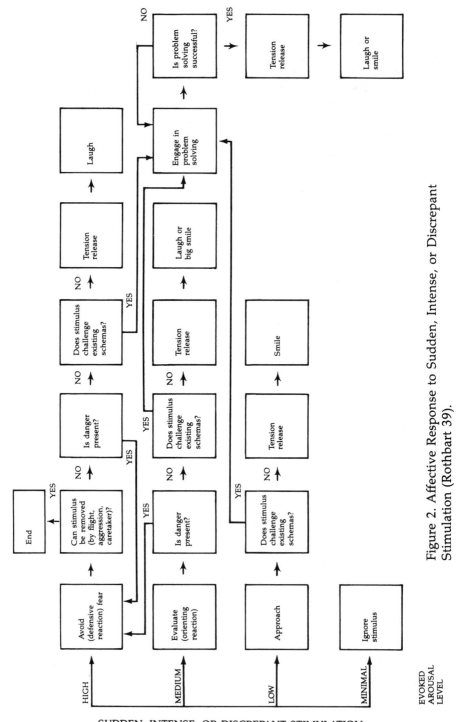

Figure 2. Affective Response to Sudden, Intense, or Discrepant Stimulation (Rothbart 39).

ferences between the experiences of terror fantasy and of natural anxiety, differences that allow for a transformation of terror into beauty.

One difference between the terror of terror fantasy and that of real anxiety is that the reader has consciously chosen to read the work and has come to its reading not only more or less intact, but also with his faculties hyper-alert. The reader who has any knowledge of tradition cannot read far into these tales without realizing that he is in the general domain of the horror thriller. The conventions of the horror thriller are, in part, instructions for the formation of the implied reader as one ready for the terrifying and alert to penetrate mysteries. In terror fantasy, both of these elements of the implied reader are traps, but they are traps for which the reader is, to some degree, prepared. The real reader who constructs the implied reader is not the sleeping ego of a nightmare, nor is he necessarily the victim of a real anxiety that surrounds him. The terror of the text wishes to surround the real reader, but the real reader possesses a defense that is less available to the person who experiences natural anxiety.

The real reader has the implied reader. The terror of the terror fantasy begins its attack by swallowing the implied reader. The real reader's desire to read, to know, to complete, sends him into the maw after his other self, to effect the rescue and carry both away. But he discovers that the trap was set for him in the first place. He discovers that rescue is impossible, and that, just maybe, death, as the loss of self, *is* possible. The sufferer from natural anxiety has no such second self prepared in advance to act as any sort of buffer between himself and his terror. If he needs such a self, he must construct it alone. His terror is his alone and, therefore, may be inescapable. But the implied reader is the real reader's savior. The implied reader may be sacrificed.

# III

The ultimate threat of terror fantasy is against the self of the real reader. The tale gestures toward capturing the real reader's self. Paradoxically, self-defense—the attempt to master the work—only strengthens the work's hold over the real reader. The overwhelming anxiety of the nightmare causes the dreamer to awaken, to reassert all the integrative powers one has learned in the process of maturation. When the real reader attempts to assert such powers, he only increases his entrapment. Responses to natural anxiety include the neurotic's attempt to preserve the self by means of the symptom and the psychotic's radical splitting of the self. As long as the real reader continues his reading, his response mirrors that of the neurotic; his reading, his being haunted, becomes his "symptom." The escape, the completion of the reading, is more like psychosis, though the differences are not insignificant.

To escape from the terror of terror fantasy is not to give in, but rather to let go of the drive for mastery: to consciously surrender a recently acquired aspect of oneself by giving up the implied reader. Driven toward his ultimate resources to deal with literary terror, the real reader turns to his imagination, the mirror in which is found the image of himself that he constructed at the behest of the tale. The tale has shown him that image and has identified him with that image. To complete his interaction with the image, the real reader must allow the image to belong to the tale. How can this be done?

The possibility of sacrificing the implied reader is suggested by the metaphor I have adopted from Wolfgang Iser, that of the actor playing a role. The actor can begin to play a role and then cease to play the role because he *knows* he is playing a role. He looks upon his part as a role he plays, not as himself, though the relations between these two may be intimate and complex. The real reader, however, does not normally conceive of himself as playing the role of implied reader. The concept of implied reader is a construct of literary theory that accounts for major phenomena of the reading experience. The real reader need not be and, in fact, usually is not conscious either of the concept or of the activity of creating the role as he reads. Terror fantasies make the already created role visible to the real reader. The role becomes visible because of terror.

Terror creates the desire, the need for escape, for disengagement from the fiction. The usual and expected means of disengagement from the horror thriller is closure. When a terror fantasy asserts anticlosure, the real reader demands closure and labors toward it. Laboring for closure, however, only intensifies the experience of entrapment and terror. At some point, in some way, the failed and terrified laborer becomes visible. The real reader, in effect, asks "Who is this obsessed reader enmeshed in this fiction?" To be able to pose this question is to be able to answer, "Not I."

At the psychological level, one's identity becomes an object of contemplation. The reader becomes able to see himself as the entity or subject that stands apart and holds itself together in the universal chaos, like Henry Adams riding his bicycle on a tightrope (433). The real reader becomes aware of himself as a process, as able to move and, therefore, as superior to the narrators who are obsessed by and trapped within their stories. This realization has many and deep implications, but for now the crucial one is that the terror of the tale moves the real reader to a new perspective in which the analogy between the implied reader and the narrator becomes visible. The reader knows himself as entrapped in the story and as having taken a critical stance as we did in examining the tales. This act in itself restores the division between real reader and implied reader that the tale had collapsed. The real reader's consciousness expands to take in a larger situation. Time and distance are the advantages that the real reader has over the narrator, distance from the reality of the narrator's obsessions, especially of the need to tell. The need to tell may be seen as the narrator's hope to achieve distance over time and to become an object for himself or herself. But the narrator's experiences involve acts in the world that entangle him or her more surely and inescapably than do the reader's acts on the text.

When the reader's consciousness expands, his aesthetic relation to the work is restored. He leaps outside the role of implied reader. It may be appropriate to say that he creates yet another implied reader, who comprehends the hesitating implied reader who, in turn, comprehends the readers of the two main alternative readings. All of these roles become samples of many roles that the real reader can play. Inevitably, this experience points at the "I," the real reader's picture of himself apart from the work, and this, too, becomes one of many possible roles, but more of this later. The key to the restoration of aesthetic distance is the establishment of psychological distance within the self, the adoption of a perspective in which one's identity as implied reader becomes an object of his own consciousness. From this perspective, one sees this identity over against the terrors of the story, locked in struggle, but undefeated. This is a victory, not over the mystery, but over the terror the mystery helps to arouse; this victory becomes a part of the work. The irresolvable indeterminacies of the text become beautiful parts of that victory and beautiful parts of the work. When the reader acknowledges and accepts that his state before the text is helplessness, that his powers of integration cannot solve the insistent indeterminacies, he discovers himself as an observer of the entrapped self before the text, and he retains identity within this new perspective. At this point the story ceases to be threatening, for the reader has withstood the threat of the story to disintegrate his personality. One naturally feels elation and power at such an accomplishment.

To experience the anticlosure that entraps the implied reader, to feel the reader split and suspended between opposing but ever insistent readings, to feel the pull of transformation as the implied reader's obsession comes to mirror the narrator's obsession, to feel the threat of transformation as the tale refuses to release the real reader from the role he has accepted—this is the terror of a terror fantasy. To become conscious of the implied reader as a construct, to abandon that role and leap into a different imaginative stance, to be released from the terror of entrapment and the tension of struggle, to see the work as a whole of which a surrendered construct of the self is a part, to master the reading by surrendering the tale—this is the pleasure of terror fantasy. To read and reread these fictions is to relive a liberation of self from self, which is a means to the end of concretizing these works. The unique pleasure of terror fantasy arises from forcing the reader to construct an appropriate closure of the reading that includes the anticlosure of the tale. As a result, the reader achieves a particularly intense experience of psychological liberation as a major component of the concretization.

It is important to understand that, even though the aesthetic experience can come to a close, the work remains unclosed. In surrendering the implied reader to the tale, the real reader surrenders mastery—the insistence upon the power of the ego to comprehend (understand and enclose the totality of) reality. The real reader, at least tacitly, admits that the conscious self is not adequate to the mystery of the text. He accepts that the tale eludes him. Without this surrender, the completion of the reading is impossible, yet paradoxically, this surrender is an admission that the tale cannot be read. In the case of terror fantasy, completing the reading, in the sense of closing the aesthetic experience, can be accomplished only by accepting the impossibility of reading the tale. The real reader becomes different in this process because he becomes conscious of himself as a performance.

Because the experience of psychological liberation from the self as a totality is so central to the pleasurable concretization of a terror fantasy, I would like to describe and explain the implications of this liberation more fully. Furthermore, at this point, the examination of terror fantasy makes connection with recent theoretical work in the general field of fantasy.

Rosemary Jackson, in her study of fantasy as a literature of subversion, has brought together recent thought on fantasy in a way quite useful to the understanding of terror fantasy. She argues that the desire of the fantastic in fiction is to express

> a longing for that which does not yet exist, or which has not been allowed to exist, the unheard of, the unseen, the imaginary, as opposed to what already exists and is permitted as "really" visible. Unlike the symbolic, the imaginary is inhabited by an infinite number of selves preceding socialization, before the ego is produced within a social frame. These selves allow an infinite, unnameable potential to emerge, one which a fixed sense of character excludes in advance. . . . [T]he most subversive fantasies are those which attempt to *transform* the relations between the imaginary and the symbolic. They try to set up possibilities for radical cultural transfor-

mation by making more fluid the relations between these realms, suggesting, or projecting, the dissolution of the symbolic through violent reversal or rejection of the process of the subject's formation. (91)

Terror fantasy may be one of the most subversive divisions of the mode of subversive fantasy because, finally, it cannot be read without *actually experiencing* the fragmentation of the self or of the symbolic.

To understand what this means, we can draw upon Jackson's working out of her readings of Jacques Lacan and his associates and followers in the elaboration and revision of Freud's ideas. Her opposition of the imaginary and the symbolic derives from these readings, specifically from the elaboration of Lacan's discussion of the mirror stage in the development of the ego. In Freud's model, the child moves from primary narcissism, through attachment to loved objects, to a reality principle that accepts the separation of the ego from the world, the laws of necessity, and the certainty of death. Lacan elaborates the transition from narcissism to the attachment to loved objects as the mirror stage.

We have glanced at this description several times in previous chapters because it seems crucial to understanding the dynamics of tales of terror. Many of the tales of terror that are most memorable seem centrally concerned with the nature of the self and the process of the formation of the self. We will remember Christine Brooke-Rose's useful summary of the three main stages of the mirror phase: "recognition of the other, recognition of the other as self, recognition of the other as self but other" (161). The child emerges from narcissism with the recognition of a wholeness in others, the distinction between his body and the body of another. The recognition merges into a desire to be the other, to be whole in the same way. The mirror, the reflection of his own physical wholeness, or the gaze of another that more directly implies wholeness of identity, reveals a relationship of self and other. The child is like the others he has distinguished. At this point begins the construction of the self, the deliberate making of the image of what the child will be. In constructing that image, the child necessarily splits. The child is the image and the child is the maker of the image. The child is the subject and the object of that subject. The object is symbolic. As we have noted earlier, to give graspable form to the image of self, the child must symbolize that image in language, the symbol systems provided by his culture. The manipulator of that image, the subject, is only known, then, insofar as it conforms to what has been symbolized. Where it does not conform, it is invisible, unspeakable, "nonexistent" within the symbol systems available in the culture: in short, it is imaginary. This is the realm of the imaginary, then, as opposed to the symbolic, the unconscious repository of all that we have chosen not to be.

The *symbolic*, then, refers to language in the widest sense, the various means by which we make present to consciousness the reality we wish to manipulate. These means are culturally determined and, hence, laden with cultural ideology. This ideology includes the culturally acceptable limits for the constitution of an "I." As the child moves through socialization, his commitment to this "I" necessitates acceptance of the social determinants of the "I" he has already chosen. In the language with which I grew up, every child buys his identity as a "pig in a poke," only to discover gradually, over years of growth, what was in the bag.

The *imaginary* consists of what the child gives up by choosing to become an identity, to become an object of his own consciousness. As the child grows, he feels a constant tearing away from himself. What he becomes is never what he hoped to become. He secretly longs for himself as subject, the self that he is never allowed by his identity to "speak." The imaginary is the unspeakable, the lost other, the unconscious.

Fantasy, according to Jackson, seeks to express the imaginary. To the extent that it succeeds in this expression in such a way as to "interrogate the category of character," fantasy is subversive of "that definition of the self as a coherent, indivisible and continuous whole which has dominated Western thought for centuries and is celebrated in classic theatre and 'realistic' art alike" (82-83).

Within the category of subversive fantasy is terror fantasy. Terror fantasy momentarily focuses upon and heightens the interrogation of the category of character by offering the "I" a new part and then requiring that it be given up. In offering a new part, terror fantasy, like most fiction, mirrors the mirror phase. It offers the reader a version of an "I" to try. Terror fantasy differs from most fiction, however, in its attempt to entrap the real reader in the role of implied reader. This entrapment is analogous to the narrowing experience of maturation, though perhaps more intense because more brief and concentrated. As the subject confines himself by conforming to the "I," so the real reader confines himself by conforming to the implied reader. When the implied reader becomes a terrifying trap, the real reader feels this confinement. When the real reader abandons the role of implied reader, he does something that, in all probability, he has rarely if ever accomplished before reading a terror fantasy. He cuts himself free from an imprisoning "I." To an adult reader, this experience promises liberation from the tyranny of the "I" because it points at the implied reader (perhaps as many as three implied readers), this recently constructed and provisional "I," as fictional, as created by the real reader and the arrangement of the language in the text. This pointing implies, at least, that the "I" that the reader brought to the work is a similarly fictional construct that may be abandoned or modified by choice. While all humans are aware, perhaps painfully, that their choices of being arise out of various views of the "I," their own and others', not all become aware that the "I" is a fiction, that it can be changed.

Terror fantasy provides the opportunity to reenact the appropriation of the image of the "I," but in a way just the opposite of the reenactment of repression that is central to the horror thriller. In the horror thriller, the forbidden is expressed to allow us to remake the decision to forbid it, to remake the decision in favor of the "I." We thereby enjoy the pleasure of creating an identity. Terror fantasy provides an opportunity to reconsider the creation of the "I," to achieve an awareness of the process of creating the "I" as in a fundamental way, voluntary. Of course, our initial experience of appropriating the other in the mirror phase seems involuntary. It is hardly a considered choice. By making possible the reconsideration of that move, terror fantasy introduces or reminds us of the voluntary element, the act of will by which we begin to become persons. In Jackson's view, the final purpose of all subversive fantasy is to reveal that character, the "I," is a fiction. This, of course, is a psychological rather than an aesthetic opinion, for from an aesthetic point of view, the final purpose, at least of terror fantasy, is to become a concretion, an aesthetic whole in the experience of its reader. The revelation of the fictionality of the real reader's "I" is a means to the end of the concretion.

Following Leo Bersani's argument in *A Future for Astyanax*, Jackson develops a historical thesis that is also instructive at this point. She sees fantasy developing historically from religious fantasy, in which the impossible is attributed to another world, toward secular fantasy, in which the impossible comes more fully to be recognized as projected from within the mind. Secular fantasy is more subversive because it tends to turn away from "supplying a vicarious fulfillment of desire and neutralizing an urge toward transgression" such as she finds generally in Gothic fiction (72). Instead, secular fantasy tries in various ways to "dissolve structures," to recover the preconscious narcissistic state, that entropic Nirvana "where all tensions are reduced" (73). She finds in the Marquis de Sade and in the Comte de Lautréamont expressions of this longing that may stimulate such longings in their readers. In much of twentieth-century fantasy, from Franz Kafka to Thomas Pynchon, she finds examples of the longing for absolute otherness and the exposure of the emptiness in the apparent but fictional fulness of the symbolic order that is public reality. While such longings may indeed be expressed in them, these tales seem significantly less effective in their interrogations of character than are terror fantasies. Kafka's major fables of anxiety seem more to challenge culture than character, though, of course, character is indirectly questioned. Kafka portrays a world that portentously refuses to speak, that claims to be comprehensive but constantly betrays its fictionality, its failure to be a total picture. Likewise, Pynchon's novels seem, as David H. Richter has argued in *Fable's End*, to move toward thematic critiques of cultural ideology rather than to involve the reader in experiencing the fictionality of his own character. By questioning cultural ideology, such works question the foundation, the language of the "I," and so express a longing for that which is not included in the language; but, without the terror of an entrapping anticlosure, they seem aesthetically tame beside *The Turn of the Screw*. The liberation of the reader, which is essential to the concretization of a terror fantasy, involves more than an intellectual realization that modern Western culture, despite its claims to the contrary, is not ALL. Kafka and Pynchon make the reader feel the oppressiveness of modern culture and so stimulate the desire for escape. Terror fantasies provide escape, insofar as it is possible, for the actual experience of the fictionality of the "I" imparts a useable conviction of the fictionality of culture.

Terror fantasies, like what I call fables of anxiety, speak to a fundamental individual and cultural need for the new, though in quite different ways. As Jackson and Bersani argue, this need has deepened as a result of the increasing cultural totalitarianism of modern Western cultures, which seem bent on concentrating all power in the "I." While Jackson and Bersani agree that there is no culture without repression or without ideology, they also argue persuasively that some of the painful oppression of this Apollonian order may be relieved by a revision of the ideas of the "I" that Dionysian fantasy can help to bring about (Jackson 178; Bersani 314-15).

In her discussion of the character of character in fiction, Hélène Cixous describes the experience of works in which character as the necessary mirror of the reader is conspicuously absent, for example, some works of E. T. A. Hoffman. Such works, she says, "unmask" character; character is: "denounced, returned to his reality as simulacrum, brought back to the mask as mask. He is given up then to the complexity of his subjectivity, to his multiplicity, to his off-centre position, to his permanent escapade: like the author, he disappears only to be multiplied, attains the self only to be, in the same instant, differentiated into a trans-subjective effervescence" (387). This passage aptly describes the experience of liberation that allows the concretization of terror fantasy. The tale exposes the "I" and hence all "I's" as fictions. Terror fantasy pulls the reader toward a perspective in which he becomes *another*, not *The Other*, or the unconscious, which threatens madness and dissolution, but *another* who stands, as it were, outside his own character, seeing it, as Cixous says, "off-centre." The reader, in the moment he takes a new perspective, stands for a moment outside the culturally, linguistically determined self in confrontation with its "invisible" antithesis. This perspective in itself is liberating, not because it frees one from choice nor because it allows one to be free of culture, but because it tends to free one *in* culture. Culture becomes visible. Of course, it always has been visible; by definition, culture is what we symbolize or make visible. Now, however, the process of making the visible, of making culture becomes visible. It is as if one saw one's culture as a new language to be learned, as if one had entered a foreign culture as an adult, with the ability to analyze and make considered choices about what he will adopt and how. Culture ceases to be an "invisible" determinant of the "I."

D. H. Lawrence seems to have seen through to this fundamental effect in Poe's tales: "Moralists have always wondered helplessly why Poe's morbid tales need have been written. They need to be written because old things need to die and disintegrate, because the old white psyche has to be gradually broken down before anything else can come to pass." Furthermore, Lawrence says, "Man must be stripped even of himself. And it is a painful, sometimes ghastly process. . . . For the human soul must suffer its own disintegration, consciously, if ever it is to survive" (Woodson 39). This is the perspective that the governess and the Poe narrators need so desperately, to let the old self die to make room for renewal. They need to surrender the drive for mastery. The reader, fortunately not fixed within the text, can surrender the drive for mastery, indeed must. In this process The Other (the unchosen selves) does not cease to exist, nor does it become visible or cease to be an object of desire, but it may be spoken of, for a moment, as tamed or blessed, for its silence becomes part of the beauty of a work of art. Alice Staverton teaches Spencer Brydon the reasons for pitying his "other," the self he has chosen not to be, in Henry James's "The Jolly Corner." The unchosen Brydon is as much to be pitied as the chosen one; furthermore, each "has" his compensations. At least part of the meaning of this tale is that when one sees oneself as chosen and the other as unchosen, it becomes possible not only to alter choices but perhaps somewhat easier to accept what one inevitably loses by choosing.

We see, then, that there is a political and a social dimension to the experience of terror fantasy. As Fredric Jameson suggests in "Magical Narratives: Romance as Genre," the liberation entailed in the aesthetic experience of terror fantasies may be psychological, aesthetic, political, and social. These tales "set up possibilities for radical cultural transformation by making fluid the relations between" the reality we choose and the imaginary that "is inhabited by an infinite number of selves preceeding socialization, before the ego is produced within a social frame" (Jackson 91). As Wolfgang Iser shows in *The Act of Reading*, the general effect of liberation is not unique to terror fantasy, for all great literature tends, through its "repertoire," to interrogate the limits of the ideologies it chooses to represent (chapter 3). Frank Kermode, in *The Sense of an Ending*, also argues that all literature, by its very existence, can remind us of the fictionality of all forms of ordering experience. Terror fantasies are unique among works of literature in their manipulation of aesthetic distance in a way that makes a particular version of the reader's self into a part of his concretion of the work, thus bringing that self in its relations to ideology before the reader's own consciousness.

# IV

At this point in the argument, a brief digression seems necessary. When I was nearly finished with the final draft of this book, I talked it over with a friend who balked at my description of terror fantasy. He argued that ordinary readers are unable to read terror fantasies in the ways I have described. In effect he said that, caught up in a love for certain authors and a passion to explain, I had forgotten ordinary readers. When I describe the workings and the pleasures of terror fantasy, do I not construct a level of experience unavailable to all real readers, except for those like myself who succumb to the obsession to explain by working out a complex and fantastic reading? Is it possible that my elaborate explanation is of an absolutely unique experience that only I have had and that no one can share?

In a sense, this is a question for other scholars to answer. I can only make my best effort to discover continuities between my experience and that of other readers and to present them clearly. The community of thought that transcends me is, perhaps, the only force that can judge whether I have succeeded. However, it is important that the question be raised. Indeed, my friend reminded me of another form in which it has been asked. In *Critical Understanding*, Wayne Booth devotes part of a chapter to *The Turn of the Screw*. He argues that we can achieve greater sanity as well as validity in interpretation if we carefully use the concept of the implied author. Booth asks whether any of the more "ingenious" interpretations of the novella correspond to what we can reasonably imagine James might attempt in writing a ghost story. Booth and my friend raise essentially the same question: do real readers read terror fantasies in the way I have described? Have real writers really written such works?

Booth attacks interpretations of *The Turn of the Screw* that fail to refer "explicitly or even by indirection, to what a human being might conceivably do if he attempted to write a story according to the new hypothesis being offered. Each interpretation springs full-bodied from an assertion of a possible *reading*, not a possible *writing*" (286). He concludes that even the most careful analysis of the governess as a mad hallucinator must assert the apparent absurdity that James set out and continued to write the novella with the purpose of concealing his true meaning from virtually all of his real readers, that his aim was not to frighten readers, but to fool them. Even more absurd, perhaps, is the conception of James as an author more interested in presenting psychological cases than in producing fine artistic effects. One of Booth's most telling points is that only a clumsy or a diabolical artist would make this particular governess the narrator: "To think of a mad governess who could and would write her own story in this way entails the absurdity of thinking that Henry James could commit such an absurdity. Think of the thousands of details that such a narrator would suppress—given the skills at suppression and distortion that she must have. . . . Why would either a mad person or a formerly mad person trouble, in telling her story, to talk about her own 'dreadful liability to impressions of the order so vividly exemplified' by the appearance of Quint and about Mrs. Grose's exemption 'from my more than questionable privilege'?" (299). On his way to this conclusion, Booth offers a reading of the novella that is closer to his conception of what James— or any intelligent writer—would most likely have intended in producing this particular text.

Booth offers his reading as a way of demonstrating one useful test of a good reading: "To pass our test, the reading . . . must account for how any writer as skillful as the James *everyone* postulates would have found it necessary or appropriate . . . to do all or most of what was done" (290). Booth accepts Douglas's statement of the effect of the governess's narrative: dreadfulness, uncanny ugliness, horror, and pain. If it has this effect on Douglas, then it would seem reasonable for it to have a similar effect on his audience and on the reader. Given this hypothetical intention, Booth works through the choices James can be seen to have made concerning his characters, the ghosts, and his narrative presentation by means of the governess. All of these explanations make good sense, and I do not dispute them.

Does this acquiescence place my reading of the novella and my theories about terror fantasy among those that fail to consider a possible writing? Naturally, I think not, but then, how do I proceed from Booth's reading to my own?

To begin, I disagree with Booth on two fundamental facts about the story. First, he argues on the basis of critical agreement that at least one of the ghosts is absolutely real (292). Unfortunately, the critical agreement for that assertion simply is not there. Every argument for the reality of the ghosts I have seen has a published counterargument. The language in which Mrs. Grose identifies the apparitions is too slippery to provide absolute confirmation, though it comes very close. I agree with Booth that James probably wanted the ghosts to seem real, but I also believe that he wanted to prevent confirmation of their reality for the very reason that Booth cites as one of the causes of critics' doubting the governess—James's apparent desire to make the governess doubt herself. Second, and more important, Booth asserts that though the governess finally "exorcises the ghosts with her courage" and saves Flora, she must endure the triumph of the ghosts when Miles dies (287). Booth omits from this summary the governess's statements that she has saved both children, the last assertion coming when Miles is dead in her arms.

These disagreements are decisive in how we read the tale. If the pointedly missing end frame and the pointed uncertainty as to whether the governess has saved or destroyed Miles do not force the reader back over the text for resolution, then this tale is much more likely to be what Booth says it is, a highly effective horror thriller. But even if I am right about how to view the text, the even more crucial question remains: would James write the reading of the novella that I have presented? I think he would and that this is precisely the sort of tale of terror he would want most to produce, one to "catch" jaded readers as well as the more ordinary ones.

Booth and I agree wholly on the apparent purpose of the work, to terrify even the most experienced readers of tales of terror. We agree on James's probable reasons for all the major choices Booth discusses: the two children as the most pathetic victims, the two sexually corrupt and convincingly—but (my qualification) not absolutely—real ghosts as the most diabolical, the vulnerable and resourceful protectress who also becomes the ideal narrator. I especially agree with Booth's characterization of the riskiness and the promise of making the governess doubt herself: "We must expose them [the children] both to the demons *and* to their hapless protectress. If we show her trying to force the children to acknowledge their communion with the demons, seeking, with less and less attention to their feelings and more and more to her own plight, for corroboration of their corruption, we shall turn the screws of horrible torture for those damned and hapless children" (295).

To this reading I add only one more observation: that the governess's self-doubt, which Booth so accurately sees her acting out with the children, persists in her telling of the tale. Because the consequences of her choices have included the death of her beloved Miles, she can never escape that self-doubt. As it haunts her, so it haunts her telling and her various readers. Because the governess herself is never absolutely certain of the reality of the apparitions she saw, the reader can never be certain either. This uncertainty explodes into prominence when the text fails to close and the reader is caught in the toils of the reading.

Whether or not James ever articulated an understanding that he had achieved this effect, we can see that it is clearly consistent with his professed aims in his preface and with the effects Douglas claims to have felt in the opening frame. James, at the height of his career, intuited the form of a tale of terror that most suited his talents and interests as a writer and produced what is to date the greatest masterpiece in the genre.

If we have a possible writing and a possible reading, do we have a description of the reading that readers really do? I have not proven that all readers read these texts the way I say they do. In fact, published criticism of the terror fantasies suggests that virtually no one reads them as I have. Rather, most readers who publish their views remain in the vibration between alternate readings or settle for one of the less satisfying closures. That my theory accounts for these responses and incorporates them into the reading of terror fantasies supports the theory, but does not prove it. Therefore, the really convincing test remains ahead. Now that a picture of "successful" reading has been drawn, will real readers recognize it?

It may help in that testing to notice and remember that an articulation of an experience is not the experience itself. This point emerges more forcefully than any other from the study of the aesthetics of terror fiction. The narrators of our three terror fantasies are trapped forever in the necessity of articulating what cannot be articulated, of trying to absolutely fix in language the unfixable reality they have suffered. We do not experience the articulation of a theory of the pleasures of terror when we read horror thrillers or terror fantasies. When I go to see *Alien* or *Psycho*, I experience the film, not a critical or theoretical discussion of the film. The test of a good articulation is how well it describes what happens to me at the film. About terror fantasy, I have argued that there are several choices for closing the anticlosed, but that the reader will be most satisfied if he finds one particular mode of closure that I call escape. Then, in concretizing the work, he will be taken out of himself in a way that may be unique in literary art, and he will receive a momentary sense of self-transcendence of immeasurable value.

## CHAPTER ELEVEN

# Conclusion: Terror and the Sublime

## I

John Aiken and Anna Laetitia Barbauld, in their essay "On the Pleasure Derived from Objects of Terror," eloquently pose the central question of this book: "But the apparent delight with which we dwell upon objects of pure terror, where our moral feelings are not in the least concerned, and no passion seems to be excited but the depressing one of fear, is a paradox of the heart, much more difficult of solution" (120). Insofar as a literary work seems intent upon arousing fear in its readers, it is aesthetically puzzling. Attempts to explain the appeal of such works have not been numerous, though some have been quite suggestive. Before considering these, it will be helpful to review the answers that have been developed in the previous chapters.

The literature of terror may be organized along a kind of branching continuum much as Tzvetan Todorov organizes fantastic literature. If successfully creating an aesthetic experience in which the real reader deals with real threats to his well-being marks the fullest development of the literature of terror, then the fully developed terror fantasies of Edgar Allan Poe and Henry James form one end of that continuum. Central to those works is the fantastic as defined by Todorov—the hesitation in the implied reader between natural and supernatural explanations of the terrifying events. The natural and supernatural sides of this hesitation come from two directions. There is a literature of terror, which seems related to tragedy, in which the marvelous has no part. Todorov calls this area the uncanny. Sensation stories such as "The Man in the Bell" and related works by authors such as Charles

Brockden Brown and Poe evoke uncanny horror. Closely related to fairy tales and that loosely defined genre called fantasy are marvelous tales of terror, those works such as *At the Mountains of Madness* in which the supernatural is accepted, however reluctantly, without questioning its reality. The uncanny and the marvelous tale of terror converge in the fantastic, in fantastic/marvelous tales, where there is fantastic hesitation in the implied reader that is eventually resolved toward the supernatural, and in the fantastic/uncanny, where this hesitation is resolved toward the natural. We see, then, a split continuum of modes of tales of terror with two parallel ends in realistic fiction and in fantasy. From these poles the continuum gradually converges toward the fantastic and ends in pure fantastic terror fantasy. Though one might trace a kind of historical development along this continuum, that would be a difficult and perhaps not a valuable enterprise, for it seems clear that works of all kinds have appeared in random order since the eighteenth century.

Along this continuum are three major highlighted areas about which it seems reasonable to center aesthetic questions. The uncanny tale of terror is distinct in the kind of pleasure it offers from the horror thriller. Within the horror thriller are all the tales that present marvelous or apparently marvelous monsters; therefore, marvelous tales, fantastic/marvelous tales, and fantastic/uncanny tales are all closely related in the pleasure they offer. Pure fantastic tales of terror or terror fantasies, though they share the characteristics of horror thrillers, are unique in exploiting the potential of the pure fantastic for anticlosure, and so they offer yet another distinct kind of pleasure.

The uncanny tale of terror in its simplest form offers vicarious risk. We are allowed to imagine being in situations we will probably never encounter, though we may well suffer analogous experiences. These may allow a kind of play or modeling, thus fulfilling the need for play that Erik Erikson describes in *Childhood and Society* (211-22). We are allowed to escape temporarily from the normal limitations of social reality and to practice or pretend mastery of some fears. This particular psychological pleasure contributes to another level of pleasure, the experience of extremes of emotion usually not available in ordinary life, for the play with fear intensifies those emotional extremes. Without actually feeling terror, we imagine what it must be like to feel the absolute terrors of physical and spiritual annihilation. Though the risk of encountering real fear in such tales is small, this risk still contributes to the aesthetic pleasure of creating a concretion of the text. Aesthetic pleasure in reading a literary text arises from the process of making a concretion or an aesthetic whole of the experience of the text and is complete when a satisfying concretion is achieved. A small amount of risk, the highly protected entertainment of fear, which becomes part of the process of concretizing the sensation story, intensifies the pleasure of completing the work by adding a small barrier to that completion.

Poe, though he wrote some sensation tales, did not find this simplest form particularly challenging and tended to parody it in pieces such as "The Premature Burial" and "How to Write a Blackwood Article." When, as in "The Pit and the Pendulum" and "The Tell-Tale Heart," he wrote in this vein, he introduced various forms of ambiguity, thereby increasing the risk for the reader at least slightly. Brown shows a similar interest in *Edgar Huntly*. Such ambiguity brings the sensation story closer to the fantastic/uncanny tale of terror.

The second major mode on the continuum of tales of terror is the horror thriller. It includes all tales of terror in which the marvelous or apparently marvelous appears, but not those that sustain fantastic hesitation throughout the whole. They are like the uncanny tales in that reading them entails taking risks. These risks tend not to be too great, in part because they arise from horror, our response to anticipating and watching harm befalling those for whom we care. Indeed, in their simpler forms, as in some tales of M. R. James, for example, their effects may hardly be distinct from uncanny tales. The important difference grows out of the new potential that is introduced when one feels free to invent supernatural monsters. When the man in the bell hallucinates, he suggests some of the possibilities that horror thrillers such as *At the Mountains of Madness* and *Dracula* develop more fully. Supernatural or apparently supernatural monsters can be made to symbolically represent unconscious psychological fears. Most recent historians and theoreticians of the Gothic tradition have recognized this possibility, and many have documented it in their examinations of Gothic fiction. Though such works present risks to the reader, they are different in kind from those of the uncanny tale. In their most fully developed forms, horror thrillers, mainly by means of their presentations of supernatural monsters, force the reader to entertain images of the forbidden, images of what a culture commands its members to exclude from their selves. Because such images are unconsciously attractive (representing parts of the self) at the same time as their meanings are forbidden entrance into consciousness, we can take a kind of illicit pleasure in the mere contemplation of these images, but ultimately they must be put back. Horror thrillers are fairly careful, sometimes indeed, elaborately careful, to create and maintain psychological distance between the real reader and the terrifying images. The reader is therefore carefully protected from the possibility of the images forcing attention away from the work to terrors in the self. The result is a highly controlled brush with the attractive/terrifying forbidden within the self. Such a glimpse seems considerably more risky than the vicarious participation in another's fear that distinguishes the uncanny tale of terror. Often, this contact with terror appears in addition to or as part of an imaginative sharing of a character's fear. The concretization of such a work is more challenging because the risk is greater. For this reason, the aesthetic pleasure of completing such works is likely to be more intense.

Another element that contributes to the intensity of a fully developed horror thriller is that completing it requires a reenactment of repression. Psychoanalysts affirm that we begin to construct our identities by forming a concept of an "I" as separate from everything else. To continue to construct that identity, we must specify the "I" in forms of language available to us: we must give up much that is part of us, for example, the desire to possess our mothers wholly or the continuous pleasure of passively receiving various stimulations. We gladly give up these things to become persons, but nevertheless we continue to long for what we have lost in the process. The forbidden images of the horror thriller offer us disguised forms of what we have given up, allow a controlled play with these images, and assist in a repetition of the original repressions by which we gave up those parts of ourselves.

There are two unique forms of psychological pleasure that contribute to the aesthetic pleasure of the horror thriller: the play with images of the forbidden and the reenactment of repression. The closer the play comes to being serious, the more recognizable the images are as representations of forbidden desire, the greater is the pleasure of controlling them with the assistance of the literary form. Aesthetic completion and the reenactment of repression coincide, thus enhancing the pleasure of the work.

The unique features of the aesthetic experience of the uncanny tale of terror and of the horror thriller seem directly related to the identity principle Norman Holland presents in *The I*. One of our unique capacities as human beings is to construct a self-conscious identity, an "I." The uncanny tale of terror allows an exploration and a testing of that identity in playing at fear. We explore our responses to intense fear, and we model our desired reactions to terrifying situations, much as Clara Wieland modeled her reactions to a threat of rape. The horror thriller requires a more sophisticated response. While modeling and testing may still be part of concretizing an effective horror thriller, the distinctive quality of this experience is the encounter, not so much with fears of physical destruction, but with images of the forbidden. These works offer opportunities to guardedly repossess the forbidden and surrendered parts of the self and then to reenact the surrender. This reenactment is analogous to the "original" acts of self-formation. We begin to achieve identities, and we continue to specify those identities by asserting and maintaining self-consciousness, by making choices to be one person and not another. This process is both pleasurable and painful; it is pleasurable to exercise our peculiarly human power of becoming a self, and it is painful to surrender potentials and desires that are not consistent with that self. While the unique pleasures of uncanny tales of terror and of horror thrillers tend to support and reaffirm the process of achieving an identity, the unique pleasures of terror fantasy take us in the opposing direction by making us *feel* the fictionality, the constructedness of our identities.

Those tales that exploit the pure fantastic without using anticlosure hover between the horror thriller and the terror fantasy, but seem finally to be highly effective horror thrillers. Terror fantasy realizes its full potential when fantastic hesitation is sustained throughout the tale and when there is anticlosure. We arrive at the end of "Ligeia," "The Fall of the House of Usher," or *The Turn of the Screw* to discover a reopening rather than a closing of the tale. The twists at the ends of these texts turn the reader back into the story by an insistent ambiguity with regard to what has actually happened. The fantastic hesitation does not end; instead it becomes the central feature of the tale, and its lack of resolution becomes a source of terror, ultimately to the real reader.

As a result of this turning back, the implied reader is split, suspended between alternate readings, and this suspension amounts to entrapment in the reading. Because the role of implied reader refuses to end, the real reader is also entrapped in the reading. His reading does not stop, and he is haunted by the work. The real reader's dilemma parallels the narrator's dilemma. Both invite the obsessive repetition of the tale. At this stage, the work ceases to behave as we expect works of art to behave. As a result, the real reader's relation to it is no longer aesthetic, but practical. The work threatens and terrifies the reader. The real reader can bring an end to his reading and to his terror, but he must do so without help from the work, except insofar as the work pushes him toward some response that might end the reading.

Several responses are possible, but only one seems satisfying. The reader can "repress" the tale, practicing a fairly simple form of flight, or he can struggle against it. Struggle might include forcing one of the alternative interpretations upon the tale, either by trivializing or by naturalizing its terrors. All of these readings are possible, and each has its rewards. Repression provides relief, a rather ragged form of the pleasure a horror thriller provides. Forcing a resolution on the tale offers a similar pleasure since it brings closure to the tale and a reenactment of repression. These responses will ultimately prove unsatisfying, especially to the reader who rereads these tales or for whom they remain vivid in memory. The repression of flight from the tale is simply an attempt to erase it from memory, which is normally impossible; repression is only *pretending* to forget, after all. And forcing closure on the tale leaves one's chosen interpretation under the critique of its alternative(s).

The more satisfying response begins with the real reader's intuitive recognition that he has created a self, an implied reader, in response to the tale and that this self is only a role that may be abandoned. If the work will not end the role, then the reader may stop playing it. When the real reader leaves his role of implied reader "in the work," the work becomes whole. The real reader unilaterally reestablishes the necessary aesthetic distance from the work, which will allow him to see it as a whole and complete work of art. Reestablishment of aesthetic distance and the completion of the reading do not resolve the narrator's or the implied reader's problems of interpretation, but they do transform them. When the real reader successfully makes the step to a critical perspective, the implied reader becomes visible as a construct of the work, entrapped in the work and suspended between the irresolvable alternatives of interpretation. The real reader thus frees himself from the role of implied reader of this text, abandoning the forever split role in the work. Having realized that the implied reader is caught in a trap from which there is no escape, the real reader surrenders the solution of the ambiguity and accepts his limitations. While horror thrillers assure the reader of his power over self and not-self, terror fantasies make him experience the limits of that power.

The rewards of this surrender of the illusion of mastery over the self and the world, the pleasures of terror in terror fantasies, are multiple. The perception of the implied reader as a fictional role and the potential perception of the implication that all versions of the self are fictional and, therefore, changeable, offer a kind of liberation. The feelings of release and freedom that may accompany these perceptions can be great indeed, occurring at psychological, social, and political levels. These perceptions are essentially intuitive and, except in a critical/theoretical effort such as this book, we are not likely to articulate them. Whether articulated or completely intuitive, the experience is intense and liberating. There is a feeling of self-transcendence, which results from the intuition that one of the selves one has been is smaller or less than the "consciousness" or the subject that created that self. This feeling meshes with and intensifies the sense of release that accompanies escape from the obsession of the implied reader. Anxiety fades, to be replaced by a dual level of exhilaration, feelings of freedom from one version of the self and from all possible versions of the self.

These feelings of release are intensified still further at the final level of aesthetics. Release from imprisonment in a fictional self and from the obsession of that self allows the reestablishment of aesthetic distance in which the reader ceases to be contained by the work and succeeds in containing it. He is able to see the work as a whole with all of its parts, including the implied reader, functionally connected and appropriate to their places and relationships. There is a kind of triumph of the perceiving subject here. "He" escapes from Usher's universe of Chinese boxes, from containment within the work, from containment within a version of the self, the implied reader, and from containment within his self, the real reader. The subject that creates the "I" is at least momentarily liberated from any particular version of that "I" and can experience himself as the creator of "I's." This escape becomes the distinctive feature of the aesthetic experience of a terror fantasy. Terror leads to liberation; liberation ends in beauty. One's future thinking about the work becomes voluntary rather than obsessive, free rather than entrapped, pleasurable rather than anxious. We may continue our contemplation of the work at our choice, without the constraints imposed upon the implied reader, and we may expect to enjoy this activity in the way we enjoy exploring the aesthetically relevant features and the implications of all great works of art.

The uncanny tale of terror and the horror thriller serve the law of the self, helping to confirm the reader in his choice of an identity. In doing so, they provide two fairly distinct sorts of aesthetic pleasure. The uncanny tale provides the pleasures of self-exploration and modeling as parts of concretization. Horror thrillers provide opportunities for the pleasurable reenactment of the repressions by which identity is chosen and maintained. Terror fantasy subverts the law of the self, helping to remind the reader that identity is a fictional construct chosen by a subject or consciousness potentially greater than any identity it might construct. The pleasure of terror fantasy, therefore, is a direct result of real terror of some degree. The real reader must truly be terrified, must experience the work as a threat (though of a special sort) to himself, and must deal with the threat not by evasion, but by altering his perspective in such a way as to separate himself from the implied reader and regain control of the aesthetic experience. This move makes possible and contributes to the successful concretization of the work and thereby becomes the distinctive feature of the aesthetic pleasure of a terror fantasy.

# II

The three distinct answers to the question about the delights of terror arise from distinguishing three modal types of tale along the split continuum between terror fantasy at one end and tales of the marvelous and the uncanny at the other. How do these answers relate to what has been suggested about the pleasures of terror?

Not much attention has been given to the problem of the pleasures of terror. Most recent writers have been more interested in the psychological, social, political, religious, and historical dimensions of the Gothic tradition. They have attempted to account for *the appeal* of works in the Gothic tradition with various hypotheses about the particular historical needs of the culture that produced them. A brief look at some of the recent hypotheses with attention to the unities among them will help suggest how they relate to the answers I have offered.

S. L. Varnado in "The Idea of the Numinous in Gothic Literature" argues that the experience of the numinous is "the essential goal of the Gothic writer" (*The Gothic Imagination* 12). G. Richard Thompson takes up this idea in his introductions to *Romantic Gothic Tales* and *The Gothic Imagination*. Thompson characterizes the numinous as metaphysical dread:

> The chief element of the Gothic romance is not so much terror as, more broadly, dread—whether physical, psychological, or metaphysical, whether of body, mind, or spirit. The Gothic romance seeks to create an atmosphere of dread by combining terror with horror and mystery. *Terror* suggests the frenzy of physical and mental fear of pain, dismemberment, and death. *Horror* suggests the perception of something incredibly evil or morally repellent. *Mystery* suggests something beyond this, the perception of a world that stretches away beyond the range of human intelligence—often morally incomprehensible—and thereby productive of a nameless apprehension that may be called religious dread in the face of the wholly *other*. (*The Gothic Imagination* 3)

Gothic writers felt the need to express such religious dread as part of a cultural response to the perceived end of the Age of Faith, the decline of the power of the Christian synthesis to unify Western civilization: "Gothic literature may be seen as expressive of an existential terror generated by a schism between a triumphantly secularized philosophy of evolving good and an abiding obsession with the Medieval conception of guilt-laden, sin-ridden man" (*The Gothic Imagination* 4-5). Deprived of a unified and unifying vision of good and evil in the cosmos and confronted by philosophies that denied the evil that they felt to be there, Gothic writers sought to express the hidden dark side of humanity by evoking metaphysical dread in the face of the wholly unknown other. In this view, the Enlightenment tended to deny the irrational, but Gothic writers, perceiving its persistence, sought to represent it and to reimagine the mind as including both the rational and the irrational. By implication, then, the readers of such works have a need to experience metaphysical dread. The Gothic novel becomes a means of appropriating experiences that the dominant culture has ruled out of reality. This sort of thinking becomes the basis of the hypotheses of David Punter and Rosemary Jackson.

Punter sees Gothic fiction as rebellion against an essentially political ideology, industrial capitalism's attempt to claim and enforce the totality of its vision of the world (411-26). Gothic fiction opposes the realistic novel's bourgeois specification of what is real, for example, family, heterosexuality, and monogamy. The Gothic expresses the alienation of those people and those aspects of all people written out of reality by such an ideology's claim of universality or totality. Gothic fiction expresses what industrial capitalism represses. It therefore responds to a need humans have to be whole, to possess themselves wholly, a need that always must resist the claim of a particular culture's values and world view to be all-inclusive.

Jackson brings together structuralist method and psychoanalysis, drawing heavily on Todorov and Lacan, among others. William Patrick Day works out a more detailed presentation of a similar view in his examination of Gothic fiction. Jackson argues that fantasy (by which she seems to mean mainly tales of terror) is ultimately subversive. In various forms fantasy questions "the category of character." She notes that many fantasies, when studied thematically, are compensatory, that is, they offer vicarious wish fulfillment (174-75). I believe she would so categorize both uncanny tales of terror and horror thrillers. They allow a temporary entertainment of the culturally forbidden, thus compensating us for giving up what was forbidden. However, she argues further that many of these same fantasies are structurally subversive; they "undermine dominant philosophical and epistemological orders" (175). These fantasies subvert cultural definitions of the real by expressing desire for the "unreal." By depicting in various ways a reversal of the process of forming the self, fantasy expresses desire for an absolute, for an expression to cover all of reality; at the same time subversive fantasy points at the failure of any given expression to communicate ALL. In an age of belief, religious fantasy can depict the union of self and other (in this case, God), but in the modern age, secular fantasies can only long for an impossible union of self and other, because the other has become the not-self hidden in the self. Modern subversive fantasy expresses our dissatisfaction with what our culture allows us to see, with the real. While it does not satisfy our desire to see the imaginary, it at least expresses our desire.

All three of these accounts of the appeal of tales of terror are insightful and helpful, especially with regard to my thinking on the horror thriller. The horror thriller, after all, includes the central forms realized by the main line of the Gothic tradition from *The Castle of Otranto* through *Dracula* to *At the Mountains of Madness*. Each of these accounts argues that the Gothic tradition emerges out of the perception of a major lack in the felt structure of modern Western culture. Todorov expresses a similar idea when he asserts that nineteenth-century fantasy "is nothing but the bad conscience of this positivist era" (168). As a particular cultural response to a particular feeling of something missing, Gothic fiction allows the expression of that feeling and an attempt, which can be only partially successful, to supply what is missing: the lost sense of religious unity and awe, the ways of living and being excluded by an industrial capitalist ideology, the hidden parts of the self surrendered in the formation of the "I" within a particular cultural/linguistic matrix (or, as Lacan would say, "patrix").

It should be immediately clear that I have leaned more on the last of these formulations, not because the others are less fruitful, but because my questions are essentially aesthetic. To treat of the unique aesthetic pleasures of modern works of fiction seems to require consideration of the individual reader's act of concretization. One naturally focuses attention on the reader's response to the text. The historical interests of Thompson, Punter, and Jackson lead them to historical hypotheses, which seek verification in what we can learn and persuade ourselves to believe about particular historical moments. I have used Jackson and those with whom she deals because of their emphasis on the personal, on the features and needs of the individual reader of a tale of terror, insofar as we are capable of knowing him. Hence, my formulations are based on what appear to be the best current insights into the formation of individual identity.

There is a sense in which one approaches the universal by this route. There is a chance, at least, that the explanations of the pleasures of terror offered here, when refined and corrected over time, may prove applicable to all tales of terror, not merely those that emerge from the Gothic tradition of a predominantly Anglo-American and modern literature. It seems likely that the emergence of a Gothic tradition in the eighteenth century may be accounted for largely in the same way we account for the emergence of the novel in the same period, in terms of economic and political changes, of the emergence of a culture-consuming middle class, and of increased literacy, among other factors. The novel was not the beginning of fiction, and the Gothic romance was not the beginning of tales of terror. Thompson and Punter provocatively explain the particular shapes the Gothic romance takes. Jackson and Todorov contribute to this explanation, but prove more helpful in trying to discover what value any individual might gain from the tales of terror that his or her culture produces. Because I take my examples from the familiar, my formulations will be limited by my gender and personality, by my culture, and by my place in history. Nevertheless, insofar as they are accurate and clear, they should point toward what an ancient Roman or a twenty-first-century Chinese would seek in the tales of terror produced at those times in those cultures.

By offering aesthetic answers to the questions of why we enjoy horror and terror in literature, I separate myself from most of the twentieth-century writers on the subject except, perhaps, for those in the popular press. Literary theory has not shown much interest in these questions since the eighteenth century, when Aiken and Barbauld formulated them so well. As Samuel Monk has shown in *The Sublime*, eighteenth-century theorists and writers were intensely interested in the problem of how the terrifying could play such an important part in the literature that was growing in importance during their century.

The general answer was "the sublime," an aesthetic effect resulting from the presentation of terrifying objects within some artistic form or from the contemplation of the awesome in a landscape. Aesthetic distance was crucial to the effect of the sublime. Edmund Burke's well-known formulation of the relation of terror to the sublime is, in fact, echoed in Edward Bullough's essay on aesthetic distance: "Whatever is fitted in any sort to excite the ideas of pain and danger, that is to say, whatever is in any sort terrible, or is conversant about terrible objects, or operates in a manner analogous to terror, is a source of the sublime; that is, it is productive of the strongest emotion of which the mind is capable of feeling. . . . When danger or pain press too nearly, they are incapable of giving any delight, and are simply terrible; but at certain distances, and with certain modifications, they may be, and they are delightful, as we every day experience" (Monk, *The Sublime* 91). According to Burke, the experience of the sublime is characterized by astonishment, "that state of the soul in which all its motions are suspended with some degree of horror. . . . [T]he mind is so entirely filled with its object, that it cannot entertain any other, nor by consequence reason on that object which employs it" (Monk, *The Sublime* 92). We can see here a route to the historical hypotheses of Thompson and Punter. The Gothic romance is a literary form that deliberately seeks to evoke the sublime. The sublime brings into aesthetic experience the irrational, the unknown, and the terrible, thereby transforming pain and danger into parts of beauty. Thompson and Punter explain why this culture would value this experience.

Burke's discussion of the sublime is helpful primarily in its recognition of the importance of aesthetic distance and of the consequences of the dissolution of that distance. His description of astonishment is also suggestive. On one hand, it might describe any number of states including the absorption of a reader in an engaging story or the uncritical taking in of any beautiful object, ranging from one's beloved to a particularly graceful shot in basketball. In no case can one quite imagine the soul with all its motions suspended, except perhaps in death. Still there is a kind of truth in the idea that something like astonishment or wonder is experienced in the horror thriller when the image of the forbidden comes closest to revealing what it veils. There is a kind of motion of contraries between attraction—the desire to really see—and fear—the desire not to know—which makes such a moment highly absorbing. We have seen how absorbing is the obsessive attempt to resolve the insistent ambiguity that erupts with the anticlosure of a terror fantasy.

Monk argues that the concept of the sublime was not fully described and clarified until Immanuel Kant took it up in the *Critique of Aesthetic Judgment* where he distinguished the beautiful from the sublime. The experience of the beautiful arises from the contemplation of the completeness and unity of closed forms. The experience of the sublime arises from the contemplation of objects that make us aware of limitlessness. Monk paraphrases Kant on the sublime: "In experiencing the sublime, the imagination seeks to represent what it is powerless to represent, since the object is limitless, and thus cannot be represented. This effort and this inevitable failure of the imagination are the source of the emotions that accompany the sublime, which achieves its effect by the opposition between the object and our faculties of knowledge" (Monk, *The Sublime* 9; see also, Guyer 264-65). Though this is quite abstract, it seems rather precisely to describe the sorts of effects we have seen in the horror thriller and, especially, in terror fantasy. There seems to be no question of an uncanny tale of terror arousing sublime emotions until it takes advantage of deliberate ambiguity, as does *Edgar Huntly*. At that point, it approaches one form of the horror thriller. Insofar as the real reader and the image of the forbidden approach each other in a horror thriller, this confrontation between the imagination and the limitless comes into play. The terrible image is a representation of what cannot be represented, of what culture and identity make invisible. Hence, the object, the image, opposes our faculties of knowledge. As Thompson, Punter, and Jackson argue, this is the central program of Gothic fiction, but as they also acknowledge, few fictions succeed in bringing about this confrontation. Indeed, the horror thriller seems elaborately structured to approach as close as possible to such a confrontation without actually allowing it to take place. Even stories such as Oliver Onions's "The Beckoning Fair One," Théophile Gautier's "The Dead Lover," or even Matthew Lewis's *The Monk*, which show characters living an alternate forbidden life, protect the reader with narrative judgments and foreground conscious alternatives (I might be someone else) rather than unconscious alternatives (I might be some*thing* else). This concern with maintaining aesthetic distance and protecting the reader is quite appropriate for a work that takes as one of its aims the pleasureable entertainment of images of the forbidden followed by a reenactment of repression, but it probably minimizes the degree to which sublime emotions can be aroused in the reader. Nevertheless, the full realization of Edward Bullough's antinomy of aesthetic distance in the presentation of the horrifying image ought to lead to some form of sublime response. The more highly charged the image itself, the more intense the response of the characters, and the more effective the rhetoric of the presentation, the more fully will the reader feel what Thompson calls metaphysical dread, the sense of impenetrable mystery, or what Ann Radcliffe in her essay, "On the Supernatural in Poetry," calls the essential "obscurity" that points to the limitlessness of that image (149-50). Probably only a few especially powerful horror thrillers such as *Dracula* and the best of those pure fantastic tales of terror such as "The Sand-Man" achieve this level of response.

Terror fantasy seems to pursue the sublime more directly. Sustained and unresolved fantastic hesitation heightened by anticlosure renders limitless the tale as a whole, forcing the imagination to try to represent what it cannot. The implied reader, the real reader's imaginative projection for the solution of this problem, is stymied. Only by recognition and acceptance of this limitlessness can the work become complete.

Kant's description of the pleasure of the sublime also seems clearly applicable to the pleasures of the horror thriller and terror fantasy. Monk paraphrases Kant's description of the sublime as a response to natural objects:

> The sublime sets the mind in motion. The motion is a vibration, a rapid alternation of repulsion and attraction produced by the same object. This is because imagination in the apprehension of the intuition is driven to the point of excess and is afraid of it, while the reason finds nothing excessive in the attempt to estimate the magnitude.
>
> The dynamic sublime is found in nature represented as might, but as might that has no dominion over us. To be dynamically sublime, nature must be a source of fear, but not at the moment of aesthetic judgment. Overhanging rocks, thunderclouds, and lightning, volcanoes, hurricanes, the stormy ocean, high waterfalls—in comparison with their might, our power of resistance is of no account. Hence they are fearful. But if we are safe from their menace, they become delightful because of their fearfulness. These objects awaken sublime feelings because, although the immensity and the energy of nature reveal our own physical limitations, we are aware that we have a faculty (reason) of estimating ourselves as in-

dependent of nature and superior to it. . . . Thus we are lifted momentarily above nature. Physically we may be dwarfed, but our reason remains undaunted, and the mind becomes aware of the sublimity of its own being. (Monk, *The Sublime* 8)

This passage needs considerable translation because Kant turns, rather naturally, to nature for objects that might impress the mind with limitlessness, because their "might" is so much in excess of any human individual's little strength.

Kant replaces Burke's stillness of astonishment with a mind in motion, specifically between attraction and repulsion. This vibration occurs because of contrary demands of different human faculties. The reason believes in wholeness and demands that the object be seen whole, but because the object exceeds the ability of the imagination to see it whole, the imagination backs away from the activity it is called upon to perform at the same time that it tries to perform it. In the most effective horror thrillers, this vibration occurs in relation to the terrifying image that demands recognition but also hides itself and refuses to be recognized. The closer it approaches being recognized without revealing itself, the fuller the experience of this vibration of attraction and repulsion, between the desire to see and the fear of knowing. Terror fantasy exhibits this quality of the sublime even more clearly. We expect, even need, the work to be a whole; we feel driven to complete a concretion of that whole. But the work resists and entraps the implied reader—our imaginary agent—by insisting upon its own limitlessness. This impasse cannot be broken until there is an alteration of perspective in which the real reader escapes the reading.

The dynamic sublime as found in these literary works is not represented as might; none is so large as to endanger us by its size or so physically powerful as to gobble us up. However, in the horror thriller, the danger is something like might. If we, by some accident, push aside the veil of the image and perceive what should not be seen, we may be overwhelmed. Hence, we fear the veiled power of that terrifying image. As long as aesthetic distance is sustained, however, we occupy a location from which an aesthetic judgment can be made. Upon completion and closure of the work, when the frightening monster has been "put back" in one way or another, we are, in a sense, lifted above ourselves, or perhaps more precisely, lifted into ourselves. The horror thriller affirms the power to create identity and the particular identity one has created. One feels strength, superiority, a sense of belonging. In *Caligari's Children*, S. S. Prawer recalls such an experience when he saw *White Zombie* as a teenager: "The whole added up to an encounter with deep-seated fears from which I felt I emerged with credit; I remember the experience with gratitude as a liberating and exhilarating one" (202).

Terror fantasy produces a perhaps stronger version of sublime pleasure. The danger in terror fantasy is not destruction or being overwhelmed by a nightmare, but obsessive entrapment before what we conceive to be the terrible, the threatening unknown and forbidden. Likewise, we are unable to simply *be* in the right location, safe from the threat we perceive in the overhanging rock or the stormy ocean. And so long as we are not in that position, aesthetic judgment is impossible. Terror fantasy requires the reader to find the safe position. Kant's formulation suggests how this might be done and parallels the argument I have made. We become aware of ourselves as having an ability to see ourselves as independent of the work and superior to it. Having "made" the implied reader, we can become aware of ourselves as creators, as superior to that particular "I" and to any other "I" we have created or will create. In short, there is a "safe location" to which we can move in imagination and from which aesthetic judgment is possible. Thus, we are lifted above the work. Though the work defeats our attempts to resolve its ambiguity, we are able to subsume it under an idea of wholeness that includes that irresolvable ambiguity. By being made aware of the limitations of "I" in relation to the apparent limitlessness of the terror fantasy, we become aware, paradoxically, of the sublimity of our own being, of the limitlessness of our essential selves as creators of our identities. Because the movement is more complex and because it covers a greater imaginative distance, requiring that we discover and recover the perspective from which to judge, the pleasure of the sublime in a terror fantasy is more intense and perhaps more profound than the sublime pleasure of the horror thriller.

It appears, then, that Kant provided the foundation for an explanation of the pleasures of terror in 1790. The horror thriller and terror fantasy prove to be possible sources of the sublime as Kant formulated it. We can see continuity between Kant's formulations of the experience of the sublime and the best of recent studies of the appeal of the Gothic romance. We can also see continuity between the sublime and the pleasures of terror fantasy. Kant's formulation suggests, in fact, that insofar as an artist understands, whether consciously or intuitively, an audience's capacity for the sublime, he might take as a goal the production of that effect in his audience. A sort of genetic hypothesis arises from this observation. Though we probably cannot show that there is any clear historical development in written literature from the uncanny and marvelous tales of terror toward the uses of images symbolic of unconscious fears, fantastic ambiguity, and anticlosure, we might still argue that this is a genetic development. Perhaps the potential for pleasure inherent in the tale of terror is fully articulated in the aesthetic effect of the sublime. If this is true, then it may also be true that all tales of terror seek in various ways to produce this effect. Finally, we might hypothesize that two of the three main modes of the tale of terror discussed in this study represent particularly satisfying ways to approach the sublime and that terror fantasies most fully realize the potentialities of the tale of terror, since they evoke the sublime most completely. That one might describe literary genres in such a way as to generalize about their potentials and to judge works according to the degree to which they realize the potentials of the genre to which they appear to belong is not a new idea. We find it in Aristotle's *Poetics*, and it pervades the practice of the Chicago school of criticism.

Certain features of this study of the pleasures of terror tend to support this genetic hypothesis. We know from childhood experience that tales of terror really can frighten us, though we may not understand why we ever listened to such stories or how we survived them. The potential for really frightening adult readers with the material of the tale is present once we symbolize the forbidden in various sorts of monsters and monstrous acts. Jerzy Kosinski's *The Painted Bird* includes episodes reminiscent of the kinds of folk tales that present such material, for example, the story of the jealous miller who spoons out a ploughboy's eyes or the story of the man who is unable to withdraw when he rapes a captured Jewish girl. Most writers of horror thrillers carefully preserve aesthetic distance when they successfully introduce such materials, presumably in part because they know that a sublime effect will result if the reader meets an impenetrable object in the story, but that the effect will probably fail if the object is penetrated. It remained for the greatest writers who took up this form to discover the possibilities of conjoining the pure fantastic and anticlosure in a tale of terror; Poe and James create formal structures that bring the reader into the presence of terrifying images and trap him there. Writers of tales of terror seem then to have made genetically, if not historically, progressive discoveries that lead from a fairly simple vicarious participation in a character's fear to a complex experience of the sublime in terror fantasy. To move from the first to that last of these forms, an artist must make certain discoveries: how to present and manipulate terrifying images, the power of fantastic hesitation, and the power of joining the pure fantastic and anticlosure. The movements from simplicity to complexity and from lesser to greater realization of the sublime suggest that the tale of terror, like tragedy, may be studied as a genre with recognizable formal characteristics. If this is true, then this discussion of the delights of terror may be a starting point for such a study.

# Sources Cited and Consulted

More inclusive bibliographies can be found in Elizabeth MacAndrew's *The Gothic Tradition in Fiction;* David Punter's *The Literature of Terror;* and Rosemary Jackson's *Fantasy.* Current bibliography is well covered by the publications of Gothic Press.

## I. Primary Sources

Adams, Henry. *The Education of Henry Adams.* 1918. Boston: Houghton Mifflin, 1973.

Bierce, Ambrose. *Ghost and Horror Stories of Ambrose Bierce.* New York: Dover, 1964.

Blackwood, Algernon. *Best Ghost Stories of Algernon Blackwood.* Edited by E. F. Bleiler. New York: Dover, 1973.

Brown, Charles Brockden. *Edgar Huntly; or Memoirs of a Sleep-Walker.* 1799. Port Washington, N.Y.: Kennikat Press, 1963.

————. *Wieland, or The Transformation.* 1798. New York: Doubleday, 1962.

Collins, Wilkie. *Tales of Terror and the Supernatural.* New York: Dover, 1972.

Faulkner, William. *Sanctuary.* New York: Vintage, 1931.

Gautier, Théophile. "The Dead Lover." In *Romantic Gothic Tales: 1790–1840,* edited by G. Richard Thompson. New York: Harper & Row, 1979.

Godwin, William. *Things as They Are; or the Adventures of Caleb Williams.* 1794. London: Oxford University Press, 1970.

Hawthorne, Nathaniel. *The House of the Seven Gables.* 1851. New York: Signet, 1961.

Hoffman, E. T. A. *The Best Tales of Hoffman.* Edited by E. F. Bleiler. New York: Dover, 1967.

Hogg, James. *The Private Memoirs and Confessions of a Justified Sinner.* 1824. New York: Norton, 1970.

James, Henry. *Stories of the Supernatural.* Edited by Leon Edel. New York: Taplinger, 1980.

————. *The Turn of the Screw*. 1898. Edited by Robert Kimbrough. New York: Norton Critical Edition, 1966.

James, M. R. *Ghost Stories of an Antiquary*. 1904. New York: Dover, 1971.

King, Stephen. *Night Shift*. New York: Signet, 1978.

Kosinski, Jerzy. *The Painted Bird*. New York: Bantam, 1972.

Lewis, Matthew G. *The Monk*. 1796. New York: Grove, 1952.

Lovecraft, Howard Phillips *At the Mountains of Madness and Other Novels of Terror*. London: Panther, 1968.

————. *At the Mountains of Madness and Other Tales of Terror*. New York: Ballantine, 1971.

Maginn, "The Man in the Bell." In *Romantic Gothic Tales: 1790–1840*, edited by G. Richard Thompson. New York: Harper & Row, 1979.

Maturin, Charles Robert. *Melmoth the Wanderer*. 1820. Lincoln: University of Nebraska Press, 1961.

Maupassant, Guy de. "The Horla." In *Classic Ghost Stories*. New York: Dover, 1975.

Mudford, William. "The Iron Shroud." In *Romantic Gothic Tales: 1790–1840*, edited by G. Richard Thompson. New York: Harper & Row, 1979.

Onions, Oliver. *The First Book of Ghost Stories: Widdershins*. 1911. New York: Dover, 1978.

Poe, Edgar Allan. *The Narrative of Arthur Gordon Pym*. 1838. New York: Penguin, 1975.

————. *Selected Prose, Poetry, and Eureka*. Edited by W. H. Auden. New York: Holt, Rinehart & Winston, 1968.

————. *The Short Fiction of Edgar Allan Poe*. Edited by Stuart and Susan Levine. Indianapolis: Bobbs-Merrill, 1976.

Radcliffe, Ann. *The Italian*. 1797. New York: Oxford University Press, 1968.

————. *The Mysteries of Udolpho*. 1794. New York: Oxford University Press, 1980.

Stevenson, Robert Louis. "The Strange Case of Dr. Jekyll and Mr. Hyde." 1886. In *Collected Works*. New York: Scribner's, 1910.

Stoker, Bram. *The Annotated Dracula*. 1897. Edited by Leonard Wolf. New York: Clarkson N. Potter, 1975.

Thompson, G. Richard, ed. *Romantic Gothic Tales: 1790–1840*. New York: Harper & Row, 1979.

Walpole, Horace. *The Castle of Otranto*. 1764. In *Three Gothic Novels*, edited by E. F. Bleiler. New York: Dover, 1966.

## *II. Secondary Sources*

Abrams, M. H. *A Glossary of Literary Terms*. 4th ed. New York: Holt, Rinehart and Winston, 1981.

Adamowski, T. H. "Faulkner's Popeye: 'The Other' as Self." *Canadian Review of American Studies* 8 (1977):36–51.

Aiken, John, and Anna Laetitia Barbauld. "On the Pleasure Derived from Objects of Terror." *Miscellaneous Pieces in Prose*. 2d ed., 119–27. London, 1775.

Alterton, Margaret. *Origins of Poe's Critical Theory.* Iowa City: University of Iowa Humanistic Studies (2.3), 1925.

Armstrong, Paul B. *The Phenomenology of Henry James.* Chapel Hill: University of North Carolina Press, 1983.

Auerbach, Nina. *Woman and the Demon.* Cambridge: Harvard University Press, 1982.

Bachinger, Katrina. "The Poetic Distance of the House of Usher." *Studies in Nineteenth Century Literature* (Salzburg, 1979):61–74.

Barbour, Brian. "Poe and Tradition." *Southern Literary Journal* 10 (1978):71–74.

Bedell, George C. *Kierkegaard and Faulkner: Modalities of Existence.* Baton Rouge: Louisiana State University Press, 1972.

Bently, C. F. "The Monster in the Bedroom: Sexual Symbolism in Bram Stoker's *Dracula.*" *Literature and Psychology* 22 (1972):27–34.

Bersani, Leo. *A Future for Astyanax.* Boston: Little, Brown, 1976.

Bettelheim, Bruno. *The Uses of Enchantment.* 1976. New York: Vintage, 1977.

Bierman, Joseph S. "*Dracula* : Prolonged Childhood Illness and the Oral Triad." *American Imago* 29 (1972):186–98.

Birkhead, Edith. *The Tale of Terror: A Study of Gothic Romance.* 1921. New York: Russell and Russell, 1963.

Booth, Wayne C. *Critical Understanding.* Chicago: University of Chicago Press, 1979.

Brooke-Rose, Christine. *A Rhetoric of the Unreal.* Cambridge: Cambridge University Press, 1981.

Broughton, Panthea Reid. *William Faulkner: The Abstract and the Actual.* Baton Rouge: Louisiana State University Press, 1974.

Bullough, Edward. " 'Psychical Distance' as a Factor in Art and an Aesthetic Principle." In *Critical Theory Since Plato,* edited by Hazard Adams, 755–65. New York: Harcourt, 1971.

Canby, Henry S. "The School of Cruelty." *Saturday Review of Literature,* 21 Mar. 1931, 673–74.

Carlson, E. W. *Poe on the Soul of Man.* Baltimore: The E. A. Poe Society and the Enoch Pratt Library, 1973.

———, ed. *The Fall of the House of Usher: Text and Essays.* Columbus, Ohio: Merrill, 1971.

———, ed. *The Recognition of Edgar Allan Poe.* Ann Arbor: University of Michigan Press, 1966.

Cawelti, John G. *Adventure, Mystery, and Romance.* Chicago: University of Chicago Press, 1976.

Cixous, Hélène. "The Character of 'Character.' " Translated by Keith Cohen. *New Literary History* 5 (1974):383–402.

Costello, Donald P. "The Structure of *The Turn of the Screw.*" *Modern Language Notes* 75 (1960):312–21.

Craft, Christopher. " 'Kiss Me with Those Red Lips': Gender and Inversion in Bram Stoker's *Dracula.*" *Representations* 8 (Fall 1984):107–33.

Cranfill, Thomas M., and Robert L. Clark. *An Anatomy of THE TURN OF THE SCREW.* Austin: University of Texas Press, 1965.

Crossley, Robert. "Poe's Closet Monologues." *Genre* 10 (1977):215–32.

Crowl, Susan. "Aesthetic Allegory in *The Turn of the Screw*." *Novel* 4 (1971):107–22.

Day, William Patrick. *In the Circles of Fear and Desire: A Study of Gothic Fantasy.* Chicago: University of Chicago Press, 1985.

Demetrakopoulos, Stephanie. "Feminism, Sex Role Exchanges, and Other Subliminal Fantasies in Bram Stoker's *Dracula*." *Frontiers* 2 (1977):104–13.

Erikson, Erik. *Childhood and Society.* 2d ed. New York: Norton, 1963.

Falk, Eugene. *The Poetics of Roman Ingarden.* Chapel Hill: University of North Carolina Press, 1981.

Felman, Shoshana. "Turning the Screw of Interpretation." In *Literature and Psychoanalysis: The Question of Reading: Otherwise,* edited by Shoshana Felman. Baltimore: Johns Hopkins University Press, 1982.

Fischer, William F. "Towards a Phenomenology of Anxiety." In *Explorations in the Psychology of Stress and Anxiety,* edited by Byron P. Rourke. Don Mills, Ontario: Longman Canada Ltd., 1969.

Fitz, Brewster E. "The Use of Mirrors and Mirror Analogues in Maupassant's 'The Horla.'" *The French Review* 45 (1972):954–63.

Freud, Sigmund. *On Creativity and the Unconscious.* Edited by Benjamin Nelson. New York: Harper & Row, 1958.

Garber, Frederick. *The Autonomy of the Self from Richardson to Huysmans.* Princeton: Princeton University Press, 1982.

Gargano, James W. "Poe's 'Ligeia': Dream and Destruction." *College English* 23 (1962):335–42.

Garmon, Gerald M. "Roderick Usher: Portrait of the Madman as Artist." *Poe Studies* 5 (1972):11–14.

Garrison, Joseph M., Jr. "The Function of Terror in the Work of Edgar Allan Poe." *American Quarterly* 18 (1966):136–50.

———. "The Irony of 'Ligeia.'" *ESQ* 60 (1970):13–18.

Griffin, Andrew. "Sympathy for the Werewolf." *University Publishing* 6 (1979):1, 17.

Grossvogel, David I. *Mystery and Its Fictions.* Baltimore: Johns Hopkins University Press, 1979.

Guerard, Albert J. *The Triumph of the Novel: Dickens, Dostoevski, Faulkner.* New York: Oxford University Press, 1976.

Guyer, Paul. *Kant and the Claims of Taste.* Cambridge: Harvard University Press, 1979.

Halliburton, David. *Edgar Allan Poe: A Phenomenological View.* Princeton: Princeton University Press, 1973.

Hallie, Philip P. *The Paradox of Cruelty.* Middletown, Conn.: Wesleyan University Press, 1969.

Heilman, Robert. "A Note on the Freudian Reading of *The Turn of the Screw*." *Modern Language Notes* 42 (1947):433–45.

Heller, Terry. "Poe's 'Ligeia' and the Pleasures of Terror." *Gothic* 2 (1980):39–48.

———. "Terror and Empathy in Faulkner's *Sanctuary*." *Arizona Quarterly* 40.4 (1984): 344–64

Hennelly, Mark M., Jr. *"Dracula* : The Gnostic Quest in the Victorian Wasteland." *English Literature in Transition* 20 (1977):13–26.

Holland, Norman N. *The I.* New Haven: Yale University Press, 1985.

Howarth, William L., ed. *Twentieth-Century Interpretations of Poe's Tales.* Englewood Cliffs, N.J.: Prentice-Hall, 1979.

Howe, Irving. *William Faulkner.* 2d ed. Chicago: University of Chicago Press, 1975.

Hume, Kathryn. *Fantasy and Mimesis.* New York: Methuen, 1984.

Ingarden, Roman. "Aesthetic Experience and Aesthetic Object." *Philosophy and Phenomenological Research* 21 (1961):289–313.

———. "Artistic and Aesthetic Values." In *Aesthetics,* edited by Harold Osborne. New York: Oxford University Press, 1972.

———. *The Cognition of the Literary Work of Art.* Translated by Ruth Ann Crowley and Kenneth R. Olson. Evanston: Northwestern University Press, 1973.

———. *The Literary Work of Art.* Translated by George G. Grabowicz. Evanston: Northwestern University Press, 1973.

Iser, Wolfgang. *The Act of Reading.* Baltimore: Johns Hopkins University Press, 1978.

———. *The Implied Reader.* Baltimore: Johns Hopkins University Press, 1974.

Jackson, Rosemary. *Fantasy.* New York: Methuen, 1981.

Jacobs, Robert D. *Poe: Journalist and Critic.* Baton Rouge: Louisiana State University Press, 1969.

James, Henry. *Theory of Fiction.* Edited by James E. Miller, Jr. Lincoln: University of Nebraska Press, 1972.

Jameson, Frederic. "Imaginary and Symbolic in Lacan: Marxism, Psychoanalytic Criticism, and the Problems of the Subject." In *Literature and Psychoanalysis,* edited by Shoshana Felman. Baltimore: Johns Hopkins University Press, 1982.

———. "Magical Narratives: Romance as Genre." *New Literary History* 7 (1975):133–63.

Jones, Ernest. *On the Nightmare.* 1931. New York: Liveright, 1951.

Kant, Immanuel. "From *Critique of Judgment.*" 1790. In *Critical Theory Since Plato,* edited by Hazard Adams, 377–99. New York: Harcourt Brace, 1971.

Kauffman, Linda S. "The Author of Our Woe: Virtue Recorded in *The Turn of the Screw.*" *Nineteenth Century Fiction* 36 (1981):176–92.

Kermode, Frank. *The Sense of an Ending.* New York: Oxford University Press, 1967.

Kerr, Elizabeth M. *William Faulkner's Gothic Domain.* Port Washington, N.Y.: Kennikat Press, 1979.

Ketterer, David. *The Rationale of Deception in Poe.* Baton Rouge: Louisiana State University Press, 1979.

King, Stephen. *Danse Macabre.* New York: Everest House, 1981.

Koelb, Clayton. *The Incredulous Reader: Literature and the Function of Disbelief.* Ithaca: Cornell University Press, 1984.

Kristéva, Julia. *Desire in Language.* Edited and Translated by Leon S. Roudiez. New York: Columbia University Press, 1980.

Krook, Dorothea. "The Madness of Art: Further Reflections on the Ambiguity of Henry James." *Hebrew University Studies in Literature* 1 (1972):25–38.
———. *The Ordeal of Consciousness in Henry James.* Cambridge: Cambridge University Press, 1962.
Lacan, Jacques. "The Mirror Phase as Formative of the Function of the 'I.' " Translated by Jean Roussel. *New Left Review* 51 (1968):71–77.
Lauber, John. " 'Ligeia' and Its Critics: A Plea for Literalism." *Studies in Short Fiction* 4 (1966):28–32.
Ljungquist, Kent. "Poe and the Sublime: His Two Short Sea Tales in the Context of an Aesthetic Tradition." *Criticism* 17 (1975):131–51.
Lovecraft, Howard Phillips. *Supernatural Horror in Literature.* 1939. New York: Dover, 1973.
MacAndrew, Elizabeth. *The Gothic Tradition in Fiction.* New York: Columbia University Press, 1979.
Mack, John E. *Nightmares and Human Conflict.* Boston: Little, Brown, 1970.
Martindale, Colin. "Archetype and Reality in 'The Fall of the House of Usher.' " *Poe Studies* 5 (1972):9–11.
Massey, Irving. *The Gaping Pig: Literature and Metamorphosis.* Berkeley: University of California Press, 1976.
Millgate, Michael. *The Achievement of William Faulkner.* New York: Random House, 1966.
Mitchell, Juliet. *Psychoanalysis and Feminism.* New York: Random House, 1974.
Monk, Samuel. *The Sublime.* Ann Arbor: University of Michigan Press, 1935.
Morris, D. Hampton. "Variations on a Theme: Five Tales of Horror by Maupassant." *Studies in Short Fiction* 17 (1980):475–81.
Murphy, Brenda. "The Problem of Validity in the Critical Controversy over *The Turn of the Screw.*" *Research Studies* 47 (1979):191–201.
Nardin, Jane. "*The Turn of the Screw:* The Victorian Background." *Mosaic* 12 (1978):131–42.
Nash, Mark. "*Vampyr* and the Fantastic." *Screen* 17 (1976):29–67.
Ostrum, J. W., ed. *The Letters of Edgar Allan Poe.* Cambridge: Harvard University Press, 1948.
Palmer, Jerry. *Thrillers: Genesis and Structure of a Popular Genre.* New York: St. Martin's, 1979.
Pease, Donald. "The Rendered and Surrendered Pose of Edgar Allan Poe." *Cithara* 20 (1980):26–43.
Pollin, Burton. "Poe's *Narrative of Arthur Gordon Pym* and the Contemporary Reviewers." *Studies in American Fiction* 2 (1974):37–56.
Porte, Joel. *The Romance in America.* Middletown, Conn.: Wesleyan University Press, 1969.
Prawer, S. S. *Caligari's Children.* New York: Oxford University Press, 1980.
———. "Hoffman's Uncanny Guest: A Reading of 'Der Sandmann.' " *German Life and Letters* 1 (1965):297–308.
Punter, David. *The Literature of Terror.* New York: Longman, 1980.
Radcliffe, Ann. "On the Supernatural in Poetry." *New Monthly Magazine,* NS 16 (1826):145–50.

Reed, Joseph W., Jr. *Faulkner's Narrative.* New Haven: Yale University Press, 1973.

Regan, R., ed. *Poe.* Englewood Cliffs, N.J.: Prentice-Hall, 1967.

Richter, David H. *Fable's End.* Chicago: University of Chicago Press, 1974.

Robinson, Douglas. "Reading Poe's Novel: A Speculative Review of *Pym* Criticism, 1950–1980." *Poe Studies* 15 (1982):47–54.

Rossky, William. "The Pattern of Nightmare in *Sanctuary;* or Miss Reba's Dogs." *Modern Fiction Studies* 15 (Winter 1969–70):503–15.

Roth, Phyllis A. "Suddenly Sexual Women in Bram Stoker's *Dracula.*" *Literature and Psychology* 27 (1977):113–21.

Rothbart, Mary K. "Incongruity, Problem Solving, and Laughter." In *Humor and Laughter: Theory, Research and Applications,* edited by A. J. Chapman and H. C. Foot. London: Wiley, 1976.

Roussel, Jean. "Introduction to Jacques Lacan." *New Left Review* 51 (1968):63–70.

Rowe, John Carlos. "Writing and Truth in Poe's *The Narrative of Arthur Gordon Pym.*" *Glyph* 2 (1977):102–21.

Saliba, David R. *A Psychology of Fear: The Nightmare Formula of Edgar Allan Poe.* Lanham, Md: University Press of America, 1980.

Salzberg, Joel. "The Gothic Hero in Transcendental Quest: Poe's 'Ligeia' and James' 'The Beast in the Jungle.' " *ESQ* (1972):108–14.

Schlobin, Roger C. *The Aesthetics of Fantasy Literature and Art.* Notre Dame: University of Notre Dame Press, 1982.

Schneiderman, Stuart. *Jacques Lacan: The Death of an Intellectual Hero.* Cambridge: Harvard University Press, 1983.

Senf, Carol A. "*Dracula:* The Unseen Face in the Mirror." *Journal of Narrative Technique* 9 (1979):160–70.

Shroeter, James. "A Misreading of Poe's 'Ligeia.' " *PMLA* 76 (1961):397–406.

Simpson, Lewis P. "Yoknapatawpha & Faulkner's Fable of Civilization." In *The Maker and the Myth: Faulkner and Yoknapatawpha,* edited by Evans Harrington and Ann J. Abadie. Jackson: University Press of Mississippi, 1978.

St. Armand, Barton Levi. *The Roots of Horror in the Fiction of H. P. Lovecraft.* Elizabethtown, N.Y.: Dragon Press, 1977.

Stahlberg, Lawrence. " 'And the will therein lieth, which dieth not': A Reconsideration of Ligeia's 'Gigantic Volition.' " *American Transcendentalist Quarterly* 43 (1979):199–209.

Stoehr, Taylor. " 'Unspeakable Horror' in Poe." *South Atlantic Quarterly* 78 (1979):317–32.

Suleiman, Susan, ed. *The Reader in the Text.* Princeton: Princeton University Press, 1980.

Tatar, Maria M. "E. T. A. Hoffman's 'Der Sandmann': Reflection and Romantic Irony." *Modern Language Notes* 95 (1980):585–608.

Telotte, J. P. *Dreams of Darkness: Fantasy and the Films of Val Lewton.* Urbana: University of Illinois Press, 1985.

Thompson, G. Richard, ed. *The Gothic Imagination.* Pullman: Washington State University Press, 1974.

————. *Poe's Fiction*. Madison: University of Wisconsin Press, 1973.

————. " 'Proper Evidences of Madness': American Gothic and the Interpretation of 'Ligeia.' " *ESQ* 18 (1972):30–49.

Thomson, Philip. *The Grotesque*. New York: Methuen, 1972.

Todorov, Tzvetan. *The Fantastic: A Structural Approach to a Literary Genre*. Translated by Richard Howard. Ithaca: Cornell University Press, 1975.

Twitchell, James B. *Dreadful Pleasures: An Anatomy of Modern Horror*. New York: Oxford University Press, 1985.

————. *The Living Dead*. Durham, N.C.: Duke University Press, 1981.

Veler, Richard P., ed. *Papers on Poe*. Springfield, Ohio: Chantry Music Press, 1972.

Wagenknecht, Edward. *Edgar Allan Poe*. New York: Oxford University Press, 1963.

Waller, Gregory A., *The Living and the Undead: From Stoker's DRACULA to Romero's DAWN OF THE DEAD*. Urbana: University of Illinois Press, 1986.

Weissman, Judith. "Women and Vampires: *Dracula* as a Victorian Novel." *Midwest Quarterly* 18 (1977):392–405.

Wilden, Anthony. "Lacan and the Discourse of the Other." In *The Language of the Self* by Jacques Lacan. Translated by Anthony Wilden. Baltimore: Johns Hopkins University Press, 1968.

Willen, Gerald, ed. *A Casebook on Henry James's THE TURN OF THE SCREW*. New York: T. Y. Crowell, 1960.

Wittenberg, Judith Bryant. *Faulkner: The Transformation of Biography*. Lincoln: University of Nebraska Press, 1979.

Woodson, Thomas, ed. *Twentieth-Century Interpretations of "The Fall of the House of Usher."* Englewood Cliffs, N.J.: Prentice-Hall, 1969.

Zink, Karl E. "Flux and the Frozen Moment: The Imagery of Stasis in Faulkner's Prose." *PMLA* 71 (1956):287–90.

# Index

## Note on the Author

Terry Heller is a member of the department of English at Coe College, Cedar Rapids, Iowa. His Ph.D. is from the University of Chicago. He is the author of several articles, which have appeared in *Arizona Quarterly*, *Gothic*, and *Thalia*.